RETHINKING ETHNICITY

RETHINKING ETHNICITY

Arguments and Explorations

RICHARD JENKINS

SAGE Publications
London • Thousand Oaks • New Delhi

First published 1997. Reprinted 1998, 2001, 2003

 SAGE Publications Ltd
6 Bonhill Street
London EC2A 4PU

SAGE Publications Inc.
2455 Teller Road
Thousand Oaks, California 91320

SAGE Publications India Pvt Ltd
32, M-Block Market
Greater Kailash – I
New Delhi 110 048

British Library Cataloguing in Publication data

A catalogue record for this book is available from the British Library

ISBN 0 8039 7677 1
ISBN 0 8039 7678 X (pbk)

Library of Congress catalog card number available

Typeset byMayhew Typesetting, Rhayader, Powys
Printed in Great Britain by
The Cromwell Press, Trowbridge, Wiltshire

Contents

Arguments

I have been working on matters to do with social identity in general, and ethnic identity in particular, for nearly twenty years. As a social anthropology student, a post-doctoral researcher, and subsequently as a university lecturer in sociology and anthropology, I have always been keenly aware of the intellectual and political importance of these topics, and the difficulties which one faces in trying to research and teach about them adequately, openly, and even-handedly.

The questions and issues that I have encountered during this time are not, however, important only in my professional, academic life. These attempts to understand better social identity – and more specifically ethnicity – are part of an ongoing dialogue with my own history and biography, and are the product of personal experience. Born in Liverpool, I moved as an infant to a middle-class suburb of Rotherham, in Yorkshire. From there, at the age of eight, I was brusquely transported to a respectable working-class housing estate on the hilly fringes of Larne, a small Northern Irish town. For various reasons, my background remains unclear in its details – perhaps a mixture of English, Irish and, to judge from the surname, Welsh – but in the years between eight and twenty-five I had to learn to understand, if not actually fully participate in or negotiate, the ethnic subtlety and bluntness of Northern Ireland. On the one hand, the boundary between England and Northern Ireland; on the other, within it, the distinction between Protestant and Catholic. While I cannot see myself as English, I am not Irish either. And being Protestant in Larne was a very different thing than it had been in Rotherham. But Larne became – and remains – home. Northern Ireland is certainly where I feel most at home. My children were born there: half me, half their Dutch-Indonesian mother. In the peregrinations that followed, they eventually came to call Swansea, in South Wales, home. In the court of final demands, they call themselves Irish, by dint of place of birth and sentiment. And as their home, and as the home of some of my dearest friends, Swansea has become in large part home to me also. As I write, however, I have returned to live within ten miles of my childhood Yorkshire home. But I have definitely not come home. I could add in further complexities, but these are sufficient to show why I am interested in identity.

There is another kind of genealogy too, which emphasizes two particular moments, and one consistent thread of indebtedness. The first occasion was in the early 1980s. The SSRC Research Unit on Ethnic Relations in

Birmingham, where I was a researcher at the time, was running a taught Master's degree and I ended up doing a few lectures on anthropological approaches to ethnicity. This made me look at issues, concerning anthropology as well as ethnicity, to which – perhaps paradoxically, given the research I was doing at the time and had already done in Belfast – I had hitherto given insufficient attention. Some of what I say in later pages was first said then. The second occasion was ten years on, in March 1992, when I was Visiting Professor in the Institute of Ethnography and Social Anthropology at the University of Aarhus, Denmark. A very great deal of the thinking which has gone into Chapters 5 and 6, in particular, dates from then. Each of these situations enabled – or required – me to revisit, and to engage at close quarters with, the work and thought of Fredrik Barth. The subsequent intellectual debt runs throughout this book.

1

Anthropology, Ethnicity

This book is about ethnicity and the social identifications that are routinely associated with it, such as 'race' and, particularly, national identity. My starting point is the view that, although the basic social anthropological model of ethnicity – most often identified with the work of Fredrik Barth – is the best way to understand ethnicity, its potential has been neither fully explored nor adequately understood. The chapters that follow will explicate this model and look at some of the ways in which it can be developed. My arguments, however, have relevance outside anthropology, because this basic, social constructionist model is rooted in an earlier, sociological literature – Weber, Hughes – and has much in common, both shortcomings and possibilities, with models of ethnicity current in sociology and elsewhere. Lessons for anthropologists in this respect are thus lessons for others too. And just because the model has become most closely identified with anthropology doesn't mean that other social scientists can't use it.

There may also be some wider lessons for anthropology as an intellectual field. Mine is an approach to social anthropology which would probably be understood by many of my disciplinary colleagues – even at a time when anthropology, certainly in the United Kingdom, seems at last to be becoming less narrowly disciplinary – as somewhat heterodox. In fact my *identity* as an anthropologist is, I know, altogether dubious in the eyes of some of them. Although formally qualified as a social anthropologist, I have spent most of my teaching career identified – by job title and by most significant others – as a sociologist. I have spent much of that career exploiting and enjoying the creative ambiguities of the disciplinary borderlands, doffing and donning affiliational caps as it suited me. Much of my research has been about topics – social class, the labour market, racism – which have been claimed by sociologists and, if they think about them at all, disavowed by social anthropologists. Theoretically, I owe huge debts to the writings of Max Weber and G.H. Mead, the two great classical theorists most markedly neglected by social anthropology. Yet despite this history, and despite frequent bouts of despair about anthropology, I have never seen myself as anything other than an anthropologist-doing-sociology (and always doing anthropology too). Fortunately sociology is a sufficiently catholic discipline to tolerate this degree of agnostic pluralism (to put it another way, sociology has always allowed me to have my cake and eat it).

If what I have to say in subsequent chapters is plausible, then the anthropological understanding of ethnicity – if no other – requires rethinking. In this case, rethinking the topic suggests some rethinking, at least, of the discipline. Echoing the words of Edmund Leach in his 1959 inaugural Malinowski Lecture (1961: 1), calls to rethink on a disciplinary scale are vulnerable to interpretation as arrogance. They certainly need to be justified. So, first, a few words about anthropology.

Locating social anthropology

The disciplinary question has two dimensions: the intellectual content of social anthropology and its relationship to cognate disciplines. One matter on which I am not going to dwell is the conventional distinction between social anthropology (largely British) and cultural anthropology (largely American). In the first place, the study of ethnicity is one of the areas in which that distinction has been of least moment. In the second, there is every reason to believe that a new global domain of socio-cultural – or, indeed, culturo-social – anthropology is emerging, in which this fault line has ceased to be of particular importance. This is a development in which European scholars have been conspicuous (one of the most conspicuous of whom has been Barth). Although my own background and training are in British *social* anthropology, and what I have to say is likely to reflect that in places, too much should not be made of this.

With respect to intellectual content, the primary emphasis in anthropology is upon understanding the cultural Other (defined, historically, from a European or North American cultural viewpoint). Historically, this fascination with the absolute elsewhere is one aspect of the discipline's roots in the colonial encounter. More interestingly, it has always called for an imaginative leap, and an epistemological daring – although some might call this a conceit – which is not always present in its nearest intellectual neighbours.

This, perhaps more than anything else, underpins the anthropological emphasis upon the personal experience of ethnographic field research. Every academic discipline is grounded in ontological and epistemological axioms that allow knowable *objects* of inquiry, and *how* they are to be known, to be taken for granted as the bedrock of disciplinary reality. The basic epistemological premise of social anthropology is that to understand Others they must be encountered. If the *sine qua non* of history is engagement with primary sources, the equivalent for anthropology is fieldwork. Long-term participant observation is the source of anthropological epistemological authority. An anthropologist's claim to know about her research site and the people who live there is typically, in the first instance, personal and experiential: 'I know because *I* was there'. Her knowledge is grounded in an ordeal of sorts; fieldwork is a professional *rite de passage*, a process of initiation. Without the 'extremely personal traumatic kind of experience' that is ethnographic fieldwork (Leach again, 1961), she is unlikely to be recognized by other anthropologists as a full member.

A comparative, essentially relativist perspective on socio-cultural diversity is central to anthropology. But perhaps the most important foundational assumption of modern anthropology – its crucial ontological premise – is that human beings, regardless of cultural differences, have more in common with each other than not. This 'psychic unity' of human-kind allows for the possibility of sufficient cross-cultural understanding for the interpretive and comparative ethnographic enterprises to be epistemo-logically defensible. Despite a minor failure of epistemological nerve recently, caused by sophisticated critiques of ethnographic research practice (e.g. Bourdieu 1990) and engagements with postmodernism during the 1980s – particularly the debate about the possibility of representation (Clifford and Marcus 1986; Marcus and Fischer 1986) – most anthro-pologists continue to do their field research in the belief that it *can* be done, however imperfectly. Although Grimshaw and Hart (1995) may be correct to diagnose a collapse of faith in *scientific* ethnography, faith in ethno-graphy – as method and as data – remains.

With respect to theory, social anthropology has always participated in the field of general social theory (although, as I have already suggested, the traditions deriving from Weber or Mead have attracted relatively few anthropological adherents). Structural functionalism, deriving from Durkheim via Radcliffe-Brown, was for a long time the accepted back-ground to most social anthropological research, certainly in Britain. It is only relatively recently, for example, that conflict and contradiction have found a central place in the anthropological world-view. Anthropology in the 1990s is more theoretically heterogeneous than at perhaps any point in its past: Marxism, transactionalism, culturalist interpretivism, structuralism, post-structuralism, feminism, and postmodern critique are all actively twinkling in the current disciplinary firmament. However, at least one remnant of structural functionalism remains at the heart of the anthro-pological enterprise. This is the emphasis – which to my mind is no bad thing – upon methodological holism: the *aspiration* to study all aspects of a situation or a group's way of life, in the belief that they are all, at least *potentially*, interconnected.

Within this holistic perspective, anthropologists have, of course, focused upon some dimensions of social life more than others: symbolism, ritual and religion, kinship and the family, morality, custom and law, micro-politics, and ethnic and communal identity are perhaps the most conspicuous and characteristic. These interests derive partly from the engagement with Other cultures, partly from the experience of data gathering within the inter-actional give and take of 'face-to-face' communities, and partly from anthropology's nineteenth-century origins in the marriage of romantic exoticism and evolutionism, within the context of European and North American colonialism (Kuper 1988). Taken as a whole, this constellation of interests may be characterized as biased in the direction of the *cultural* and the *everyday*:

> Anthropologists . . . have always derived their intellectual authority from direct experience of life . . . That is, they knew the exotic Other and their readers did not. Within that framework of bridging the gap between civilized and primitive, they emphasized the salience of the everyday, the ordinary. (Grimshaw and Hart 1995: 47–8)

The world is changing rapidly, however, and anthropology has to some extent changed with it. Additional subjects and issues have been taken up by some anthropologists in the last two or three decades: these include urbanization (typically in the 'developing world'), socio-economic change and 'development', health care and illness, nutrition, the impact on indigenous communities of tourism, literacy and processes of literization, migration, and nationalism. What remains characteristic of the anthropological point of view, however, is its holistic emphasis on understanding local meanings (culture) using data (about everyday life) gathered via participant observation.

A further important development within the discipline has been a modest shift in its relationship to the exotically Other. This has occurred in three phases. First, as early as the late nineteenth century, but more commonly from the mid-twentieth century onwards, the metropolitan peripheries offered accessible and relatively exotic alterity, in the shape of residual hunters, fishers and nomads, or peasants. Subsequently, second, the exotic Other migrated to the metropolitan homelands of anthropology to become ethnic minorities; anthropologists followed them home. Third, and perhaps most radically, anthropologists have begun to pay more attention to their own cultural backyards (Jackson 1987; Forman 1994).

These trends – theoretical and topical diversification, and a widening of cultural and/or geographical scope – reflect anthropology's attempts to negotiate the post-colonial, post-1945 (perhaps even the post-modern) world. They have brought with them, however, problems in disciplinary boundary maintenance. It is, for example, no longer as easy as it might once have been to distinguish anthropology from sociology, its closest sibling and most obvious rival, simply by reference to method or area. Sociologists are increasingly enthusiastically embracing participant-observation ethnography (although, in fact, ethnography as a research tradition is at least as long-standing within sociology as within anthropology: remember the Chicago School?). On the other side of the coin, some anthropologists have been using quantitative and other non-ethnographic methods since at least the 1950s (Epstein 1967; Pelto and Pelto 1978). And the comparative method – witness Max Weber if no one else – is every bit as sociological as anthropological.

In terms of area and setting, sociologists have been working in the 'developing world' for a long time, and the two disciplines have always competed in the rural areas of industrial societies. Industrialization and globalization have between them conspired to produce a degree of planetary social convergence: in some sense *all* societies may now be thought of as industrial societies. Anthropology no longer has a territorial preserve that it can unambiguously call its own (a situation which has been further encouraged by the post-colonial disrepute in which anthropology is held in some places). On top of this – in part in response to it, indeed – anthropologists are, as I have already commented, 'coming home' to look at 'their own' societies.

This particular fault line has become further confused as sociology, moving now in a fully global arena, has itself engaged with a widening topical agenda. The sociology of culture, in particular, deserves mention in this respect. The development of interdisciplinary feminism as a unifying intellectual field of critical discourse has also contributed to the blurring of boundaries, as has the debate about, and the influence of, postmodernism. Nor is sociology the only problematic boundary: social psychology, social geography and social history might also be mentioned here.

In some other respects, however, anthropology has been moving further away from sociology. As a consequence of the institutional specialization that has encouraged the growth of separate departments within universities and colleges, heightened competition for dwindling resources, the partial abandonment by both disciplines of the shared theoretical heritage of structural functionalism, and the perceived threat posed by the modest convergence of the disciplines in terms of field and topic, boundary maintenance has become more assertive. Competitive or entrepreneurial assertions of the distinctiveness and virtue of anthropological approaches to topics outside the traditional disciplinary spheres of competence have become ever louder. The difference between anthropology and sociology seems to matter more than it did thirty or forty years ago. Despite the fact that personnel and, even more important, *ideas* do cross disciplinary boundaries – most usually, at least in Britain, from anthropology into sociology – those boundaries remain. Sociology – bigger, less specialized, more intellectually promiscuous and pluralist, recruiting from and training within less elitist social and institutional fields – may not be not as sectarian as social anthropology, but *both* disciplines are intellectually impoverished by the communication gap that has opened up between them.

So, where does this leave social anthropology? One analogy which has been used with some success to understand relationships between disciplines – and which is peculiarly appropriate to this discussion – is that of 'academic tribes' (Becher 1989). In this view social anthropology and sociology can be seen as two neighbouring and historically related academic 'tribes' (or ethnic groups). With environmental change they are increasingly competing – with respect to limited research and teaching opportunities – in and for the same ecological niches. Bearing in mind that anthropological studies of ethnicity suggest that ethnic identity is often hierarchically segmentary, it is plausible to argue that while social anthropology excludes sociology, sociology includes social anthropology; while sociology embraces all of the methods and most of the concerns of anthropology, the reverse is not true. Social anthropology can thus be analogized as an exclusive and specialized sub-section or clan of the greater sociological tribe.

Lest this view be thought too extreme, or perhaps even flippant, consider the following definition of sociology, offered by the late Roy Wallis, writing in the *The Times Higher Education Supplement* on 18 April 1986, a time when sociology was having to justify itself in an altogether hostile British political climate:

> Sociology is not only about translating the manners and mores of alien life and sub-culture into the language and sensibility of the rest, it is about making strange and problematic what we already know, questioning the assumptions long held in our community deriving their strength from prejudice and tradition rather than open-minded observation. And making the strange, the foreign, obvious, enabling us to see how reasonable people starting from the point they do, could come to live and think this way; and making what has hitherto seemed obvious in our own society problematic, to question how and why it is done, providing the opportunity for reappraisal or greater understanding of our own behaviour, seems to me a socially and morally worthwhile purpose.

This is, admittedly, only one view of sociology. Any such definition, in a discipline famous for differences of opinion if not discord, must be. But it sketches out a broad intellectual enterprise with which most – if not all – social anthropologists would feel utterly at home. In the context of the present discussion, it eloquently emphasizes the essentially sociological character of social anthropology.

This doesn't mean, however, that sociology and social anthropology are the same thing. They clearly are not (quite). The differences of emphasis between them, when taken together, constitute a specifically anthropological point of view:

> Our emphasis on pluralism, our understanding of culture, our appreciation for the informant's perspective . . . add up to a distinctive perspective. (Blakey *et al.* 1994: 302)

A minimalist disciplinary model of this kind is what I have in mind when I persist in seeing myself as an anthropologist: comparative, epistemologically relativist, methodologically holistic, focusing on culture and meaning, stressing local perceptions and knowledge, and documenting the routine of everyday life. This is the specifically anthropological version of the sociological imagination.

However, if the notion of anthropology as a segment of sociology is right, and given the situation in which it finds itself, we need to do more than establish sufficient differences between sociology and social anthropology to allow the latter a distinct intellectual identity. Anthropology is still faced with a problem, which the following summarizes nicely:

> it is not a crisis of *representation* which now threatens our discipline but a problem of *relevance*. Social anthropology as we know it is in danger of becoming marginalized and redundant unless it adapts to the changing world

which now threatens to undermine its cherished theories, methods and practices, This means, above all, re-evaluating its conventional objects of study and developing new domains and methods of inquiry that are commensurate with the new subjects and social forces that are emerging in the contemporary world . . . anthropology's image as a discipline still primarily concerned with exotic, small-scale disappearing worlds must be complemented – perhaps even supplanted – by greater concern with 'emerging worlds', the culture of the 'colonizers' as well as those of the colonized, and on subject areas that cannot be defined by traditional fieldwork methods alone. (Ahmed and Shore 1995: 14–16)

Apart from wanting to insist that the problem of anthropological relevance is neither new nor even particularly recent – a small minority of anthropologists, some of them eminent within the discipline, have been pursuing the approach advocated by Ahmed and Shore for many years now – this, it seems to me, pretty much hits the nail on the head.

The rest of this book should be read, therefore, not only as a rethinking of ethnicity, but also as a contribution to the rethinking of anthropology. To the development of an anthropology that is unapologetically at home in large-scale, metropolitan, industrialized societies. An anthropology that is sure of its epistemological ground when using survey methods, archival sources, relying on secondary material, or whatever. A discipline that is defined not by its methods or by its places of work, but by its *concerns* and, above all, by its *point of view*.

Locating ethnicity

So, what do anthropologists mean when they talk about ethnicity? What does anyone mean when they talk about ethnicity? The word comes from the ancient Greek *ethnos*, which seems to have referred to a range of situations in which a collectivity of humans lived and acted together (Østergård 1992a: 32), and which is typically translated today as 'people' or 'nation'. Since the early decades of this century, the linked concepts of ethnicity and ethnic group have been taken in many directions, academically (Stone 1996) and otherwise. They have passed into everyday discourse, and become central to the politics of group differentiation and advantage, in the culturally diverse social democracies of Europe and North America. With notions of 'race' in public and scientific disrepute since 1945, ethnicity has obligingly stepped into the gap, becoming a rallying cry in the often bloody reorganization of the post-Cold-War world. The obscenity of 'ethnic cleansing' stands shoulder to shoulder with earlier euphemisms such as 'racial hygiene' and 'the final solution'.

So it is important to be clear about what our subject – ethnicity – is and about what it is not. An early and influential sociological reference to ethnic groups, and the ultimate rootstock of the argument which I will develop in subsequent chapters, can be found in Max Weber's *Economy and Society*, first published in 1922 (1978: 385–98). An ethnic group is based, in this view, on the *belief* shared by its members that, however distantly, they are of common descent. This may or may not derive from what Weber calls 'anthropological type' (i.e. 'race', embodied difference or phenotype):

> race creates a 'group' only when it is subjectively perceived as a common trait: this happens only when a neighbourhood or the mere proximity of racially different persons is the basis of joint (mostly political) action, or conversely, when some common experiences of members of the same race are linked to some antagonism against members of an *obviously* different group. (1978: 385)

Perhaps the most significant part of Weber's argument is that:

> ethnic membership does not constitute a group; it only facilitates group formation of any kind, particularly in the political sphere. On the other hand, it is primarily the political community, no matter how artificially organized, that inspires the belief in common ethnicity. (1978: 389)

Weber seems to be suggesting that the belief in common ancestry is likely to be a *consequence* of collective political action rather than its *cause*; people come to see themselves as *belonging* together – coming from a common background – as a consequence of *acting* together. Collective interests thus do not simply reflect or follow from similarities and differences between people; the pursuit of collective interests does, however, encourage ethnic identification.

In terms of collective action, this sense of ethnic communality is a form of monopolistic social closure: it defines membership, eligibility and access. Any cultural trait in common can provide a basis and resources for ethnic closure: language, ritual, economic way of life, lifestyle more generally, and the division of labour, are all likely possibilities in this respect. Shared language and ritual are particularly implicated in ethnicity: mutual 'intelligibility of the behaviour of others' is a fundamental prerequisite for any group, as is the shared sense of what is 'correct and proper' which constitutes individual 'honour and dignity'. By this token, an ethnic group is a particular form of *status group*. Finally, Weber argues that since the possibilities for collective action rooted in ethnicity are 'indefinite', the *ethnic group*, and its close relative the *nation*, cannot easily be precisely defined for sociological purposes.

The next significant sociological contribution to our understanding of ethnicity came in an undeservedly somewhat neglected short paper by the Chicago sociologist Everett Hughes, first published in 1948 (1994: 91–6). Hughes had clearly read Weber, and he rejected a commonsensical or ethnological understanding based simply on distinctive 'cultural traits':

> An ethnic group is not one because of the degree of measurable or observable difference from other groups: it is an ethnic group, on the contrary, because the people in it and the people out of it know that it is one; because both the *ins* and the *outs* talk, feel, and act as if it were a separate group. This is possible only if there are ways of telling who belongs to the group and who does not, and if a person learns early, deeply, and usually irrevocably to what group he belongs. If it is easy to resign from the group, it is not truly an ethnic group. (1994: 91)

His argument can be paraphrased thus: ethnic cultural differences are a function of 'group-ness', the existence of a group is not a reflection of cultural difference. Furthermore, ethnic groups imply ethnic relations, and ethnic relations involve at least two collective parties, they are not unilateral. Identity is a matter of the *outs* as well as the *ins*. A concomitant of this point of view is the injunction that we should not, for example, study a *minority* group – which is, after all, a relational notion – without also studying the *majority*:

> if the groups in question have enough relations to be a nuisance to each other it is because they form a part of a whole, that they are in some sense and in some measure members of the same body. (1994: 95)

In Weber and Hughes we can see the early sociological emergence of the social constructionist model of ethnicity which anthropologists have so strikingly made their own. From this point of view, ethnic groups are what people believe or think them to be; cultural differences mark 'group-ness', they do not cause it (or indelibly characterize it); ethnic identification arises out of and within interaction between groups.

The notion of ethnicity did not, however, come into widespread anthropological use until the 1960s, beginning in the United States. Within American anthropology, the increasing use of an ethnicity model was part of a long-term, and gradual, shift of analytical framework, from 'race' to 'culture' to 'ethnicity' (Wolf 1994). It can also be interpreted as a change – about which more in Chapter 2 – in the conceptualization of one of the basic units of anthropological analysis, from the 'tribe' to the 'ethnic group'. More recently, the unit of analysis in this respect has widened further, to reflect a growing concern with the 'nation' and the processes whereby ethnic groups and categories are incorporated into states (Eriksen 1993a; Verdery 1994; B. Williams 1989). It is now anthropological common sense to consider ethnicity and nationalism in the same analytical breath, although 'race', as we shall see, is more problematic. The study of ethnicity – and nationalism – has become one of the major growth areas within the discipline, 'a lightning rod for anthropologists trying to redefine their theoretical and methodological approaches' (B. Williams 1989: 401).

Being a growth area has encouraged a healthy diversity: the anthropological model of ethnicity is a relatively broad church which allows a wide range of phenomena under its roof. What is more, it remains firmly grounded in empirical research. In this field as in others, social anthropologists are most concerned to get on with writing in detail about everyday life in specific local contexts. This is what anthropologists see themselves as doing best (and in this they are probably right). There is little in anthropology to compare, for example, with the abstraction of a recent sociological debate about the relationship between 'race', racism and ethnicity (Anthias 1992; Mason 1994). At the level of meta-theory, however, it is perhaps worth noting that ethnographic texts about specific localities contribute, even if only by default, to the perpetuation of an axiomatic view of the social world as a mosaic of discontinuous and definite cultural *difference*, rather than a seamless web of overlapping and interweaving cultural *variation*.

The strong ethnographic tradition notwithstanding, there is social anthropological theory and there are definitions. Perhaps the most general is the notion of ethnicity as the 'social organization of culture difference' originally proposed by Fredrik Barth's symposium *Ethnic Groups and Boundaries* (1969b), the seminal text from which stems much current anthropological conventional wisdom about ethnicity. In his 'Introduction' to that collection, Barth (1969a) outlined in detail a model of ethnicity which was intended as a corrective to the structural functionalist understanding of the social world – which was at that time still dominant within anthropology – as a system of more or less unproblematic, more or less firmly bounded societies or social groups, which existed as 'social facts', and were, *pace* Durkheim, to be treated or understood as 'things'.

Barth began with what actors believe or think: ascriptions and self-ascriptions. He focused not upon the cultural characteristics of ethnic groups but upon relationships of cultural differentiation; specifically upon contact between collectivities thus differentiated, 'us' and 'them' (Eriksen 1993a: 10–12). The emphasis is not so much upon the *substance* or *content* of ethnicity – what Barth called 'the cultural stuff' – as upon the social processes which produce and reproduce, which organize, boundaries of identification and differentiation between ethnic collectivities:

> we can assume no simple one-to-one relationship between ethnic units and cultural similarities and differences. The features that are taken into account are not the sum of 'objective' differences, but only those which the actors themselves regard as significant . . . some cultural features are used by the actors as signals and emblems of differences, others are ignored, and in some relationships radical differences are played down and denied. (Barth 1969a: 14)

Barth emphasizes that ethnic identity is generated, confirmed or transformed in the course of interaction and transaction between decision-making, strategizing individuals. Ethnicity in *Ethnic Groups and Boundaries* is, perhaps before it is anything else, a matter of politics, decision-making and goal-orientation (and this is the ground over which Barth has been most consistently criticized: as materialist, individualist and narrowly instrumentalist).

Shared culture is, in this model, best understood as generated in and by processes of ethnic boundary maintenance, rather than the other way round: the production and reproduction of difference *vis-à-vis* external others is what creates the image of similarity internally, *vis-à-vis* each other. Barth and his collaborators ushered in an increasing awareness on the part of many anthropologists that culture is a changing, variable and contingent property of interpersonal transactions, rather than a reified entity, 'above' the fray of daily life, which somehow produces behaviour. As Barth has recently suggested, this point of view can be seen as anticipating the postmodern view of culture (Barth 1994: 12). Whatever one might want to make of *that* idea, his understanding of ethnicity has certainly been central to subsequent anthropologizing about ethnicity.

Like Hughes, Barth had clearly read Weber. Having been a student at the University of Chicago in the late 1940s it is likely that he was also familiar with Hughes's work (and he acknowledges the influence of Erving Goffman, one of Hughes's students). Whatever the source – because intellectual lineage is never straightforward – the above quotation from Barth illustrates the striking affinities that the *Ethnic Groups and Boundaries* model of ethnicity has with earlier sociological discussions of ethnicity. It can, in fact, be understood as their development and elaboration.

But Barth's arguments also had more strictly anthropological antecedents. Leach (1954), for example, talked about Kachin identities in Highland Burma as flexible rather than fixed over time, questioning the general utility of the notion of the 'tribe'. Later, Moerman's (1965) discussion of the situational variability of ethnicity in Thailand implicitly anticipated much of Barth's model, and Yehudi Cohen's apparently independent discussion of 'social boundary systems' (1969) is a good example of the extent to which the contributors to *Ethnic Groups and Boundaries* were part of a developing head of disciplinary steam.

Thus, although his is the most systematic model in depth and detail, the most securely grounded in wider theoretical arguments about social forms and social processes (e.g. Barth 1959, 1966), and has certainly been the most influential, Barth was not alone in establishing the current anthropological understanding of ethnicity. Nor is his the only anthropological model of ethnicity to have been influenced by Weber. Reflecting, on the one hand, the ethnographic concern with the everyday lives of concrete subjects – their 'actually existing' social relationships (Radcliffe-Brown 1952: 190) – and, on the other, the pursuit of *verstehen* ('understanding') advocated by Weber and Simmel, Clifford Geertz has elegantly defined ethnicity as the 'world of personal identity collectively ratified and publicly expressed' and 'socially ratified personal identity' (1973: 268, 309). In this view, which will receive further consideration in subsequent chapters, ethnicity has to mean something – in the sense of making a difference – not only to *the people* one is studying, but also to individual *persons*.

What I have called 'the 'basic social anthropological model of ethnicity' can be summarized as follows:

- ethnicity is about cultural differentiation – although, to reiterate the main theme of *Social Identity* (Jenkins 1996), identity is always a dialectic between similarity and difference;
- ethnicity is centrally concerned with culture – shared meaning – but it is also rooted in, and to a considerable extent the outcome of, social interaction;
- ethnicity is no more fixed or unchanging than the culture of which it is a component or the situations in which it is produced and reproduced;

- ethnicity as a social identity is collective and individual, externalized in social interaction and internalized in personal self-identification.

A word about culture – and a minor caveat – is appropriate before going further. The implicit understanding of culture upon which this model depends is considerably narrower than the general-purpose model of culture – as the definitive characteristic of human beings, the capacity for which unites us all in essential similarity – to which neophyte anthropologists are quickly introduced, often in the shape of Sir Edward Tylor's famous and time-honoured omnibus definition. Here, instead of *culture*, we find a model of different *cultures*, of social differentiation based on language, religion, cosmology, symbolism, morality, and ideology. It is a model that leads occasionally to the problematic appearance that culture is different from, say, politics or economic activity (when, in fact, they are all cultural phenomena). In this, the model is revealed as the analytical analogue of everyday notions of ethnic differentiation. This should be borne in mind in reading the discussions of 'the cultural stuff' in subsequent chapters.

The general model of ethnicity I have outlined is supported to some degree by most social anthropologists interested in the topic. I will elaborate upon it in subsequent chapters, and introduce some important qualifications and modifications. However, it is not my intention to provide a comprehensive survey of the expanding anthropological literature about ethnicity. Several, generally complementary, essays into this territory are already available (Banks 1996; Cohen 1978; Eriksen 1993a; B. Williams 1989) and little would be served by competing with them. However, the fact that lots of anthropologists are talking to each other about ethnicity, combined with the disciplinary enthusiasm for detailed ethnography rather than theory, may lead to some things being taken for granted. Among these things are the definition of anthropology, and, more important, the definition of ethnicity, both of which have already been discussed. A further problem, however, is the perpetual need to struggle against our tendency to reify culture and ethnicity. Although we talk about them in these terms endlessly, neither culture nor ethnicity is 'something' that people 'have', or, indeed, to which they 'belong'. They are, rather, complex repertoires which people experience, use, learn and 'do' in their daily lives, within which they construct an ongoing sense of themselves and an understanding of their fellows.

One possible consequence of this reification is the construction of ethnicity as typically – or even only – an attribute of the Other. Ethnicity thus becomes something which characterizes other people rather than ourselves. We need, however, to remind ourselves all the time that each of *us* participates in an ethnicity – perhaps more than one – just like *them*, just like the Other, just like 'the minorities'. Some of us, members of those 'ethnic minorities', perhaps, or coming from ethnically marked peripheries – such as, in the British Isles, Wales, Ireland, or Scotland – may know this only too well. However, for others it can be a very difficult thing to appreciate. Yet its appreciation is arguably the first step towards understanding the ubiquity and the shifting salience of ethnic identification. Recognizing that ethnocentrism is routine and understandable, as routine and understandable as the invisibility of one's own identity, does not absolve us from the need either to struggle against it, or to make ourselves more visible (*to* ourselves).

Although, as good social scientists, we may pooh-pooh its reality or distance ourselves from it by recourse to irony, our national identity or 'character' may be easier to perceive than our ethnicity. Nationalism and the construction of national identity are, after all, explicit projects of the state. If nothing else, we have passports. The contours and contents of national identity are likely to be more visible, as are the contexts of its uses and justifications. And even if, as good anthropologists, we may not have to remind ourselves of the socially constructed character of national identity and sentiment, there is certainly a job to be done in keeping that idea as firmly in the public eye as possible.

Because that idea is undoubtedly important. Although it is welcome, we should not really *need* Eric Wolf's argument (1994) that 'race', 'culture' and 'people' are 'perilous ideas'. We *should* know this. Newscasts if not history should have taught us it long ago. Which is what makes anthropological research and teaching about ethnicity both urgent and troublesome. Because of its comparative global reach and its local-level research focus, its emphasis upon culture as well as social construction, its capacity to see individual trees as well as the collective wood, anthropology offers a promise to the world beyond the academy: to relativize notions about ethnicity and to resist the naturalization or the taking for granted of ethnic identity and nationalist ideology.

There is still some way to go, however, and some conceptual clarification, before we can live up to that promise. This book is offered as a contribution to that clarification. It should be read as part of an ongoing enterprise. It is, hence – and perhaps all theoretical texts should declare themselves in this way – self-consciously provisional (although this doesn't mean that it is merely tentative). I hope that the fact that it is something of a *bricolage* – a computer-age assemblage, manipulation and reconstruction of an existing body of papers – has not resulted in too much repetition or overlap in the arguments, and that the reader will bear with me where they occur.

2

From Tribes to Ethnic Groups

Until relatively recently, social anthropologists studying ethnicity and inter-group relations have typically concentrated upon ethnicity as a corporate social phenomenon. They have oriented themselves to the identification and understanding of ethnic groups, as distinct-from-each-other culture-bearing collectivities. This approach still characterizes the working practices of many anthropologists, even if only tacitly. This ontology of the social world emerged from the social anthropological preoccupation – itself a legacy of the long-standing and disproportionate theoretical sway exercised by structural functionalism during the discipline's formative years – with social groups and their systematic interrelationships, and with social order and integration.

To an audience that has, perhaps, allowed itself to become over-impressed by the postmodern fluidity and evanescence of the social world and its conventions, these concerns may appear to be *passé* or quaint. However, they continue to inform many of the presumptions and founda-tional axioms of anthropology as a generalizing study of human social life. Nor are they in themselves either stupid or disreputable. The social world is, among other things, a world of institutionalized social groups; in that world there is system; nor are order and integration absent or insignificant. It is the preoccupation with, and the taking for granted of, these dimen-sions of the social world, to the exclusion or marginalization of other things – non-corporate collectivities, transient and heterodox improvisation, disorder, disintegration, conflict – which is problematic. The preoccupation and the taking for granted were what Barth was writing against in the 'Introduction' to *Ethnic Groups and Boundaries*.

During the colonial and immediately post-colonial periods, social anthro-pology's theoretical preoccupation with corporate groups and integrated social systems was manifest in an orthodox assumption that the subject matter of the discipline – 'primitive' peoples (Firth 1958: 6) – was most commonly organized into tribal groups. Indeed, as in the following quotation from one of the founders of the ethnographic method, the notion of 'the tribe', as a real, perduring social entity, was central to the theoretical and the methodological development of social anthropology:

> [The modern ethnographer] with his tables of kinship terms, genealogies, maps, plans and diagrams, proves the existence of an extensive and big organisation, shows the constitution of the tribe, of the clan, of the family . . . The Ethno-grapher has in the field, according to what has just been said, the duty before him of drawing up all the rules and regularities of tribal life; all that is permanent and

fixed; of giving an anatomy of their culture, of depicting the constitution of their society. (Malinowski 1922: 10, 11)

In one move, the concept of the tribe accomplished two important things: in the first place, it distanced tribal society from civilized society, in both commonsensical and analytical discourse; in the second, it provided the anthropologist with a theoretical model of the nature of 'non-civilized' social organization which could serve both to organize ethnographic data and function as a framework for the cross-cultural comparison of 'primitive social organization'. Thus, while on the one hand the difference between 'them' and 'us' was being established, on the other, the basic similarity between different sorts of 'them' was being proclaimed.

One of the earliest anthropologists to cast doubt upon the usefulness of the notion of the tribe was Edmund Leach, in his study of inter-group relations in northern Burma. To paraphrase, Leach argued that tribes as discrete bounded entities were essentially analytical models – developed by anthropologists or other outsiders, for their own purposes – rather than locally meaningful principles of everyday social organization in practice:

the mere fact that two groups of people are of different culture does not necessarily imply – as has nearly always been assumed – that they belong to two quite different social systems. (Leach 1954: 17)

Locals might talk about themselves *as if* there were clear-cut collective identities and entities, but everyday interaction and organization revealed a more complex pattern of overlap and variation, the reality of which was *also* recognized by locals. While hinting at a more general theoretical problem (1954: 281–2), Leach attributed the difficulty in the first instance to ethnographic specifics: anthropology 'in the classic manner which treated culture groups as social isolates' was impossible in the Kachin Hills, due to the fact that 'named groups culturally or partly distinct' were often 'all jumbled up' (1954: 60).

By the 1960s the notion of 'the tribe' was beginning to be replaced by the, perhaps less embarrassingly colonial, 'ethnic group'. However, the underlying presumptions had not necessarily changed. The event which most clearly marked the paradigm shift within social anthropology from the study of 'tribal society' to the social constructionist model of 'ethnic groups' which is current today, was the publication of *Ethnic Groups and Boundaries* (Barth 1969b). For Barth, the issue was not whether local ethnography fitted the model. The problem was inherent in the presumption of 'distinct named groups'. In saying this his argument was in harmony with a growing body of critique which, *contra* structural functionalism, had begun to explore the important place of non-corporate collectivities in social life: networks (Barnes 1954; Mitchell 1969), non-groups (Boissevain 1968), and action sets and quasi-groups (Mayer 1966), for example.

Barth identified four theoretical features of the conventional, taken-for-granted model of the corporate, culturally distinct ethnic group (1969a:

10–11). First, such a group was biologically self-perpetuating; second, members of the group shared basic cultural values, manifest in overt cultural forms; third, the group was a bounded social field of communication and interaction; and, fourth, its members identified themselves, and were identified by others, as belonging to that group:

> This ideal type definition is not so far removed in content from the traditional proposition that a race = a culture = a language and that a society = a unit which rejects or discriminates against others . . . we are led to imagine each group developing its cultural and social form in relative isolation . . . a world of separate peoples, each with their culture and each organized in a society which can legitimately be isolated for description as an island to itself. (Barth 1969a: 11)

It would be wrong to present the tribe-group model that Barth was criticizing as an explicit analytical framework. It wasn't; it was implicitly embedded in most ethnographic studies, never being examined or seriously questioned. But it was there, and the kind of problem that this taken-for-granted understanding of collective identity has bequeathed to latter-day interpreters of the classic ethnographies is well illustrated by the controversy surrounding the question of whether the Nuer of the southern Sudan – as documented by Evans-Pritchard (1940) – are, in fact, really the Dinka (Newcomer 1972), or whether they are both distinct components of a single plural society (Glickman 1972).[1]

In Barth's model, ethnicity, the boundaries of ethnic groups, and hence their ontological status as collectivities, are not to be treated as 'hard' or accepted uncritically as a fixed aspect of the social reality in question. Barth insisted that ethnic identity, and its production and reproduction in routine social interaction, must be treated as essentially problematic features of social reality, emergent properties of everyday life. The ethnographer must examine the practices and processes whereby ethnicity and ethnic boundaries are socially constructed. And the starting point for such an examination must be an acknowledgement that 'ethnic groups are categories of ascription and identification by the actors themselves' (Barth 1969a: 10).

To make use of a distinction first developed by Raymond Firth (1961: 28), it appears that Barth and his colleagues had shifted the theoretical emphasis, from the evocation of tribal identity as a defining feature of *social structure*, to a recognition of ethnic identity as an aspect of *social organization*. In addition, as Ronald Cohen pointed out (1978: 384), while the earliest anthropological notions of ethnic groups still typically implied that such groups were isolated, primitive-atavistic, or non-Western, the shift of emphasis signalled by *Ethnic Groups and Boundaries* involved 'fundamental changes in anthropological perspectives', from a Western interest in the uncivilized peoples of the colonies and ex-colonies, to a more equitable concern with the heterogeneity of all societies.

Returning to the terms of Barth's critique of the traditional model, several features of the emergent alternative analytical framework are worth highlighting. In the first place, the analysis of ethnicity starts from the definition of the situation held by social actors. Second, the focus of attention then becomes the maintenance of ethnic boundaries: the structured interaction between 'us' and 'them' which takes place across the boundary. Third, ethnic identity depends on ascription, both by members of the ethnic group in question and by outsiders. Fourth, ethnicity is not fixed; it is situationally defined. Fifth, ecological issues are particularly influential in determining ethnic identity, inasmuch as competition for economic niches plays an important role in the generation of ethnicity.

The origins of this understanding of ethnicity can be traced as far back as Max Weber, as argued in the previous chapter. In laying it out as explicitly as he did, introducing it to a new audience, and developing it within an anthropological context, Barth sketched out the essentials of the model of ethnicity that has dominated discussion of the topic within European and North American anthropology in subsequent decades:

> there is little doubt that Barth's introduction to *Ethnic groups and boundaries* holds a special place. More than any other text, it has become the symbolic marker of the changes to which it contributed substantially . . . The shift from a static to an interactional approach was accomplished by differentiating the notion of ethnicity from that of culture. Barth presented ethnicity or ethnic identity as an aspect of social organization, not of culture. (Vermeulen and Govers 1994: 2)

In British social anthropology, the development of the ethnicity model can be exemplified by looking at the work of Michael Banton and Sandra Wallman. In his original formulations Banton (1967) argued that 'race'[2] is used as a role sign. Social groups are unities which appear in response to various stimuli to alignment, and 'race' is a visible marker of status and role as functions of group membership. The notion of ethnicity is here combined with a status-attainment model of stratification. The emphasis is upon inter-ethnic behaviour as transactional, albeit within a social context of stratification and/or coercion. Subsequently, Banton developed a 'rational choice' model of inter-ethnic relations (1983), which sought to integrate the study of ethnicity and nationalism with the study of 'race relations'. This analytical framework is founded on four premises: one, human beings act in order to maximize their net advantage; two, social action has a cumulative effect, inasmuch as present actions limit or constrain subsequent actions; three, actors utilize physical or cultural differences to generate social groups and categories; and, four, when relationships between groups which are held to be physically distinctive are determined by an imbalance of power, 'racial' categories are created.

Banton's ideas rest on many of the same underlying assumptions as Barth's, and presumably share some of the same Weberian roots. However, the relation between the analyses of Barth and Wallman is a good deal more intimate (Wallman 1978, 1979, 1986). Locating her arguments explicitly within the Barthian framework, Wallman argues that:

> ethnicity is the process by which 'their' difference is used to enhance the sense of 'us' for purposes of organisation or identification . . . Because it takes two,

ethnicity can only happen at the boundary of 'us', in contact or confrontation or by contrast with 'them'. And as the sense of 'us' changes, so the boundary between 'us' and 'them' shifts. Not only does the boundary shift, but the criteria which mark it change. (Wallman 1979: 3)

By this definition ethnicity is transactional, shifting and essentially impermanent. Ethnic boundaries are always two-sided, and one of the key issues becomes the manipulation of perceived significant differences in their generation. Furthermore, Wallman considers it 'useful to set the ethnic/ racial quibble aside and to consider simply how social boundaries are marked' (1978: 205); having once done so, there is an effective concentration in her work upon the mobilization of social (ethnic) identity as a resource with respect to social support, solidarity, communication and economic cooperation.

Moving away from the narrow orbit of specifically British social anthropology, the ethnicity paradigm was usefully developed by Don Handelman (1977), in an article which speaks to a number of the issues with which this book is concerned. Handelman began by acknowledging the Barthian importance of boundaries and the situational negotiability of ethnic membership. However, he criticizes Barth for confusing 'the idea of "group" with the ascription of social categories which are everpresent features of the process of interaction' (1977: 187), a comment which is similar to an earlier sceptical assessment of Barth by Abner Cohen: 'At most, what we are establishing . . . is the simple fact that ethnic categories exist' (1974: xiii). Handelman further suggests that Barth, in assuming or overstressing the necessity of 'group-ness' to ethnic identification, is failing to appreciate that:

'Cultural stuff' . . . and ethnic boundary mutually modify and support one another. The former establishes and legitimizes the contrast of the boundary; while the latter, often in response to external conditions, modifies or alters the relevance to the boundary of aspects of the former. (1977: 200)

Thus, for Handelman, the cultural content of ethnicity is an important aspect of its social organization: a crude dichotomy between the cultural and the social is misleading. Acknowledging the influence of Boissevain's discussion of 'non groups' (1968), Handelman argues further that ethnicity is socially organized or incorporated in differing degrees of intensity and territoriality – differing degrees of group-ness, if you like – on which depends its salience and importance in individual experience. Moving from 'the casual to the corporate', Handelman distinguishes the *ethnic set*,[3] the *ethnic category*, the *ethnic network*, the *ethnic association* and the *ethnic community*. Ethnic identities can, for example, organize everyday life without ethnic *groups* featuring locally as significant social forms.

Handelman is also concerned with the relationship between ethnicity and other identities. He distinguishes 'lateral' from 'hierarchical' arrangements of categorical membership. Laterally arranged identities are of more or less equal significance and individuals may be categorized in different ways in different situations: their occupation or class may be most important in one situation, their religion in another, and their ethnicity in another. In a hierarchical arrangement, however, one category will tend to dominate or colour all others. 'Race' is a potent example of a hierarchically dominant ethnic category set (1977: 193).

In reviewing the social anthropological ethnicity paradigm, its positive aspects and its achievements require emphasis first. Inasmuch as it stresses social processes and the practices of actors, the approach has encouraged a move away from various strands of determinism which were influential during the 1970s and early 1980s. Similarly, the emphasis upon the social construction of ethnic or 'racial' categories discourages the intrusion of biologically based conceptions of 'race' into social analysis. Finally, the importance that is attached to the views and self-perceptions of social actors themselves – the folk view of ethnic identity – should lead us away from the taken-for-granted ethnocentrism of much social science. These are all important gains; an emphasis on looking at ethnicity from an inter-actional perspective marked a useful departure from previous approaches to the study of inter-group relations, and remains central and valuable today.

However, the ethnicity paradigm – the 'basic social anthropological model of ethnicity' outlined in Chapter 1 – seems often to have suffered at the hands of those who have most wholeheartedly embraced it. Pursuing a theme similar to Handelman's, Ronald Cohen (1978: 386–7) argues that, in stressing concepts such as 'group', 'category' and 'boundary', and processes of 'maintenance', Barth, despite his obvious intentions to the contrary, has contributed to the further reification of the ethnic group as a perduring corporate entity. In particular, the notion of the 'boundary', with its spatial and physical overtones, allows the superficial or the careless to celebrate the situational flexibility of ethnicity without taking on board the more difficult questions – about the nature of collective social forms – in which Barth is interested. In their enthusiasm for processes of boundary maintenance, negotiation and strategizing, many of those whose analyses owe much – if not everything – to Barth have taken for granted what he did not, i.e. the 'group' that is the object of the research.

Four other criticisms are worth brief consideration at this point. First, there is the apparent difficulty experienced by many anthropologists in handling the distinction between the ethnic and the 'racial'. Banks suggests (1996: 97–100), that the most typical anthropological response to this problem is either to ignore it, or just to mention it in passing. It is certainly not sufficient to adopt Wallman's solution, and simply dismiss the distinc-tion as 'a quibble'. John Rex has argued, for example, that we must pay attention to the importance and significance of folk 'racial' categorizations, because:

> a far wider set of situations are based upon cultural differentiation of groups than those which are commonly called racial and . . . few of them have anything like the same conflictual consequences that racial situations do. (Rex 1973: 184)

Since Rex wrote that, events have somewhat caught up with the second part of his argument: the Balkans, Northern Ireland – one could doubtless cite other ethnic conflicts which seem to give it the lie. But it is really only *somewhat* and only *seem*. Ethnicity is still a wider classificatory or organizational principle than 'race', and it remains true that few ethnic conflicts are as bloody as 'racial' ones (the comparison between the former Yugoslavia and Rwanda is depressingly instructive here).[4] Furthermore, the boundary between 'race' and ethnicity is historically variable; what was 'racial' before 1945 may be more publicly acceptable as 'ethnic' today.

This is not just an issue concerning the categories with which social anthropologists – perhaps because of an ex-colonial collective guilt complex – feel comfortable. It leads on to the second criticism of the anthropological approach to ethnicity: the unease which many anthropologists appear to feel when forced to recognize the question of power imbalances. This seems to be the basis for the anthropological celebration of ethnicity as a positive social resource. This criticism is related to the first: to take Banton's point – and Rex's – 'racial' categories and racism are characteristic of situations of domination. It is not, however, an inescapable theoretical weakness of the general approach: one of the papers in *Ethnic Groups and Boundaries* was, for example, concerned with ethnic identity as a social stigma (Eidheim 1969). A third criticism is similarly bound up with the previous two: the relative lack of theoretical attention which has been given to the points of difference and similarity between ethnicity, on the one hand, and class and stratification, on the other (cf. Eriksen 1993a: 50– 4). Finally, it is worth pointing out that stressing, as Barth does, the orientations, values and goals of actors – particularly members of ethnic minorities – can seem to be somehow blaming the victims for their own disadvantage (Bourne and Sivanandan 1980: 345). Which is, of course, paradoxical: the very point of view which can offer a powerful counter-weight to ethnocentrism may, at the same time, appear to admit prejudice by the back door. This point resembles closely those criticisms of Barth which indict him in general terms for an a-sociological individualism, a neglect of power and 'structural' constraints, and an overemphasis on narrow instrumentality (e.g. Evens 1977; Kapferer 1976; Paine 1974; for a response, see Barth 1981: 76–104).

None of these, however, is an inherent flaw in the ethnicity paradigm, about which nothing can be done. Quite the reverse in fact. If they are indeed weaknesses, they derive from aspects of social anthropology – a preoccupation with social integration and consensus, and the theoretical constitution of the social world in terms of corporate groups – which have long been contested within the discipline itself,[5] and against which Barth's arguments were originally formulated. A solution to both of these problems may be found in the theorization of the distinction between groups and categories in the context of inter-ethnic relations, a distinction which is elided in the bald assertions by Barth and Wallman that ethnicity depends on ascription from *both* sides of the group boundary. It is important to distinguish in principle between two analytically distinct processes of ascription: *group identification* and *social categorization*. The first occurs *inside* the ethnic boundary, the second *outside* and across it.

Social categorization, in particular, is intimately bound up with power relations and relates to the capacity of one group successfully to impose its categories of ascription upon another set of people, and to the resources which the categorized collectivity can draw upon to resist, if need be, that imposition. To acknowledge the significance of the distinction between the group identification and categorization is to place relationships of domination and subordination on the theoretical centre-stage. By so doing, it seems likely that the problem of 'blaming the victim' can be more easily avoided.

Similarly, reference to the distinction between groups and categories may allow us to clarify, even if only to some extent, the contrast between ethnicity and 'race'. Banton has argued that ethnicity is generally more concerned with the identification of 'us', while racism is more oriented to the categorization of 'them' (1983: 106). From this point of view ethnicity depends of necessity upon group identification, while 'race' or racism is most typically a matter of social categorization. Such an understanding is only helpful, however, if qualified. If nothing else, the point must be made that group identification and social categorization are inextricably linked: logically, inasmuch as similarity entails difference, and inclusion entails exclusion, and processually, with respect to individual as well as collective identities (Jenkins 1996). Furthermore while, on the one hand, hostile categorization with reference to putative ethnic or cultural criteria is commonplace, on the other, groups may come to identify themselves positively in 'racial' terms, as in the more or less supremacist ideologies of societies such as Imperial Britain, Nazi Germany, Japan pre-1945, or the South Africa of apartheid.

Thus although group identification and social categorization are distinct processes, each – and to insist on this is to make a partial return to the conventional wisdom of the ethnicity paradigm – is routinely implicated in the other. Ethnicity may, for example, be strengthened or generated as a response to categorization; similarly, an aspect of one group's ethnicity may be, indeed is likely to be, the categories with which it labels other groups or collectivities. In each of these cases the absolute centrality of power relationships – a centrality which many ethnicity theorists have been reluctant to include in their analyses – must be acknowledged.

To return briefly to the quotation from John Rex, it appears that ethnicity is a more general social phenomenon than racism or 'racial' categorization. It is equally clear that ethnicity, although its emphasis may conventionally be thought to fall upon group identification, is routinely implicated, through the signification of cultural or ethnic markers, in processes of categorization. Bearing these considerations in mind, racism may be understood as a historically specific facet of the more general social phenomenon of ethnicity. As such, it characterizes situations in which an ethnic group dominates, or attempts to dominate, another set of people and, in the course of so doing, seeks to impose upon those people a categorical identity which is primarily defined by reference to their purported inherent and immutable differences from, and/or inferiority to, the dominating group. Viewed from this perspective, the distinction between ethnicity and 'race' is indeed something more than a quibble; it is deserving of the most serious attention (cf. Miles 1982: 44–71; Rex 1986: 18–37; M.G. Smith 1986: 188–94).

Despite the criticisms of the basic social anthropological model of ethnicity which I have discussed in this chapter, it remains – in its generic emphasis upon social construction, its recognition of fluidity as well as solidity, and its refusal to biologize or naturalize what are socio-cultural phenomena – arguably the best approach to the topic. Before exploring some possible avenues for its development, there are questions which require further introductory attention: the interrelationship of different ethnic identities within one societal framework, the relationship of ethnicity to other kinds of social identity with which it might be thought to have affinities, and, following on from these, the 'nature' of ethnicity.

3

Myths of Pluralism

Just as the conceptual replacement of the 'tribe' by the 'ethnic group' was central to a post-colonial shift in the moral and philosophical centre of gravity of social anthropology, so the development of the notion of the 'plural society' also reflected the loss of empire and a changing post-war world. And, once again, the model emerged out of social anthropology's linked concerns with social groups as the basic unit of analysis and with processes of social integration.

The notion of pluralism or the 'plural society' was a response to two distinct, if not dissimilar, problems. Colonial territories, for example many British possessions in Africa and elsewhere, were often governed by means of a system of indirect rule, through native courts and chiefs. Different collectivities – 'tribes' – were integrated into the colonial administrative framework through different sets of institutions and administered according to localized and conflicting bodies of custom and law. How was one to conceptualize the convergence of these separate institutional systems – one (or more than one) for the tribespeople, another (or others) for the Europeans and the urbanized intermediate groups – into a coherent and integrated social system?

A very different situation pertained in those colonial territories which were, by contrast, basically unitary institutional systems for the purposes of politics and government. In these systems the indigenous peoples, although contained within and controlled by the state, were rarely, if at all, considered to be jurally adult members of the polity. As the twentieth century drew towards its mid-point this situation began increasingly to exhibit signs of change. Black people, in short, were moving from subjection to citizenship. The meek, it appeared, were about to (re)inherit their particular bits of the earth. But what would be the political structure of the resultant new nation-states?

Both of these questions spoke to the same historical trend: the creation, by the European powers, of colonies or other dependent territories – and, later, emergent new states – whose internationally recognized boundaries bore little or no resemblance to the local spatial arrangements of ethnic identity or cultural continuity and discontinuity. As such, they lacked the clear-cut homogeneous national identities which at that time still seemed to characterize the established states of the Old World. Social anthropologists had to develop a new analytical model in order to understand the changing situation.

In fact, they didn't develop a new model. They turned to political science instead. The notion of 'pluralism' and the concept of the 'plural society' have their origins in Furnivall's analysis of colonial policy in South East Asia in the 1940s (Furnivall 1948). The social anthropologists who are perhaps most closely associated with the elaboration of his ideas are M.G. Smith, in the context of West Africa and the Caribbean (Smith 1965, 1974), and Leo Kuper, in his studies of South Africa and other African states (Kuper 1971; Kuper and Smith 1969). A number of sociologists have also found the plural society model attractive and useful: Schermerhorn (1978: 122–63) and van den Berghe (1967, 1981) are perhaps deserving of particular mention.

When these writers talk about pluralism, they mean the institutional incorporation of different ethnic groups or collectivities into one societal or state system. In other words, as opposed to the homogeneous nation-state, there is the heterogeneous plural society. Even though the model's initial formulation significantly predated *Ethnic Groups and Boundaries*, the concept of pluralism, as both Barth (1969a: 16) and Cohen (1978: 398) have recognized, sits reasonably comfortably beside the ethnicity paradigm. Logically and theoretically, the progression from an awareness of the importance of ethnicity to the identification of a pluralist social system is an obvious, although not a necessary, step to take. Although relatively few social scientists have been concerned with the theoretical elaboration of formal models of pluralism, the word 'pluralism' has carelessly passed into the lingua franca (or pidgin?) of social anthropologists and others, as a loose and apparently useful descriptive term for labelling all multi-ethnic societies.

There are, however, those who have been concerned with precision in the concept's usage. M.G. Smith (1974: 108–10, 205–39, 341–2) distinguished three types of pluralism. The first of these is *cultural pluralism*, in which, although a society is composed of different ethnic groups, these are not relevant in the political sphere or as a criterion of citizenship. Examples of such a situation are Brazil or, arguably, the United Kingdom. Second, there is *social pluralism*; in this situation, although ethnicity is relevant in terms of political organization, it does not affect citizenship, the incorporation of individual members of ethnic groups into the state. Here one can point to the West Indies, the USSR as was, or Belgium as examples. Finally, Smith talks about *structural pluralism*, where ethnic identity directly affects citizenship and the incorporation of collectivities into full membership of the state, as in the South Africa of apartheid, Israel, the USA (with respect to native Americans), and Burundi. These different kinds of pluralism correspond in an approximate fashion to what Smith describes as different *modes of incorporation*, the principles on the basis of which individuals or collectivities are incorporated into membership of the society: uniform or universalistic, equivalent or segmental, and differential (1974: 333–7). In a later discussion (1986: 194–8), he identifies differential incorporation with *hierarchic plurality*, equivalent/segmental incorporation with *segmental plurality*, and the mixture of both modes of incorporation with *complex plurality*. Finally, to complicate – or confuse – the matter further, Smith also talks about *the* plural society as a generic type, in which cultural diversity is associated with the rule of a dominant minority through the medium of a state system (e.g. 1974: 214).

R.A. Schermerhorn has also attempted to conceptualize pluralism and its varieties with a degree of rigour (1978: 122–5). He distinguishes between *normative pluralism*, which is a political ideology in its own right, *political pluralism*, which describes a society with a multiplicity of political interest groups, *cultural pluralism*, which relates to a multi-ethnic society, and *structural pluralism*, a society which is institutionally internally differentiated in a manner which reflects the differentiation of its population. Although cultural and structural pluralism are analytically distinct, 'they have a dialectical relation of mutual implication in the empirical world' (1978: 127). Since Schermerhorn understands ethnic relations as intimately bound up with relationships of integration and conflict, and with processes of group identification and categorization, cultural and structural pluralism are, from his point of view, necessarily interconnected. In adopting this position his debt to social anthropology is plain; his attempt to analyse conflict in a framework which also explicitly emphasizes an integrative dimension owes something to Max Gluckman's analyses of 'custom and conflict' (Gluckman 1956, 1965).[1] It remains important, however, to distinguish between the models of pluralism put forward by Schermerhorn and Smith; for Smith there is no necessary association 'in the real world' between structural pluralism and cultural pluralism.

Such differences notwithstanding, Smith and Schermerhorn are clearly working within a broad theoretical framework of shared understandings about 'plural societies'. As such there are a number of general criticisms to which they – and other authors such as Kuper and van den Berghe – are equally vulnerable. The most basic of these, following Ronald Cohen (1978: 399), is that the notion of pluralism implies that cultural or political homogeneity – 'monoism', to coin an unlikely neologism – is the social norm. This, of course, harks straight back to the anthropological atom of comparative analysis, the bounded tribal society, discussed in the previous section. In fact, it is poly-ethnic collectivities, with fluid and permeable boundaries, which appear to have been the norm. Neither the isolated tribal group nor the ethnically homogeneous nation-state, to take the extreme 'monoist' theoretical alternatives, is much in evidence in the historical or the contemporary sociological and anthropological records.

A second criticism is that, ultimately, the notion of pluralism is theoretically vapid. The best which can be said is that it is merely profoundly descriptive, going no further than the extensive cataloguing of concrete situations by reference to a classificatory scheme of ideal-typical plural societies, an approach exemplified by van den Berghe (1967: 113–15, 132–48). The classificatory quagmire into which this approach can beguile the analyst is clear from my account of Smith's work, above. A further, related, criticism is that the model resists the incorporation of other principles of stratification – such as class – or of international relations.

Finally, there is a set of trenchant criticisms of the pluralist model made by Heribert Adam, a sociologist who has written extensively about the South Africa of apartheid (Adam 1972; Adam and Giliomee 1979: 42–50). Although not all of these criticisms need detain us here, three are particularly serious. First, Adam argues that the pluralism approach overestimates the autonomy of the segments of a supposedly plural society. It neglects to examine the necessary degree to which they are all reciprocally implicated in a societal framework of common political, social and economic institutions. This is an implicit criticism of the pluralism model which can also emerge from a reading of Gluckman's analysis of inter-ethnic relationships in South Africa (1956: 137–65). Second, the emphasis on cultural and political diversity as the primary sources of heterogeneity ignores the role and importance of economic disparities and inequalities – from Adam's point of view capitalism – in the production of social cleavages. Finally, with respect to Smith's general notion of *the* plural society, Adam denies that there is a necessary association between cultural diversity within the political boundaries of one state and domination by a cultural minority; he argues that such a condition could, in theory, lead just as easily to a system which granted each cultural segment equality of representation.

These criticisms amount to a heavyweight challenge to the pluralist perspective – so substantial that there seem to be no compelling reasons for insisting upon its continued usefulness in the analysis of ethnicity and 'race relations'. This is especially true of the 'strong' version of the pluralist model, articulated by Smith or Kuper, for example. Even with respect to the 'weak' version of the notion – the everyday, almost casual, usage which equates plural societies with multi-ethnicity – if the above criticisms are admissible there are irresistible grounds for removing the word from the social science vocabulary altogether: if, in this sense, all societies are to some extent plural societies, from what is pluralism actually being distinguished?

And, finally, there is another reason, not yet discussed, for dismissing altogether the plural society model. Schermerhorn, as we have already noted, recognizes the ideological or normative uses of the notion; similarly, Adam has highlighted the uses to which the pre-Mandela South African state put the notion of pluralism in legitimizing its apartheid and 'homeland' policies (Adam and Giliomee 1979: 45). This is all the more reason for treating the concept with caution in academic discussions of inter-ethnic relations. If we cannot talk about pluralism without potentially importing into our discourse ideological baggage of this kind, then perhaps we are better not talking about it at all. At the very least, the word deserves to live out its days in the inverted commas which, as with 'race', denote a degree of dissension or controversy.

This does not, however, seem about to happen. If for no other reason, this is because anthropologists[2] continue easily and descriptively to equate pluralism or the 'plural society' with multi-ethnicity (e.g. Barth 1984; Doornbos 1991; Maybury-Lewis 1984; Rapport 1995). But there is another – frequently implicit – notion of pluralism afoot in current debates. This quasi-analytical and normative model, different from the one I have been talking about so far, has enjoyed a vogue under the sign of various strands of postmodern critique. The word 'pluralism' may not always be used, but the impulse and the concerns are unmistakable.

The key to this new discourse of 'pluralism' is a celebration of *difference*: as the site of resistance to Eurocentric and androcentric meta-narratives of history and progress; as a bulwark against fundamentalist images of the world; as an assertion of the rights to autonomous (co-)existence of peripheralized, marginalized, minority-ized peoples; as the inspiration for ethics and politics of representation and diversity which challenge the centralization, the homogenization, the integration, and the domination of – it will come as no surprise after *that* list – the nation, or more particularly the nation-state (e.g. Rutherford 1990).

This multi-faceted strand of argument and debate is an acknowledgement that the world is a less straightforward place than – with the naïvety of a post-war generation which (mis)took the particular world in which it grew up to be the norm rather than the historical exception – we perhaps once thought it was. An acknowledgement which is a reaction to the material and political uncertainties of the post-1989 world, and an attempt to read meaning into the apparently unravelling intellectual project of the Enlightenment. It is a response to the ambiguities and contradictions of relativism, in postmodernism no less than in its immediate ancestor, liberal humanism. It is, finally, a recognition – whether belated or timely is a matter of viewpoint – that culture is definitively socially constructed and arbitrary (Barth 1994: 12).

All of which is welcome. Viewed from such a point of view, cultural and ethical pluralism is a humane and attractive aspiration. But this particular understanding of it is not without problems. Stuart Hall is among the debate's most characteristic and consistent voices. To pay him a doubtful compliment by treating him as an exemplar of key features of a (post)modern discourse with which he may not wholly identify, let us look at his position (see also Hall 1990, 1991). The topic he is addressing is the resurgence of nationalism, apparently against the grain of history:

> Since cultural diversity is, increasingly, the fate of the modern world, and ethnic absolutism a regressive feature of late-modernity, the greatest danger now arises from forms of national and cultural identity – new or old – that attempt to secure their identity by adopting closed versions of culture or community, and by the refusal to engage with the difficult problems that arise from trying to live with difference. (Hall 1992: 8)

A couple of paragraphs later, Hall describes the peoples of the diasporas of 'the South' as:

products of the cultures of hybridity. They bear the traces of particular cultures, traditions, languages, systems of belief, texts and histories which have shaped them . . . They are not and will never be unified in the old sense, because they are inevitably the products of several interlocking histories and cultures, belonging at the same time to several 'homes' – and thus to no one, particular home.

He finishes with a rousing declaration of the need to recognize, and to meet the challenge of, the fact that 'in the modern world identity is always an open, complex, unfinished game – always under construction'.

Running through all of this is the strong suggestion that negotiable, socially constructed identities and cultural diversity – difference, pluralism – are somewhat new phenomena, 'the fate of the modern world'. The mirror image of this is a vision of the past as homogeneous: 'unified in the old sense'. Although he refers approvingly (1992: 6) to Welsh Nationalist politician Dafydd Elis Thomas's view that the 'old' nation-states of the West have always been 'ethnically hybrid – the product of conquests, absorptions of one people by another', what Hall actually offers is a historicism which imagines a pre-modern world of stable culturally unified societies being progressively replaced by a shifting culturally plural modernity. The image of primordial, original 'cultural purity' is further emphasized by Hall's use of 'racial' metaphors such as 'hybridization' and, borrowed from Salman Rushdie, 'mongrelization'.

The arguments against ideas of this kind are in some respects pretty much the same as the critique of the more analytically formal models of pluralism offered earlier. Once again, a model of ethnicity as socially constructed sits easily alongside an understanding of societies as culturally plural. And the reality of 'monoism' which the latter assumes – of a social world which is, or was, an archipelago of discrete, bounded, culturally distinctive and homogeneous units – is no more plausible here than it was there. What is more, the account of modernity which is on offer seems to be blinkered with respect to the past and cross-cultural variation; unsupported by the historical or ethnographic records, it appears to have more rhetorical than analytical power.

South and west Wales as a case in point

The Stuart Hall paper I have just discussed was originally given in Cardiff as the 1992 Raymond Williams Memorial Lecture. There is, therefore, a tidy appropriateness in looking at the issues in a Welsh context.[3] It is even more appropriate given that Wales has actually been characterized, by Giggs and Pattie (1992), as a 'plural society' in terms of ethnicity and class. They argue that this long-standing pluralism is the result of four 'tidal waves' of in-migration from England and elsewhere, beginning in the early Middle Ages. The implication is that before that time Wales was culturally and socially relatively homogeneous. Taking as my particular focus south and west Wales, the geographical bottom half of the Principality which is in many respects distinct from north Wales, I want to argue that the *region* – because to talk about 'Wales' as an entity becomes more and more anachronistic the further back in time one looks – has always been culturally and ethnically heterogeneous, always a 'plural society'.

It has been a very long time since the people of south and west Wales have been able to live their lives solely within the horizons of their local preoccupations and concerns, if indeed that has ever been the case. During the extensive period to which archaeology and history allow us access, the inhabitants of this small part of the world have been in regular contact with the inhabitants of other small parts of the world. Isolation, whether cultural, political or economic, has not been the Welsh lot, nor has cultural homogeneity. As far back as it is possible to look with any clear-sightedness, one finds unambiguous evidence of migration, trade, and extensive cultural diffusion or assimilation.

Following the gradual recession of the glaciers of the last great Ice Age, some time before 12,000 BP (10,000 BC), the area must have been gradually colonized from the south to the north in the first of many successive waves of immigration. These processes of migration have, over the subsequent millennia, resulted in the present-day population of Wales. Perhaps the first immigrants to single out for mention, insofar as they loom so large in the national consciousness of all the peoples of western Britain and Ireland, are the Celts, Iron Age farmers from continental Europe – and originally even further east – who settled in Wales in successive waves between the seventh century BC and the period immediately before the arrival of the Romans. Their mark has perhaps most strikingly been left in the great hill forts and promontory forts of this era: Llanmelin (Gwent), y Bwlwarciau (Mid Glamorgan), Cil Ifor (West Glamorgan) and Carn Goch (Dyfed) are among the better-known examples. In this period may also be found the deepest roots of the modern Welsh language.

In south and west Wales it was the Celtic tribes of the Silures and the Demetae who resisted the Roman campaigns of AD 74 and 78, the second stage of the Imperial subjugation of Britain. Southern Wales was successfully Romanized to a degree unknown in the north. Caerwent, Caerleon, Cardiff, Neath, Loughor and Carmarthen were Roman centres of differing degrees of importance; the mines at Dolaucothi, Dyfed, provided Welsh gold for export to the Imperial heartland. Here and there one can still follow a Roman road; in other places the modern road does so. The linguistic influence has perhaps been most enduring and most significant: more than a thousand modern Welsh words have their origins in the Latin of the Roman occupation.

From the late third century AD, Roman Britain came under pressure from the barbarians of the east and the north. A process of gradual Roman withdrawal culminated in 410, when the Emperor Honorius finally abandoned the pretence of Imperial dominion – the last Roman troops had departed for Gaul in 407 – and bade Britain see to its own defences against the Anglo-Saxons. And with the Anglo-Saxons lay much of the future of

Britain. Romano-British culture and society – the civilized Celts and their descendants – survived only on the western and northern margins. To the victorious barbarian immigrants went the spoils in the shape of the fertile English lowlands; the mountains of the west were the refuge and the punishment of a defeated population. They were also the anvil upon which a distinctly Welsh identity was to be forged, in the creation and consolidation of kingdoms such as Dyfed, Brycheinlog and Glywysing (later known as Morgannwg, the present-day Glamorgan), and in the persistence of a distinctly Celtic Christianity. That religious distinctiveness survives, still significant, today (Harris 1990).

Early medieval Welsh society – beginning in the period we somewhat misleadingly call the 'Dark Ages' – was neither isolated nor safe. Anglo-Saxon Mercia was a particular threat, its raiding forces regularly sallying forth from behind the safety of Offa's Dyke to devastate Welsh land, livestock and settlements. But there were also alliances – of convenience, or necessity, or simple self-interest – to be struck with the English. The border zone became an extensive and imprecise area in which Welsh and English lived beside and among each other. There were contacts, especially religious contacts, to be maintained with Ireland and the wider Christian communion of the north Atlantic seaboard. And there were also the Norse sea-raiders, the people who we today call the Vikings, to be traded with and defended against. The ecclesiastical settlement of St David's, Dyfed, was particularly vulnerable in this last respect, but it was not the only local object of the northern pirates' attentions.

The Normans, the next major invaders and originally of course Scandinavian raiders themselves, conquered England between 1066 and 1070. Wales took a little longer. Starting in 1067, Norman control was not finally established until Edward I's second campaign against the kingdoms of Gwynedd and Deheubarth in 1282–3. The earliest (and easiest) Norman gains, however, had been made on the border and in the southern coastal areas of Gwent, Glamorgan, Gower and Pembroke. These are still the most Anglicized parts of Wales, replete with the family names of its conquerors, and with their castles: Caerphilly, Cardiff (built right on top of a Roman fort), Kidwelly and Pembroke are now prime sites on the 'heritage' trails of tourism.

The overlordship of England was to prove no less permanent than the stones with which these castles were constructed and no more glorious. Despite the best efforts of Owain Glyndŵr between 1400 and 1408, Wales was henceforth to be an integral part of its more powerful neighbour. The political ties binding the two countries were tightened further when a Welsh noble, Henry Tudor, took the English throne in 1485 after his victory at Bosworth Field, founding a dynasty which has coloured many of our basic expectations of the British monarchy.

The Norman conquest and subsequent political incorporation into England of Wales did not mark the end of large-scale migration into or out of south and west Wales. The nineteenth century saw population movements in both directions: Welsh folk joining the drive to populate the Empire with white settlers, people from England, Ireland and as far afield as Spain coming to the industrial valleys of south Wales, with their promise of employment in mining and metal manufacture. Irish migration has continued throughout the twentieth century and there was, early on in the century, an equally distinctive wave of Italian settlement. The size of the Irish community is easy to gauge from a Swansea or Cardiff telephone directory: O'Sullivans, Murphys, Maloneys, Flynns, they are all there. As for the Italians, they are now sufficiently well established to have provided a member of the 1990 Welsh rugby union team, Mark Perego from Burry Port, Dyfed.

In this brief overview of a rich and complicated history, I have tried to make three points. First, that the region that is now south and west Wales has been part of the ebb and flow of cultural, economic and political relations between the peoples of the western maritime margins of Europe for a very long time. Second, that, as a consequence, there is no point in searching, ever further back in time, for a period when Wales *was* Wales, free from outside influence and interference.[4] Not only was there never such a time, but what we know as Welsh culture has its roots in a past which is as Roman as it is Celtic (British). And neither Celts nor Romans can be identified as anything approaching autochthonous. Third, that the development of Welsh society – whatever that might *mean* – continues to be a definitively plural and international process, enriched internally and externally by contacts with other cultural traditions. It is only within those plural and international contexts that a defensible sense of 'Welshness' – whatever *that* might mean – is likely to be articulated.

To bring the story more up to date, south and west Wales in the 1980s and early 1990s continues to illuminate the themes of this discussion. With respect to culture, perhaps the most salient thing upon which to focus is the Welsh language. Without wishing to pre-empt the discussions of subsequent chapters, there are two trends to bear in mind (C.A. Davies 1990; Day and Rees 1989). On the one hand, the language has been, and continues to be, in a long-term decline in *y fro Gymraeg*, the traditionally Welsh-speaking rural areas of the west and north; on the other, however, as a consequence of a complex of educational, labour-market and political factors, Welsh is experiencing a modest but not insignificant resurgence in the Anglicized south-east. In different ways and with strikingly different connotations, both areas are becoming more 'pluralized'.

Looking at 'external' factors, the United Kingdom's membership of the European Union (EU) and other European organizations is increasingly a significant factor in the constitution of everyday life in south and west Wales. The pressure of European competition has been an important factor in the restructuring – or devastation, each word contains more than a grain of a complicated truth – of the local steel industry (Mainwaring 1990). Llanwern, Ebbw Vale, Port Talbot and Llanelli – these are plants and communities that bear painful witness to the various meanings of 'rationalization'. Nor is agriculture beyond the reach of the EU (Hutson 1990). The Common Agricultural Policy has had enormous consequences: the imposition of milk quotas, following a long period of subsidized expansion in milk production, brought many small farmers to absolute ruination or close during the 1980s. As I write – Spring 1996 – many small farmers in the region are discovering the power of the EU to intervene dramatically in their livelihoods, in the shape of the ban on British beef because of scientific and public concern about BSE. And it is not just the EU: Welsh farming is increasingly vulnerable to the eddies and currents of decision-making within a global arena (Midmore *et al.* 1994).

Being 'in Europe' is not wholly to the region's detriment, however. There is, for example, the important role of various relationships with European institutions for the promotion of equality of opportunity and enhanced employment rights, particularly for women workers (Charles 1990). The EU has also contributed, via regional aid and the European Social Fund, to the improvement or development from scratch of a range of projects, from by-pass roads to theatres. No less significant, perhaps, is the availability of an alternative – if perhaps relatively ineffective – forum within Europe for the publicization and articulation of Welsh grievances, and the promotion of local interests.

But why should such an alternative political forum be necessary? This is a reasonable question to ask: Gwent, the Glamorgans and Dyfed are an integral part of one of the oldest democracies in the world, a pioneer welfare state, and a land where individual liberties are said to be so firmly enshrined in the common law as to render a written constitution nearly unthinkable. The answer is that government from Westminster, Whitehall and, given the specific party political circumstances of the period since 1979, the Welsh Office, has increasingly been seen and experienced as an alien imposition by many South and West Walians. The legitimacy of the present constitutional arrangements for the government of Wales has been called into serious question over the last decade.

There are at least two related reasons for this (Stead 1990). First, there has been a long spell of government by a party, the Conservatives, which is a minority party, by a very long head, within Wales. This difficulties of this situation are strikingly exemplified in the appointments of a succession of Secretaries of State for Wales – Peter Walker, John Redwood, William Hague – without any Welsh connections at all. And although Peter Walker, for example, was locally seen to have Welsh interests at heart – as a conscious demonstration on his part, perhaps, of the continuing virtues of 'wet' Conservatism – his party and his leader were emphatically not seen in the same light. His replacement, David Hunt, was indeed Welsh by birth, but it was the same party, the same leader and the same problem. About *his* replacement, John Redwood, perhaps the only thing of which I need to remind the reader is the wonderful spectacle of his gallant attempt to sing *Mae hen wlad fy nhadau, yn annwyl i mi* – the (unofficial) Welsh national anthem – at a Welsh Conservative Party Conference.

Second, the late 1980s saw the imposition of a new system of local government finance – first, the poll tax or Community Charge, and subsequently the Council Tax – which may suit a relatively affluent electorate in areas with high rateable values, but does not suit the majority of Welsh people. Nor is Wales seen to have provided an electoral mandate for the new system. And this is to say nothing, for reasons of space, about local perceptions of other Conservative policies, such as the privatization of public utilities.

There may, therefore, be an incipient 'internationalization' of the politics of the United Kingdom (although not necessarily the 'break-up' that Tom Nairn [1981] predicted). Leaving the particular situation of Northern Ireland aside for the moment, the Scots have spent some time reconsidering their constitutional options, in the work of the Constitutional Convention and in the policy reviews of the Scottish Nationalist Party and the Labour Party. Opinion and events in Scotland have so far moved faster and further than in Wales (and Hollywood has yet to give Owain Glyndŵr the star treatment it has accorded William Wallace). But even the Labour Party – in Wales and Westminster – has finally, if altogether grudgingly, come to acknowledge that constitutional issues, with respect to both electoral reform and the structure of the state, will at least have to be addressed (if not actually confronted). In Wales, opinion polls have suggested that there may again be popular support for a form of devolved government (although it should not be forgotten that similar poll results preceded the referendum vote *against* devolution in 1979).

And spheres of activity other than politics must be taken into account. Inward investment – particularly, but by no means exclusively, from the United States and Japan – has been important in replacing some of the jobs lost in the traditional extractive and manufacturing industries. However, the investment decisions of Ford, Hitachi, Hoover, Sony, or whoever, are taken in the context of a global complex of economic and political factors, within which the needs and priorities of Wales – or of any region within Wales – have (at best) to take their place alongside a host of competitors. Much the same can be said about the strategies of British companies. Nor is it simply the financing of manufacturing employment which has been internationalized. Cardiff is fast becoming – or indeed may have become – the second most important financial centre in the United Kingdom. The prosperity which is in part attendant upon this transformation is locked into the international telecommunications networks of global markets. Similarly, the capital required for major civil engineering programmes such as the Cardiff Bay project is, by and large, to be found neither in the local arena nor in the public purse, but in those same international markets.

Telecommunications are important in other respects as well. At the same time as Sianel Pedwar Cymru (S4C, the Welsh Channel Four television station) has provided the Welsh language with a new and resolutely non-traditional forum, the wonders of the satellite dish have been unleashed. It is now possible to watch ten, twenty, or more different television channels, from all over the world, offering a varied fare of movies old and new, sport (everything from Sumo wrestling to professional ten-pin bowling), and news commentary. In homes, social clubs and pubs, and whether for good or ill, television and satellite technology has made a difference. Over Christmas and New Year 1989–90, for example, we sat down in Wales to watch a revolution in progress in Romania, at one end of the world, and the US invasion of Panama, at another. It is a trite cliché to observe that television has made the world smaller, but it is only trite and clichéd because it is so true.

There are, of course, other things that have simultaneously narrowed and broadened our horizons, in south and west Wales as elsewhere. It is no longer the case, for example, that the emigration of daughters and sons means a *de facto* final farewell. Where thirty or forty years ago a holiday for a family from Bargoed might have been, at best, a week at Barry Island, it is now more likely to start with a journey to Rhoose, to Cardiff-Wales Airport. From here or from Bristol, there is a choice, summer and winter, of package tour destinations in the Mediterranean, North Africa, and North America. At one time I would have included the Balkans in that list, but times change. It is no longer an object of community amazement to hear of somebody going for a holiday to Florida; quite the reverse, Disneyland is now an ordinary destination, not much to shout about, even if it remains out of the economic reach of many.

The cutting edge of tourism cuts, of course, both ways. The development of an organized tourist industry in the region – not just the marketing of existing 'traditional' resources, but the the creation and promotion of 'heritage', the manufacture of attractions and facilities in post-industrial areas such as the Valleys, the recognition of the central significance of tourism to the Welsh economy as a whole – may turn out to be one of the most diagnostic trends of the late twentieth century. Despite the doubtful contribution such ventures have made to the prosperity of most Valleys people, it seems likely that they are here to stay. Those who can no longer mine or make must, if they are lucky, serve.

Neither travel nor television necessarily liberates the imagination or undermines localized chauvinism and parochial smugness. The reality of the low-cost Mediterranean resort, or (for example) BSkyB Television, is different. Mean-minded, crass, lowest-common-denominator commercial-ism is unlikely to be the best vehicle for improving – even if it were transparently clear what that word might mean in this context – under-standing and relations between people internationally. Nonetheless, there are two sides to this story: on the one hand, McDonald's and Coca-Cola in Moscow, on the other, many thousands of people sitting round their televisions in Welsh households on a Sunday afternoon in February 1990, waiting to see Nelson Mandela walk out of imprisonment (and, just as significant, millions more in households around the world). It has become increasingly difficult *not* to acknowledge that the women and men on the streets of São Paulo, Warsaw, Soweto or Llandysul share many similar fears, basic needs and aspirations. In a sense, the fact of their obvious – and equally important – differences only serves to make their similarities clearer.

Many of those fears, needs and aspirations are no respecters of international boundaries, and nor are the problems to which they relate. The environmental movement is, by definition, global in its concerns and in its activities and organization. Global warming, the depletion of the rain forests, whale hunting, marine pollution, Chernobyl and Sellafield, toxic waste, food additives, etcetera, etcetera. The list is long, and all of it matters to Wales. Much of it – for example Welsh sheep which, ten years to the week after Chernobyl as I write, are still unfit to eat, or crude oil fouling the beaches of Dyfed in early 1996 – ends up, quite literally, on Welsh doorsteps. As with constitutional reform, these are issues which politicians locally – whether their new green hue is dyed in the wool or merely a cheap paint job – can no longer afford to ignore. Welsh concerns entail global issues. They are issues in the pursuit of which the narrow focus of local self-interest must, of necessity, combine with a wider perspective.

The last decade or two have seen south and west Wales become ever more firmly tied into a widening international context. Although this is neither a new phenomenon nor a radical departure from a parochial past, it is a trend which has gathered speed and momentum and shows no signs of slowing down. And the context has broadened and deepened to the point where it is genuinely global. Whether in terms of national identity, culture and language(s), the popular view of the world, the economic realities of trade and employment, the preservation or improvement of the environment, or the institutional framework of politics, the future is one in which what it means to be Welsh, and what it is to live in Wales, will reflect, to a large degree, what goes on in the outside world. And it really will be the outside *world*.

There is an obvious affinity between social constructivist approaches to ethnicity and models of society as culturally plural, heterogeneous and diverse. It is a pity, therefore, that both the formal theorists of 'pluralism' and the recent (post)modern celebrants of 'difference' suggest – if nothing stronger – that plural diversity is a relatively modern phenomenon, presumably a development and progression from previous conditions of bounded cultural homogeneity. This essentially historicist model – from simple to complex, closed to open, absolutist to relativist, static to dynamic – is, if only on the evidence of south and west Wales, implausible. This chapter raises two questions. Can 'pluralism' be a defensible analytical – rather than a simply commonsensical or descriptive – category? And if, as I am arguing, it is routine, everyday, and nothing more than the expected state of social affairs, should we continue to talk about 'difference' as if it were something distinctive or special, worthy of comment or in need of explanation? My own answers are 'no' to both: emphatically in the first case, more equivocally in the second.

Cultural and ethnic diversity (pluralism) is nothing new. The secure hermetically bounded group is an imaginative, somewhat romanticized, retrospect. But, as the excursion to south and west Wales also illustrated, the social world of the late twentieth century *is* different in some respects from what went before. It is different in the *scale* of the meaningful arenas within which people see themselves and others. To draw on a set of notions from the work of Alfred Schutz (1967; Schutz and Luckmann 1973) the 'life-world' has widened and deepened. The immediate everyday social world of our 'fellows' has expanded because of improved communications of all sorts: it is now possible for people to remain in immediate and intimate contact at enormous distances – globally – and travel over global distances is no longer difficult or impossibly expensive. As Giddens has argued (1984: 110ff.) time and space are no longer bound up with each other to the degree that they used to be. The more abstract and socially distant world of our 'contemporaries' has changed too.

These changes are, before they are anything else, *quantitative*: we know about many more people who we do not know personally than we did even as recently as a generation ago, and we know more about them. We also know about them more immediately: telecommunications, in particular, have been responsible for a blurring of the distinction between our fellows and our contemporaries that is one aspect of globalization. The spreading ripples of globalization are enlarging the scale of the social arenas in which identities are forged and maintained. The amount of information about Others is expanding and becoming more immediate. But these changes do not represent discontinuity and radical novelty; they are differences of degree and of emphasis. The difference between our fellows and our contemporaries remains. We should not lose sight of the fact that most of us, most of the time, continue to live in practical life-worlds that are primarily what they have always been, small-scale arenas, peopled largely by those who we know face to face (which is not the same thing as knowing them well or intimately). This is not to deny the significance or reality of globalization, merely to put it into everyday perspective.

A propos difference and 'pluralism', taking seriously the ongoing behemoth of globalization can also put another spin on the ball. If anything, we might plausibly insist that the modern world is in some respects becoming ever *more* homogeneous. Step off the plane in New York, the New Hebrides or Novaya Zemlya, and, increasingly, the similarities may be as striking as the differences. Nor is it simply a matter of technology: the global convergence of business, tourism and, to some extent, culture and politics is a phenomenon to be reckoned with. In terms of values – particularly with the apparent triumph of capitalism – the cultures of the world are now divided at least as much by what they hold in common as by their differences. While too much can be made of this, it should not be dismissed as trivial. Nor can we deny that diversity and fragmentation are 'real': they are certainly no *less* real than they ever were. As Ulf Hannerz argues (1992: 217–67), the 'global ecumene' involves convergence *and* polycentric variety.

Between the global arena and the everyday world there arise tricky questions about analytical levels, and about categories of identification. What, for example, is the relationship, and how do we distinguish, between local identities and ethnic, regional and national identities? These issues, among others, are broached in Chapter 4.

4

Ethnicity etcetera

In Chapter 1 I outlined a basic social constructionist model of ethnicity that commands a considerable amount of support within anthropology. To reiterate, the model's four elements are as follows:

- ethnicity emphasizes cultural *differentiation* (although identity is always a dialectic between similarity and difference);
- ethnicity is *cultural* – based in shared meanings – but it is produced and reproduced in *social* interaction;
- ethnicity is to some extent *variable* and *manipulable*, not definitively fixed or unchanging; and
- ethnicity as a social identity is both *collective* and *individual*, externalized and internalized.

That this is the basic model, and that it is widely agreed upon, does not mean – as indeed we have already seen – that it is uncontroversial. Some of the most interesting controversies bear upon questions about how ethnicity is to be differentiated from, or related to, other bases of communal attachment or identification with which it appears to have much in common. Hence the 'ethnicity etcetera' of this chapter's title. Looking at these issues leads almost inexorably to questions, which are probably always lurking somewhere in the background, about what ethnicity actually *is*, about the *nature* of ethnicity in some kind of basic ontological sense.

The communal, the local, the national, the global

Inasmuch as it is situational, ethnic identity is also likely to be segmentary and hierarchical. Although two groups may be differentiated from each other as A and B, in a different context they may combine as C in contrast to D (with which they may combine in yet other circumstances). One of the best illustrations of this model can be found in Moerman's classic paper dealing with Thailand (1965). The model is straightforward to communicate, and we can all relate on the basis of own own experience. But it does precipitate an interesting problem. When does an identity in the segmentary hierarchy of comparison and contrast become local or communal rather than ethnic? Consider the very incomplete classificatory sequence shown in Figure 4.1, which harks back to the case study of south and west Wales in the previous chapter:

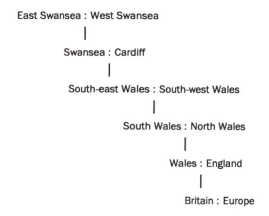

Figure 4.1   *A hierarchy of Welsh identity*

Precisely where in this sequence does an identity that is based on community or locality become an identity that is based on ethnicity? Is the difference between, for example, a South Walian and a *Gog* (an epithet for a North Walian, derived from the Welsh *gogledd*, meaning 'north') an ethnic difference? And where does ethnicity become national identity? And why? And what, indeed, is the difference? After all, each of these identificatory contrasts reflects 'the social organization of culture difference' (Barth) and involves 'socially ratified personal identities' (Geertz).

One way to understand the Welsh illustration might be as a hierarchy of *nominal* identifications which overlap and intermesh in complicated ways, depending upon the *virtualities* of each. Nominal identification is a matter of name and classification; virtual identification encompasses the consequences of name and label (i.e. what the nominal *means*, in terms of experience). From this perspective, the difference between, say, the communal and the local, or the local and the ethnic, lies in the consequences of each: in terms, for example, of rights and responsibilities, or access to social and economic resources, or social recognition. Shared locality does not entail the same kind of mutual interpersonal recognition that is ideally presupposed in communality. In terms of administration and bureaucracy, locality involves political rights and responsibilities – the payment of local taxes, the right to vote in local elections – which are not entailed in ethnicity. And so on.

Questions about the relationship between ethnic and other identities are also thrown into sharp relief by the work of Anthony Cohen on cultural identity and the symbolic construction of community and communal boundaries (Cohen 1982, 1985, 1986). There is a clear similarity between the ideas of Cohen and his collaborators and the Barthian, social constructionist view of ethnicity. Indeed, many of the contributors to the edited volumes (Cohen 1982, 1986) make the connection explicit, as does Cohen himself. What is more, the subtitles of the edited collections invoke the idea of 'British cultures', a minor reification which hints that each of the local research sites documented by the ethnographers concerned can be conceptualized, anthropologically at least, as a distinct domain of bounded cultural difference. Perhaps not quite ethnic groups or tribes, but almost:

> 'Community' thus seems to imply simultaneously both similarity and difference. The word thus expresses a *relational* idea: the opposition of one community to others or to other social entities . . . the use of the word is only occasioned by the desire or need to express such a distinction. It seems appropriate, therefore, to focus our examination of the nature of community on the element which embodies this sense of discrimination, namely, the *boundary*. (Cohen 1985: 12, original emphasis)

Substitute for 'community' the words 'ethnicity' or 'ethnic group', as appropriate, and this would be a perfectly sensible set of propositions, that would not look out of place in Barth's 'Introduction' to *Ethnic Groups and Boundaries*. Cohen's further emphasis upon the role of symbolism in the social construction of community boundaries is, suitably modified, a powerful contribution to our understanding of ethnicity.

But this still leaves the question of whether, and how, it is possible to distinguish the ethnic from the communal or the local. Nor is the question confined to locality or community. Heading in the other direction, towards the more macro and the more abstract, when does ethnic identity become national identity, and what is the relationship between them? This question is also posed by the Welsh illustration in Figure 4.1. From a different angle, Eriksen (1993a: 116–18) draws upon his Mauritian ethnography to raise the possibility of a 'non-ethnic nationalism'. Which turns the argument somewhat on its head: when does nationalism *cease* to be ethnic? Does it, indeed, make any sense to talk about a non-ethnic nationalism? Two things seem to be in need of conceptual clarification here. The first has to do with levels of abstraction and analysis, the second with the developing character of nationalism in the modern world. These are matters to which I will return.

Talking about the nature of the modern world raises again some of the issues discussed in the previous chapter. Regardless of what one wants to call the historical juncture at which we presently find ourselves – 'postmodernity', 'high modernity', 'late modernity', or whatever – one consistent theme, about which there is a broad consensus among academics and other commentators alike, is that something called 'globalization' is happening or has happened. The nation-state economies of the world are becoming ever more interdependent and ever more subservient to the eddies and currents of a thoroughly internationalized economic system. New technology has facilitated a shift in the nature, amount and communicative immediacy of information which is available to us. Cultural homogenization and creolization seem in some respects to be the order of the day, alongside diversity and 'pluralism'. International travel, whether it be migratory or temporary, occupational or recreational, has become an accepted part of the way of life of ever-larger sections of the world's population. The result – globalization – is believed to be a qualitative break with the past (Robertson 1992) . . . or not: there are those who locate the present situation firmly within a much longer-term evolution of a world social and economic system (Frank and Gills 1993). Whichever option we choose, a range of commentators are agreed that globalization has consequences, one way or another, for ethnicity as a social phenomenon (Hannerz 1990, 1992; Friedman 1990, 1994; Hall 1991; Waters 1995: 133–9).

It is, however, painfully clear that globalization doesn't necessarily broaden the mind. Globalization and heightened localization, far from being contradictory, are inter-linked: the world is becoming smaller and larger at the same time, cultural space is shrinking and expanding. Localism and ethnicity are conceptualized as two sides of the same coin, and each may (re)assert itself either as a defensive reaction to, or a result of, the increasingly global context of social life.

The debate about globalization raises a number of concerns. Perhaps the most important is whether the 'global' can ever be an appropriate or useful unit of analysis, particularly with respect to cultural matters. Is it possible to say anything about it other than the glib or the superficial? Another concerns the way in which the local and the global are juxtaposed; there are a number of 'layers' in between which require considerable attention as well: nations, regions, ethnic groups, which have not diminished in importance. The notion of globalization also seems to take for granted more than it should the close implication of the ethnic in the local. The jury is still out with respect to the shape which all of these issues will assume in the medium term, but, in the anthropological here and now, the discipline is still only beginning to shape a response with respect to either theory or method (e.g. Eriksen 1993a: 150–2, 156–62; Marcus 1992; Miller 1995).

Globalization notwithstanding, I find it difficult to imagine a future in which the notion of ethnicity does not continue to be necessary as a way of talking about one of the most general and basic principles of human sociability (Carrithers 1992): collective identification, a sense of 'us' and 'them', socially constructed with some reference to cultural similarity and difference. By this token, the communal, the local, the national and the 'racial' are to be understood as historically and contextually specific social constructions on the basic ethnic theme, allotropes of ethnic identification. One can also talk about ideologies of identification such as communalism, localism, nationalism, racism and ethnicism. Whether or not we can look forward to talking about global*ism* remains to be seen (although, in the dream of socialism, it may already be something about which we can, regrettably, only be nostalgic). Unresolved for the moment, these issues remain on the table, questions which must be broached in our research and theorizing and in our teaching. Fundamentally concerned with the theoretical constitution of the topic and the pragmatic definition of the field for research purposes, they could not be more important.

The primordial versus the instrumental

Over the years this has turned into a perennial and argumentative debate about the nature of ethnic identity. Is ethnicity a fundamental, primordial aspect of human existence and self-consciousness, essentially unchanging and unchangeable in the imperative demands it makes upon individuals and the bonds it creates between the individual and the group? In other words, is ethnicity an aspect of 'human nature'? Or is it, to whatever extent, defined situationally, strategically or tactically manipulable, and capable of change at both the individual and collective levels? Is it wholly socially constructed?

This argument takes its place alongside a range of theoretical controversies about the capacity of humans to intervene in their own lives, to determine or to be determined. But the primordial model also has deep historical roots in the Romantic reaction to Enlightenment rationalism. Finding some of its more respectable voices in the work of Herder and Hegel, this is more than an academic point of view, providing the intellectual charter for a great deal of terrible – to the point of murderous – ethnic chauvinism and nationalism. The ideology of primordialism naturalizes ethnic groups and justifies chauvinistic ethnic sentiments. It can, for example, be identified at play in the ongoing debate about the modernity and nature of nationalism (Bauman 1992; Smith 1994).

Within anthropology, the name that is most often identified with a primordial model of ethnicity is Clifford Geertz (1973: 255–310). Drawing upon the work of Edward Shils, Geertz, originally writing in 1963, was concerned to understand the obstacle that 'primordial attachments' – deriving mainly from kinship, locality and culture, and encompassing much more than ethnicity – posed to the development of the modern political sentiment of citizenship, in the emergent post-colonial 'new states' in particular:

> [the] crystallization of a direct conflict between primordial and civil sentiments – this 'longing not to belong to any other group' – . . . gives to the problem variously called tribalism, parochialism, communalism, and so on, a more ominous and deeply threatening quality than most of the other, also very serious and intractable, problems the new states face. (1973: 261)

This quotation provides a neat bridge between the present discussion and the issue of 'levels of analysis' raised in the previous section. It is also a timely reminder that the problem is not new.

In opposition to this position one is generally offered the 'instrumentalist' or 'situationalist' perspective, deriving in the main from Barth. As we have already seen, this model of ethnicity emphasizes a degree of plasticity in ethnic identification and in the composition of ethnic groups: that people (and peoples) can and do shift and alter their ethnic ascriptions in the light of circumstance and environment. The pursuit of political advantage and/or material self-interest is the calculus which is typically held to inform such behaviour.

The dispute is, however, not as clear-cut as it seems, and it is hard to resist the conclusion that more heat than light has been its outcome. To begin with, both positions arguably have at least as much in common as not (Bentley 1987: 25–7). Whether that is the case or not, the protagonists are certainly usually misrepresented, sometimes to a remarkable degree. For example, as Eriksen reminds us (1993a: 54–6) even Barth has been accused, by Abner Cohen, of the sin of primordialism:

> Barth . . . [sees] ethnic categories as classifying persons in terms of their 'basic most general identity' . . . Some writers attribute primordiality to this basic identity.
> Ethnicity tends to be conceived by this school of thought as an essentially innate disposition. Barth goes so far as to attribute to it an existence of its own, separate from any social 'content'. (Cohen 1974: xii)

Geertz too is often widely caricatured, as the purveyor of

> a picture of underived and socially-unconstructed emotions that are unanalysable and overpowering . . . A more unintelligible and unsociological concept would be hard to imagine. (Eller and Coughlan 1993: 187)

However, turning to what he actually wrote, Geertz explicitly recognizes not only the role of culture in defining the primordial 'givens', but also that the

> strength of such primordial bonds, and the types of them that are important, differ from person to person, from society to society, and from time to time. (Geertz 1973: 259)

Further, Geertz is perfectly clear that what matters analytically is that ties of blood, language and culture are *seen* by actors to be ineffable and obligatory; that they are *seen* as natural. He is concerned with the terms in which attachments are understood and mobilized locally; with what people *believe*. Later in the same piece (pp. 269–70) – making a point which in all its essentials was reiterated by Anthony Cohen (1985: 117), with respect to the effect of national integration on local, communal identities – Geertz further argues that in some respects these putative 'primordial attachments' are actually likely to be stimulated and quickened by the political modernization of nation-building.

Barth, for his part, has never neglected the power and stability of ethnic identifications: the 'organizing and canalizing effects of ethnic distinctions' (1969a: 10). As much concerned with the persistence of ethnic boundaries as with their flux, his argument was that in certain, not uncommon, circumstances ethnic change *can* happen, not that it *must*. More important perhaps, Barth's point of view is often presented fossilized in its 1969 *Ethnic Groups and Boundaries* incarnation. Since then he has explored the importance of ongoing and historically relatively stable 'streams of tradition' or 'universes of discourse', within the constraints of which ethnic identities are produced and reproduced in practice (Barth 1984, 1989). Most recently, in a discussion which explicitly refers to the 'privacy of . . . hearts and minds' (1994: 29), he acknowledges the need to add micro and macro levels of analysis to the intermediate level upon which his original arguments concentrated. This means looking at what ethncity means for individuals.

There are other reasons for becoming impatient with this debate. In the evocative words of one teaching text, it offers a contrast between 'ethnicity in the heart' and 'ethnicity in the head' (Banks 1996: 185–7). This alerts us to the need to acknowledge affect and emotion in our considerations of ethnicity (cf. Epstein 1978). But there is no necessary contradiction between instrumental manipulation, and sentiment. They may even go hand in hand. They may also, of course, conflict. But so may different sentiments, or opposing instrumental goals. And when they do, difficult decisions – precisely of the kind which are the staple of political manoeuvre and manipulation – are the result.

Taking another tack, there is good cause to reject totally any strongly primordialist view. Too much ethnographic evidence exists of the fluidity and flux of ethnic identification, and of the differing degrees to which ethnicity organizes social life in different settings, for any other position to be sensible, and the theoretical argument in favour of a constructionist view is too well founded. Nor, as the discussion in Chapter 1 showed, did Barth 'invent' this understanding of ethnicity, and nor does its utility seem to be confined to a limited range of cultural contexts. Leach's classic study of Shan and Kachin in highland Burma (1954) is an ethnographic precursor of the social constructionist position in important respects, and many, many other studies could be cited to make the point: recently, for example, a range of work about pastoralists in East Africa has offered a similar view (e.g. Schlee 1989; Spear and Waller 1993).

However, we cannot deny the longevity and stubbornness, in certain circumstances, of ethnic attachments. Pondering the relative failure of the project of social and cultural 'integration' with respect to 'ethnic minority' migrants in Britain – and the same point could be made to differing degrees about other European states – John Rex comments that:

> despite the very strong pressure in complex societies for groups to be formed on the basis of congruence of interest, many individuals do in fact stubbornly continue to unite with those with whom they have ties of ethnic sameness, even though such alliances might run contrary to patterns of group formation determined by shared interests. (Rex 1991: 11)

But to acknowledge this point doesn't necessitate embracing a notion of primordiality or abandoning the social constructionist perspective. It is not stretching the point to regard ethnic differentiation – the social construction of 'us' and 'them', marked in cultural terms – as a ubiquitous feature of human sociability, and hence of all human societies. The only possible exception to this might be an imaginary and altogether unlikely society existing in total isolation (the implausible 'monoism' criticized in Chapter 3). The debate about whether or not ethnicity is 'situational' or 'primordial' has confused the *ubiquity* of a social phenemenon such as ethnicity with 'naturalness', implying fixity, determinism and some kind of pre-social power of causation. To suggest that ethnicity is ever-present as one of the 'givens' of human social life is *not* to endorse any of the arguments of the primordial point of view.

An individual's sense of ethnic membership may – depending upon context – be internalized during early primary socialization, along with many of the markers of ethnicity such as language, religion, non-verbal behaviour, etc. (Bentley 1987). During this period the primary, deep-rooted social identities of selfhood, gender and humanness are entered into (Jenkins 1996). In these senses, identity is an aspect of the emotional and psychological constitution of individuals; it is, correspondingly, bound up with the maintenance of personal integrity and security, and may be extremely resistant to change. In a social setting where ethnic differentiation is sufficiently salient and consequential to intrude into the social world of children, ethnicity may be acquired in this way, as an integral part of the individually embodied point of view of selfhood. Thus, ethnicity may, *under local circumstances*, be characterisable as a *primary*, although not a primordial, dimension of individual identity.

Internal or self-identification – whether by individuals or groups – is, however, not the only 'mechanism' of ethnic identity formation. People are not always in a position to 'choose' who they are or what their identity means in terms of its social consequences. Power differentials are important here. As will be explored in later chapters, external categorization is an important contributor to ethnicity, not least during primary socialization but also in a range of other settings.

So the visibility of ethnicity within primary socialization is likely to be a product of local contingencies of place and time. Growing up in Denmark in 1994, for example, is not the same as growing up in Northern Ireland in 1994. And – to return to the distinction between the nominal and the virtual which was proposed earlier – growing up in Denmark in 1994 is not the same as growing up in Denmark in 1944. Ethnicity, or at least an awareness of it, is likely to figure in different ways, with different social costs and benefits (consequences) attached, in each place and at each time. Other processes of ethnic categorization – which is, after all, what is going on in primary socialization: children know who they are, in large part, because others *tell* them – also vary with context in their effectiveness and intrusiveness. Thus, although ethnicity *may* be a primary social identity, its salience, strength and manipulability are situationally contingent (to say which is to come very close to Geertz's position, outlined above). No matter how apparently strong or inflexible it may be, ethnicity is *always* socially constructed, in the first instance and in every other.

If the primordial position is so unconvincing, that may be because, as an analytical model, it is largely a straw man. The debate about 'instrumentalism' and 'primordialism' exaggerates the differences between, for example, Geertz and Barth; it does neither justice. It is tempting to agree with Eller and Coughlan (1993) that the notion of the 'primordial' should be banished from the social science lexicon. However, the debate remains important and it would be irresponsible to forget it altogether. Crude primordialism is essentially a common-sense view, with enormous power in the world. In sheep's clothing it occasionally makes an academic showing, indirectly in the guise of sociobiology (van den Berghe 1981, 1995) and, more explicitly, in a recent paper about territoriality (Grosby 1995). Even though these views are not widely supported they cannot simply be ignored. In response, an anthropological perspective – rooted in the social constructionist assumptions of the discipline – has much to offer as a critique of the naturalization of chauvinism and ethnic conflict.

Culture and biology

The controversy about the relationship between culture and biology is in many respects homologous to the debate about instrumentality and primordiality. It is at least as important, and for largely similar reasons: common sense continues to assert the reality and significance of 'race' and racism remains a blight. Building upon the example set by Boas (1940), social and cultural anthropology have long offered an important challenge to dubiously scientific notions of 'race' (Benedict 1983; Lévi-Strauss 1952). Unfortunately, an ironic consequence of the ascendance of the social constructionist model of ethnicity as – to borrow a notion from Kuhn – a normal science paradigm within the discipline, has been that the problem of 'race', of the relationship between biology and culture, has receded from the anthropological agenda. Sandra Wallman, as we saw earlier, dismisses the debate about the distinction between 'race' and ethnicity as a 'quibble' (1978: 205). Elsewhere (1986: 229) she argues that phenotype or physical appearance is just one potential ethnic boundary marker among many. A strikingly similar position is taken by Thomas Hylland Eriksen in his recent textbook: 'Ideas of "race" may or may not form part of ethnic ideologies, and their presence or absence does not seem to be a decisive factor in interethnic relations' (1993a: 5)

The adoption of such a view seems, at least in part, to be a laudable refusal to risk the inadvertent validation of biological models of ethnic difference. Interestingly, however, the naturalization of ethnicity within a sociobiological framework can lead to a similar position. In van den Berghe's terms, for example, ethnicity is an extension of kinship, a manifestation of an adaptive nepotism between kin which has essentially genetic foundations. Van den Berghe argues that 'race' has become nothing more than a 'special marker of ethnicity', a visible folk test of likely common ancestry (1981: 240). By this token, it is racism rather than 'race' which matters, as an adaptive stratagem of 'biologically-rooted nepotism' (although it is instructive to observe the conflation of 'race' and racism in his writing: see van den Berghe 1995).

There are, of course, anthropologists who neither gloss over the relationship between 'race' and ethnicity, nor submerge the one in the other. As illustrated by the discussion in Chapter 2, one such is Michael Banton, who has written at length about the history of theories of 'race' (1987), and consistently explored and theorized the two concepts and the relationship between them. His basic argument is that 'race' is a categorical identification denoting 'them', based on physical or phenotypical characteristics, while ethnicity is the cultural group identification of 'us' (Banton 1983: 1–14; 1988: 1–15). Ethnicity is thus voluntarily embraced, while 'racial' identifications are imposed. Although Banton is clear that both – albeit perhaps with different force – are socially constructed, Wade (1993) has criticized him for taking phenotypical variation somewhat for granted, neglecting the social processes of categorization that denote and signify the differences which make a difference. In Wade's view physical differences of 'race' are always highly – if not *completely* – socially constructed.

A closely related issue is the anthropological perspective on racism. The reader may be weary by now of my reiteration of the anthropological celebration of ethnicity as a 'good thing', as a cultural and social resource rather than a liability. Anthropology has also concentrated on minority rather than majority ethnicities. Each of these biases derives in part from the anthropological romance with exotic Otherness, in part from the interpretive cross-cultural advocacy role assumed by many anthropologists, and in part from the continuing legacy of structural functionalism and the theoretical underplaying of conflict. There is an increasing number of exceptions to these generalizations, and clear evidence that world events – in the Balkans, Amazonia, Indonesia, the list would have to be a very long one – in tandem with the developing anthropological concern with nationalism, are finally effecting shifts in these respects within the discipline that are likely to prove durable.[1] Nonetheless, racism remains an aspect of the social construction of ethnic differentiation which is relatively little discussed by anthropologists (and, when it is, it is not always done well: see La Fontaine 1986 and Jenkins 1987).

The arguments about the spurious nature of 'race' are too well known to require rehearsal here. The complexities of how one might theorize the relationship between 'race' and ethnicity are discussed in subsequent chapters. My intention at this point is simply to suggest that the 'problem of race' is currently underplayed within anthropology and that adopting a social constructionist model of ethnicity neither requires nor entitles us to indulge in such a neglect. Anthropology has, after all, for many years specialized in the study of classificatory systems. To reiterate Wade's point (1993), whatever else it is, 'race' is a set of classificatory social constructs of considerable historical and contemporary significance. An exemplary study of the social construction of 'racial' categorization – although one not undertaken by an anthropologist – is Dikötter's monograph dealing with modern China (1992). Racism, as an ideology of ethnic identification and a folk cosmology, is also socially constructed, an everyday version of the primordial model. As such it, too, is an appropriate object for the anthropological attention which, at the moment, it receives all too infrequently.

Redrawing the boundaries

A social constructionist approach to ethnicity and cultural differentiation involves, of necessity, an appreciation that ethnic identity is situationally variable and negotiable. It also involves recognizing the central emphasis which must be accorded to the points of view of actors themselves if we are to understand how processes of social construction and negotiation work. None of the reservations about the anthropological model that have been expressed cast doubt on these basic points of departure. However, the criticisms and reservations suggest that some qualifications to these foundational principles are necessary. These qualifications are, in large part, restatements or developments of the original arguments of Weber, Hughes and Barth.

For example, with respect to cultural differentiation, the arguments of Chapter 3 must be re-emphasized: diversity – with respect to ethnicity – is nothing new, it is altogether the 'norm'. It is an expected dimension of human sociality. Inhabited social arenas are routinely multi-ethnic: as far as the archaeological, historical and anthropological records can tell us, bounded, homogeneous 'societies' or 'cultures' are exceptional (if they can be said to exist at all). This is what ethnicity – collective identification that is socially constructed in the articulation of purported cultural similarity and difference – is all about. The increasing scale, density and extensiveness of modern social life, allied to rapidly evolving technologies of the intellect – to borrow a useful expression from Jack Goody – *may* have upped the tempo of, and increased opportunities for, differentiation. But, even if this is so, to suggest that this represents something qualitatively new or radical is probably to fall victim to one of the many conceits of modernity.[2]

Thus we should neither problematize difference *in itself*, nor celebrate it as a departure – and a liberation – from the past. It *is*, and there is no reason to expect that matters could be otherwise. Adopting this sceptical position does not, of course, prevent us problematizing either *how* difference is socially constructed, or the relative *salience* of difference from one context to another. The Barthian theme that seems to have been most comprehensively forgotten by anthropologists who have looked at ethnicity in the wake of *Ethnic Groups and Boundaries* requires emphatic reiteration here. 'Group-ness' is not to be reified; 'groups' are not distinct 'things' in any positivist sense. They are contingent and immanently changeable, an emergent product of interaction and of classificatory processes (the definition of 'us' and the categorization of 'them'). Human society is best seen as an ongoing and overlapping kaleidoscope of 'group-ness', rather than a 'plural' system of separate groups.

There is more to difference, of course, than the simple fact of diversity: there is also temporal and situational difference, the flexibility and negotiability of ethnic identity. One of the central lessons of the anthropology of ethnicity is that there is nothing new or distinctively modern – let alone *post*modern – about the possibility of a degree of shape-shifting, whether it be collective or individual, with respect to ethnicity (and a similar point could be made about other identifications). There is, however, a further point to be underlined here. To say that ethnic identity is transactional and changeable, is really to say that it *may* be; it doesn't mean that it *always* is, or *has* to be. This is the sensible point that emerges from the debate about situational ethnicity versus primordiality. The recognition that ethnicity is neither static nor monolithic should not be taken to mean that it is definitively and perpetually in a state of flux. There are questions to be asked about how and why ethnicity is more or less flexible in different places and times.

In the chapters which follow, these arguments will be given shape and direction through the exploration of three inter-related themes. The first of these is the role of *social categorization* in the construction of ethnic identifications. This directs our attention away from the 'group' as the atom of ethnicity, and also highlights relationships of power and domination. Second, there is the relationship between ethnicity and other analogous or homologous principles of identification. This involves looking not only at *classificatory* models such as 'race' or nationality (or, indeed, class and religion), but also at the role of *ideology*. Finally, I want to begin to explore the *individual* or personal aspects of ethnicity. To turn Geertz's definition on its head, this is to problematize the processes whereby social identity becomes personally ratified. Why does ethnicity seem to matter to some people(s) – in some situations – but not to others? And why, when ethnicity matters, does it seem to *really* matter?

5

Categorization and Power

One of the important insights offered by the basic social anthropological model of ethnicity is the notion that ethnicity is not an immutable bundle of cultural traits, which it is sufficient to enumerate in order to identify a person as an 'X' or a 'Y' or to locate the boundary between ethnic collectivities. As Barth has consistently argued, ethnicity is situationally defined, produced and reproduced in the course of social transactions which occur at or across – and in the process help to constitute – the ethnic boundary in question. Ethnicity is fundamentally political, and ethnic boundaries are, to some extent at least, permeable and osmotic, existing despite the flow of personnel or interaction across them. Thus criteria of ethnic ascription and subscription are variable in their nature and salience.

Although his overall concerns have remained grounded in the theoretical concerns of his 1966 *Models of Social Organization* project – how to theorize 'the constraints and incentives that canalize choices' and the ways in which social 'patterns are generated through processes of interaction and in their form reflect the constraints and incentives under which people act' (1966: 1, 2) – Barth's point of view on ethnicity has developed over the last three decades. His recent discussions of the routine cultural pluralism of complex societies emphasize the importance of history, as well as the transactional immediacy of everyday life and its negotiations (Barth 1984, 1989). History is invoked in two different senses: as the ongoing progress of events which constitutes the context and content of the here-and-now, and as 'streams' of 'tradition' – the reference to Redfield is explicit – within which people are to differing degrees located and of which they differentially partake. Stressing history has produced a shift of emphasis away from the individualistic voluntarism of his earlier writings, for which he has been so consistently criticized, towards a Weberian acknowledgement of the unintended consequences of action. Further, recognizing the centrality of history entails a search for pattern, influence and effect within a wide social and geographic arena; attention must be given to factors both within and without the social setting, local community or region which is the object of analytical interest.

In all important respects, however, Barth has remained true to the original perspective of *Ethnic Groups and Boundaries*, not least in according primacy to the perceptions and definitions of actors themselves. I shall concentrate upon this in what follows, focusing on the issue of *which* actors? Rather than offer an alternative which pretends to radical novelty, I shall draw out some elements of the anthropological model of ethnicity, interpreting their implications in the context of a set of general arguments about the production and reproduction of social identities (see Jenkins 1996).

Groups and categories

If ethnicity is transactional, those transactions are of two basic kinds. First, there are processes of *internal definition*: actors signal to in- or out-group members a self-definition of their nature or identity. This can be an ego-centred, individual process or a collective, group process, although it only makes sense to talk of ethnicity in an individual sense when the identity being defined and its expressions refer to a recognizable collective identity and draw upon a repertoire of culturally specified practices. Although conceptualized in the first instance as internal, these processes are necessarily transactional and social (even in the individual case) because they presuppose both an audience, without whom they make no sense, and an externally derived framework of meaning.

On the other hand there are processes of *external definition*. These are other-directed processes, during which one person or set of persons defines the other(s) as 'X', 'Y', or whatever. This may, at its most consensual, be the validation of the others' internal definition(s) of themselves. At the conflictual end of the spectrum of possibilities, however, there is the imposition, by one set of actors upon another, of a putative name and characterization which affects in significant ways the social experience(s) of the categorized.

This process of external definition may, in theory, be an individual act, in which person A defines person or persons B as, say, 'X' or 'Y'. For two reasons, however, it is difficult to think about external definition as solely an individual process. In the first place, more than an audience is involved: the others here are the object(s) of the process of definition, and implied within the situation is a meaningful intervention in their lives, an acting upon them. Thus external definition can only occur within active social relationships, however distant or at however many removes. Second, the capacity to intervene successfully in other people's lives implies either the power or the authority to do so. The exercise of power implies competitive access to and control over resources, while authority is, by definition, only effective when it is legitimate. Power and authority are necessarily embedded within active social relationships.

This distinction between internal and external definition is, of course, primarily analytical. In the complexity of day-to-day social life, each is chronically implicated in the other in an ongoing dialectic of identification. The categorization of 'them' is too useful a foil in the identification of 'us' for this not to be the case, and the definition of 'us' too much the product of a history of relationships with a range of significant others (Hagendoorn

1993). Which is, of course, one of Barth's original claims. Ethnicity – the production, reproduction and transformation of the 'group-ness' of culturally differentiated collectivities – is a two-way process that takes place across the boundary between 'us' and 'them'. At the individual level, in the ongoing production of personal identities, much the same can be said. Individual identity is located within a two-way social process, an interaction of 'ego' and 'other', inside and outside. It is in the meeting of internal and external definition that identity, whether collective or individual, is created.

It may be objected that the suggested homology between collective identity and individual identity is misleading, that the boundaries of the self are secure and unproblematic in a way that is not, for example, true of social groups, particularly inasmuch as selfhood is embodied. There are a number of reasons for persisting with an approach that treats individual and collective identities as similar in important respects. First, it seems clear that a relatively secure sense of the boundaries of individual selfhood is *acquired*, as the infant separates itself psychologically from the significant other(s) in its life through an early interactive process of being defined and defining (Dunn 1988; Kaye 1982; Stern 1985). Second, there is a well-established understanding of adult personal or self-identity which sees its content(s), boundaries and, most critically, security as *variable* over time in interaction with changing circumstances (Giddens 1984: 41–92). Finally, even if the boundaries of the self are, most of the time, stable and taken for granted, this is only true as long as it *is* true. When it is not, when the boundary between the self and others weakens or dissolves, the result is a range of more or less severe, and not uncommon, disruptions of secure selfhood which, in Western cultures, are conceptualized as psychiatric disorder (for one understanding of which, within a model analogous to the distinction between external and internal definition, see Laing 1971). To extend the logic of this last point, the boundaries of collective identity are also taken for granted until they are threatened.

The contrasting processes of identity production, internal and external, can be illuminated further by drawing upon concepts derived from the methodology of social research. Basic to the sociological and anthropological enterprises is the classification of human collectivities. One of the most enduringly useful distinctions we employ for this purpose is that between *groups* and *categories*. A group is a collectivity which is meaningful to its members, of which they are aware; a category is a collectivity which is defined according to criteria formulated by the sociologist or anthropologist. A group is a self-conscious collectivity, rooted in processes of internal definition, while a category is externally defined. This distinction is, in the first instance, concerned with the procedures which sociologists and anthropologists employ to constitute the social world as a proper object for systematic empirical inquiry and theorization. As such, it is relevant beyond the study of ethnicity and ethnic relations. Debates about social class, for example, are often characterized by disagreement about which principle of definition is most appropriate for the adequate constitution of classes as objects of/for analysis.

However, social groups and social categories can also be understood as different kinds of collectivities *in the actual social world*, and not just in the abstracted social world conjured up by social scientists. A vivid example of this can be found in Marx's famous contrast between 'a class in itself' (a category) and 'a class for itself' (a group). In this understanding of the development of class consciousness, the working class(es) – a social category that was initially defined, with reference to their immiseration and alienation from the means of production, and to their threat to the established order, by others such as capitalists, agencies of the state or socialist activists – becomes a social group, the members of which identify with each other in their collective misfortune, thus creating the possibility of organized collective action on the basis of that identification.

Social categorization – the identification of others as a collectivity – is no less a routine social process than the collective self-identification of the group. Whereas social groups define themselves, their name(s), their nature(s) and their boundary(ies), social categories are identified, defined and delineated by others. All collectivities can be characterized as, to some extent, defined, and thus socially constructed, in both ways. Each side of the dichotomy is implicated in the other and social identity is the outcome of a dialectical process of internal *and* external definition. Whether, in any specific instance, one chooses to talk about a group or a category will depend on the balance struck between internal and external processes in that situation. It is a question of degree.

Although social anthropology, inasmuch as it has considered *individual* identity at all, has privileged social or external knowledge over self- or internal knowledge (A.P. Cohen 1994), the emphasis of the post-Barthian anthropology of ethnicity and *communal* identity has tended to fall on the other side of the internal–external dialectic: upon processes of group identification rather than social categorization (e.g. A.P. Cohen 1982, 1985, 1986; Eriksen 1991; Wallman 1978, 1986). To go over some old ground, there are at least three reasons why this is so. First, anthropology, in its enthusiasm for 'Otherness' and its (still) essentially non-conflictual model of the social world – regardless of internal theoretical debates or the impact of various threads of postmodernism – tends to celebrate ethnicity as a social resource. This is at the expense of paying sufficient attention to ethnicity as a social liability or stigma. Second, this is reinforced by the fact that enthusiasm for a transactional model of social life – ethnicity as *process* – has typically been accompanied by a view of social relationships as rooted in reciprocation, exchange and relatively equitable negotiation. Finally, anthropology's continued emphasis upon participant observation as the discipline's methodological *sine qua non* has led its practitioners to concentrate on the collection of data during face-to-face encounters or through direct observation. Processes of collective internal definition may be easier to study using such an approach than their external counterparts. This bias is, however, entailed neither by the Barthian model nor, indeed, by anthropology. The exploration of processes of ethnic and other forms of categorization is an extension, refinement and development of the anthropological model rather than an alternative to it.

There is one important further point that has so far only been implicit. In talking about the names, characteristics and boundaries of groups and categories, there is a strong suggestion that identity is 'made up' of a number of distinct strands, even if they are only analytically distinguishable. Two of these strands, in particular, are significant here. Social identity, whether it be ethnic or whatever, is both *nominal*, i.e. a name, and *virtual*, a practical meaning or an experience (Jenkins 1996). This contrast is implicit in the distinction between boundaries and their contents, and very approximately analogous to the well-worn distinction between 'status' and 'role'. It is an important contrast because one can change without the other doing so; similarly one can be the product of internal processes of identification, the other of categorization. For example, although categorization may not necessarily change the name or boundary of an identity, it may have considerable potential to define what it means to bear it, the consequential experience of 'being an X'. I will explore the implications of this below.

Social categorization

Distinguishing between internal and external definitions, and between groups and categories, allows us to think about ethnic identity at a number of different 'levels' – not a good word, but it will have to do – within a unified analytical framework. The basis for this framework is what I have called elsewhere (Jenkins 1996) *pragmatic individualism*: the recognition that the social world is peopled in the first and last instances by embodied individuals.

Taking inspiration, *inter alia*, from Erving Goffman (1969, 1983) and Anthony Giddens (1984: 1–40), it is possible to talk about whatever it is that we call society as a set of relationships within and between three orders of phenomena:

- the *individual order*, the world of embodied persons, considered as individual organisms, and 'what-goes-on-in-their-heads';
- the *interaction order*, the world of co-presence and relationships between embodied individuals, of 'what-goes-on-between-people';
- the *institutional order*, the world of systematized, patterned, organized, and symbolically templated 'ways-of-doing-things'.

This scheme is only a way of *thinking about* society. It simply says that society can be thought of as made up of individuals, as made up of the interaction between individuals, and as made up of institutions. It also says that it *cannot* be thought of as any of these in isolation from the other two.

This an ideal-typical model for representing a complex actual reality: it is not meant to suggest that there are *really* three separate social domains, analogous, for example, to ecological zones or different states of physical matter.

Each order is founded in and on the same basic constituents: embodied individuals. And embodiment is one of the keys to understanding the model. Each of the three orders is *distinctively* materialized: in individual bodies; in the collective space of 'set and setting' and the interactional practices which take place between embodied individuals; and in the institutionalized appropriation of space in buildings, territories, visible symbolism, etc. The use of the word 'order' is deliberate, to indicate both distinctive 'domains of activity', and the ordered and orderly nature of the social world (Goffman 1983: 5). But words such as 'world' and 'domain' are apt to mislead: the orders overlap completely. Each is iredeemably implicated in each of the others, and none makes sense without the others.

The internal–external dialectic of identification can be seen at work in all of these orders. Before looking at each in greater detail, a number of basic points of departure need to be outlined. The most fundamental is that internal and external identification do not exist in isolation. Identification is never a unilateral process: at the very least there is always an audience. This principle can be established in a number of ways. First, categorization – external definition – is a basic dimension of internal definition. The process of defining 'us' demands that 'they' should be split off from, or contrasted with, 'us'; group identification is likely to proceed, at least in part, through categorizing others positively or negatively. Second, external definition – by others of us – undoubtedly has an impact upon our internal definition(s). Finally, pre-existing established internal definitions may provide a defence against the imposition of external definitions. The experience of categorization may strengthen existing group identity through a process of resistance and reaction. Thus, the experience of being categorized as 'A' may, only apparently paradoxically, contribute to the reinforcement, or even perhaps the formation, of group identity as 'B' (although the ways in which it will do so are largely a matter for empirical investigation rather than theoretical prediction). Arguments analogous to all the above can also be offered with respect to individual identity.

To talk about the *individual order* is to talk about mind, selfhood and embodiment. I will leave the issue of the social constitution of mind for discussion elsewhere (Jenkins 1996) and concentrate on embodied selfhood here. A conceptual device which is well worn in this respect is the distinction between *I* and *me*. Inspired ultimately by William James, it derives its sociological formulation from G.H. Mead (1934: 173–226), a theorist who has been 'curiously unacknowledged by social anthropology' (A.P. Cohen 1992: 226). To paraphrase Mead, the 'I' is that active aspect of the self which responds to others, whereas the 'me' comprises the attitudes and responses of significant others, as they are incorporated into the self. Mead's 'me' is intimately bound up with what he called the 'generalized other', the voice of the individual's community of membership. Mead's self is embodied, not in a crude physiological sense, but in the notion that selfhood is the social organization of individual consciousness. To put this another way, the self fills the space between embodied mind and (embodied) social interaction, and is inextricably a part of each. Hence *Mind, Self,* and *Society* as the building blocks of his theoretical framework.

The distinction between the 'I' and the 'me' can be interpreted as homologous in many respects to Freud's famous formulation of the 'ego' and 'superego', as fundamental aspects of individual personality. And it shares at least one of the Freudian model's major shortcomings: the ongoing embodied unity of selfhood is vulnerable to misrepresentation as an assembly of more or less separate bits: 'as if an ordinary person is really some sort of committee or team of persons, all laced together inside one skin' (Ryle 1963: 181). That criticism aside, Mead's model of the self is useful here, in that it leaves no room for doubt about the social character of selfhood, or the centrality to it of an internal–external dialectic of identification.

In the course of earliest socialization each human being develops a unique personality, a sense of self which, although it may not always be available to us consciously, is one of the bedrocks of our 'ontological security' (Giddens 1984: 50ff.; 1991: 36–46). Much of this 'sense of self' is located in that embodied hinterland of routine and unreflexive habit – neither conscious nor unconscious – that is the generative site of practices which Bourdieu calls the *habitus* (Bourdieu 1990: 53–97). This 'sense of self' is not simply a 'mental' phenomenon but is intimately bound up with the physical integrity of the individual. Selves are located within bodies, and that embodiment is one of the sources of the unity of selfhood. A sense of self is created in the course of the early verbal and non-verbal dialogue – a complex interaction of separation *from* and identification *with* – between the child and significant others. Typically parents in the first instance, the voice of these others becomes internalized as what Mead calls the 'me', and Giddens (1984: 8) the 'moral conscience'. A voice which tells the child both who she *is* and what she should *do*, each being an aspect of the other.

We know who we are because, in the first place, others tell us. This is the interactional learning process of primary socialization, which works at the conscious and less-than-conscious levels, and which creates an internal relationship – whether harmoniously 'adjusted' or not – between the individualized demands of the self and its internalized social expectations (which may also be thought of in this context as representing culture). It is in the initial and continuing dialectic between the internal and the external that basic selfhood – the individual's sense of who she is, and her embodied point of view on the 'rest of the world' – is constituted.

It is easy to imagine how primary socialization may – depending on local circumstances and the salience of ethnicity – include an ethnic component. Cognitively, if nothing else, the child will develop a point of view on a social world which is axiomatically organized in terms of ethnic classifications. She will learn not only that she is an 'X', but also what this means: in terms of her esteem and worth in her own eyes and in the eyes of others; in terms of appropriate and inappropriate behaviour; and in terms of what it means *not* to be an 'X', what it means to be a 'Y' or a 'Z' perhaps (Epstein 1978). This is emphatically the case, for example, in social contexts where 'racial' categorization is a powerful principle of social organization and stratification (Goodman 1964; Milner 1975; Troyna and Hatcher 1992).

The *interaction order* is where *self-image* meets *public image*. Self-image is the way we see ourselves and, perhaps even more important, the way we would *like* to be seen by others. The starting point for any attempt to understand how this works in social interaction is Goffman (1969). In the context of this discussion, Goffman's most important arguments about the 'presentation of self' are: first, that identity is a matter of performance; second, that in interactional terms, there is no necessary consistency in selfhood, but rather a range of partial aspects or *revelations* of self, depending on the social situation; third, that management of the awkward relationship between the desired presentation of self and other, counter-vailing aspects of one's biography and present situation is of great importance; and fourth, that validation of the performance by others, if not their complicit collaboration, is central to successful impression manage-ment. The homology between Goffman's view of social selfhood as performative and processual and Barth's model of ethnicity as transactional is obvious.

The third and fourth points, above, direct our attention to public image, the vexed question of how others see us. It goes without saying that there is no necessary equivalence between self-image and public image. What is more, it is not always easy to know how others see us anyway. Apart from the obvious epistemological issue – the old philosophical problem of 'other minds' – there are a number of reasons why this should be so. The audience may attempt to conceal its opinion of both actor and perform-ance. The actor may, for various strategic or tactical reasons, attempt to present something other than their 'true' self-image. There may be poor communication between the two sides, for various interactional, institu-tional or other external reasons. The personal psychology which is integral to selfhood may, in the event of major disagreement between self-image and public image, block acknowledgement of the threatening public image.

However, allowing for these qualifications, there will usually be at least *some* interaction between self-image(s) and public image(s), some process of conscious or unconscious adjustment in the ongoing making and re-making of social identity. An example may clarify the point. Occupational identities are among the most important of social identities. For many people they provide the basis on which their livelihood is secured. They are also closely connected to social status. This was so in the pre-modern world and it remains so today. In modern industrial societies, there is an element of election involved in the assumption of an occupational identity. Choice, however, only operates within strict limits and is generally bilateral: other people, gatekeepers of one sort or another within the education system and the labour market, play a crucial role in validating (or not) occupational aspiration. In order to pursue occupational goals and ambitions, qualifications must be obtained, jobs must be applied for and the cooperation of more powerful others obtained. In the process, there is for many young people, first in school and subsequently in the world of employment and unemployment, a gradual convergence of aspiration and outcome, self-image and public image, which is recognized culturally as 'realism' and is one source of stability in a visibly inequitable system (Jenkins 1983; Willis 1977).

It is not just aspirations which are adjusted because of their public reception and evaluation; identity is also variable and vulnerable. For example, the labelling perspective in the sociology of deviance suggests that deviant identities can become internalized as a consequence of the individual concerned being publicly categorized as a law/rule breaker and treated accordingly (Becker 1963; Lemert 1972; Matza 1969). Similarly, identities are imposed upon individuals in school (Cicourel and Kitsuse 1963; Rist 1977) and in the labour market, in a dialectical process of internal and external definition. The individual is identified in a particular way by significant others, who by virtue of their power or authority are in a position to make their definition of the person and the situation count, and thus to constitute that person's subsequent career in terms of the identity in question. That individual's experience of the consequences of being categorized may, over time, lead to an adjustment in her self-image in the direction of the stigmatizing public image. For example, an individual who is defined as 'unreliable', and is not only distrusted but *publicly* distrusted and denied access to occasions where reliability is expected and could therefore be demonstrated, may, as a consequence, become as unreliable as she or he is purported to be. The notion of unreliability may then become an important dimension of her or his self-image.

A point which is made less often is that similar processes are likely to operate with respect to positive or socially valued categorizations. Labelling is not just a negative phenomenon. Inasmuch as the external social world is at least as much a source of self-esteem as it is a threatening environment of hostile labelling, this basic model can also be applied to the incorporation of positive public images into self-imagery.

The implications of these examples for ethnicity is apparent if we look at discrimination in the labour market and the depression or encouragement of aspiration – either effect being possible – among those ethnic minorities who find themselves on its receiving end. The cumulative outcome of this kind of situation, if left unchallenged by currents of resistance within the ethnic community or communities concerned, may, at best, be the development of ethnic occupational niches and a communally and individually accepted ceiling on occupational mobility. At worst, the self-image of a stigmatized and discriminated-against minority will interact with discrimination and exclusion in a vicious circle of cumulative decay and disadvantage, as in many black urban neighbourhoods in North America (Anderson 1978; Hannerz 1969; Liebow 1967) and elsewhere. 'Realism' becomes, in part at least, constitutive of 'reality'. This general process is not in any sense peculiar to 'race' either: a similar argument can be made, for example, with respect to class (Jenkins 1983; MacLeod 1987; Willis 1977).

Ethnic disadvantage in the labour market may seem far removed from the micro-interactional concerns of Goffman. A better example for our purposes might, perhaps, be the subtlety with which people in Northern Ireland purport to 'tell' the difference between Catholic and Protestant in social interaction (Burton 1978: 37–67; Jenkins 1982: 30–1). However, the principles involved are essentially the same. The 'labour market' is, after all, nothing more than an abstraction from a myriad encounters in which the strategies of job-seekers are subject to categorizing decisions about who should get which jobs (Jenkins 1986a). Although, for the moment, a question is begged here – that of *who* is authorized to make the decisions and to make those decisions count – the example serves to connect the micro-interaction of self-image and public image with the *institutional order* of groups and categories.

The important thing to emphasize is that ethnic groups, indeed all groups, are institutions: patterns of social practice identifying persons that have become established over time as the 'way things are done' in a particular local context, and of which people in that context are conscious. Institutions are aspects of local social reality in terms of which and with reference to which decisions are made and behaviour oriented. Social categories may not be institutions – although it is not impossible – but ethnic categorization is likely to be, at least in part, institutionalized.

Most discussions of ethnicity are pitched in terms of *social groups,* the emphasis being upon collective internal definitions of distinctiveness: 'ethnic groups are categories of ascription and identification by the actors themselves' (Barth 1969a: 10). While it is clear from Barth's discussion that the 'actors themselves' can signify actors on both sides of the ethnic boundary, it is equally – if only implicitly – clear that explanatory or analytical priority is accorded to identification *within* the ethnic boundary. And there is a sense in which this is as it should be. A claim to ethnic identity must be validated by an audience of outsiders or Others – because without such an audience the issue would not arise – but it seems to make little sense to talk about an ethnicity which does not, at some point, and no matter how weakly or tenuously, recognize itself as such.

When the issue is expressed thus, the anthropological emphasis upon internal group identification becomes apparent. Leaving aside the massive body of work on caste and hierarchy in India and elsewhere, because it is not concerned with ethnicity as such, there are relatively few examples in the anthropological literature on ethnicity of an explicit concern with processes of *social categorization*. Those examples which can be found, however, testify to the value of such an approach. For the reader who

wishes to survey the diversity of ways in which it can be done, these
include: Hugh Brody (1986) on relations between the Beaver Indians of the
Canadian sub-Arctic and white trappers; Elizabeth Colson (1953) on
Makah native Americans and reservation life; the theoretical arguments of
Jean and John Comaroff (1992: 49–67); Frederick Erickson (1976) discussing gatekeeping encounters and 'race' in the schools of Chicago's West
Side; Ralph Grillo (1985) on encounters between French bureaucrats and
(im)migrants; my own work (Jenkins 1986a) on racism and employment
recruitment in England; Carola Lentz (1994) on the colonial and post-
colonial creation of ethnic identities in Ghana; and Jill Nash and Eugene
Ogan (1990) on mutual categorization in Papua New Guinea. To this list
I would also want to add David Howell's anthropologically informed
historical study (1994) of the categorization of the Ainu by the Japanese
during the early modern period.

For the purposes of illustration, one such will do (Stuchlik 1979).
Looking at the history of European colonial expansion into Chile, the
Spaniards came into contact relatively early – in the sixteenth century –
with an indigenous people known today as the Mapuche. Milan Stuchlik,
using documentary sources, identifies five distinct ways in which the
Spanish, and subsequently the Chileans, categorized the Mapuche in the
course of the centuries which followed: as 'brave and fearless warriors',
'bloodthirsty bandits', 'lazy drunken Injuns', 'the white man's burden' and
'gentle savages who lack education', in historical sequence. The main thrust
of this analysis – which while it does not tell us directly about the impact of
categorization on Mapuche group identity, does suggest some of its consequences for Mapuche life – is that these categorical models of the Mapuche
are not a reflection of 'factual' knowledge about the Mapuche. Rather, they
tell us about native policies, the goals of the Spanish and the Chileans with
respect to the Mapuche. Hence they tell us about the *categorizers* – how
they see themselves and their objectives – more than the *categorized*. It is
Chilean ethnicity that is under construction as much as anything else.

A more general point can perhaps also be made about the anthropological enterprise itself, particularly with respect to notions of 'primi-
tiveness' as a categorization of other cultures (Boon 1982; Kuper 1988).
The constitution of individual Others as sufficiently *similar* to us to be
comprehensible human beings has been one of modern anthropology's
greatest achievements. It has, however, proceeded, much of the time, hand
in glove with powerful assumptions and discourses about collective *difference*. Fortunately, unlike Spanish colonizers or Chilean administrators and
politicians, the capacity of anthropologists to make their definitions count
for those whom they categorize has generally been modest, although their
indirect influence should not be underestimated.

The three social orders – the *individual*, the *interactional*, and the
institutional – have been distinguished only for purposes of explanation.
They are thoroughly intertwined with each other; occupying the same space
and each made up of embodied, socialized, individuals. The unitary sense

of self lies behind self-image. Self-images meld with public images in the complex negotiation of shared meanings, understandings and practices that constitutes group identity. Group identification and categorization combine in situationally specific relations of resistance or reinforcement to produce the social reality in historical time and space of ethnicity and institutionalized ethnic collectivities. I could, of course, as easily have approached these interrelationships from the other end, beginning with the relationship between groups and categories. The traffic on this street flows in both directions. Making this point re-emphasizes the internal–external simultaneity of processes of ethnic identification: individually, interactionally, and institutionally. None has precedence, whether conceptually, historically or developmentally. Nor can any of them be imagined in the absence of the others.

Contexts of ethnic categorization

Identity is produced and reproduced during social interaction, and interaction is always situated in context. I will now look at some of the specific contexts and processes of social categorization. Although the emphasis will be upon *ethnic* categorization, the overall picture is generalizable to other kinds of social identity. This section will begin to draw out the implications of my arguments for a research agenda concerned with ethnicity and ethnic identity. It will also relocate the theoretical discussions so far, into the everyday contexts of social life in which we do our research.

The basic shape of the empirical agenda is presented schematically in Figure 5.1. It is not intended to be exhaustively inclusive; it is simply an attempt to sketch in some of the flesh which can be hung on the bones of my argument. To keep the discussion manageable, two simplifying assumptions are implicit in what follows: that ethnic categorization is likely to be more often pejorative, negative or stigmatizing than not; and that there are no contemporary social settings in which the formal–informal distinction does not have some relevance. The contrast between the formal

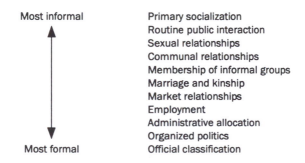

Figure 5.1   *Contexts of ethnic categorization*

and the informal is not a sharp distinction. It is, rather, a continuum of emphasis. The degree to which *primary socialization*, for example, is the private domestic responsibility of the child's immediate caretakers – unsupervised by state or local community – and the degree to which it is formally organized and regulated, is a matter of enormous variability. So too is the relationship between primary socialization and subsequent formal education. Similarly, *routine public interaction*, although typically informal, can also, in specific circumstances, be formalized (as in the case of inter-'racial' public encounters in the South Africa of apartheid). At the other end of the spectrum, *administrative allocation* and *organized politics*, for example, are shot through with informality in every aspect of their organization. If for no other reason, this is because informality is not conceptualized as a residual category: as whatever is left in the absence of formality, or once the formal dimensions of a situation have been identified. Formality and informality are specific kinds of social relation which have developed, historically, side by side: 'The formal is simultaneously an absence and a presence within the informal, and vice versa' (Harding and Jenkins 1989: 137). Each depends upon and takes part of its meaning from the other (see Figure 5.1).

The importance of *primary socialization* in the social construction of identity has already been alluded to, and will be discussed again. Suffice it to draw attention briefly to a number of points here. First, there is no necessity that ethnicity will feature explicitly in primary socialization; much depends here upon local circumstances and histories. If it does, however, ethnicity may take its place alongside the primary identities of human-ness, gender and selfhood (Jenkins 1996): deeply rooted in first encounters and the egocentric taken-for-granted constitution of the social world that is the embodied individual point of view, and resilient to easy transformation. Finally, primary socialization is an exchange of communication between infant and others, but in the first instance, and for quite a time thereafter, it is an exchange in which information *in* dominates: if we know who we are, it is because, a long time ago, beyond the reach of conscious recall, other people told us (Dunn 1988; Kaye 1982; Richards 1974). Primary socialization is the realm of categorization, and sets patterns for our receptiveness to being categorized in the life that follows.

Routine public interaction is the face-to-face interaction which occurs, much of it outside ongoing social relationships, within the gaze of others. Informal ethnic categorization organizes 'relations in public' in a number of ways. First, there are the verbal and non-verbal cues which are used to allocate unknown others to an ethnic category. In some cases, these cues are a dimension of group identity, explicit signals of ethnic identity: language, clothing, bodily adornment, etc. Others, however, including many aspects of non-verbal behaviour, are likely to be involuntary or unconscious (and here we see again the importance of habit and the body, *pace* Bourdieu). Items of behaviour are appropriated by others as criteria of ethnic categorization, without those who 'own' them participating in this identification (or even, perhaps, being aware of it). Aspects of physical appearance – whether 'real' or imaginary and typically crystallized in ethnic stereotypes – are also a staple of anonymous public categorization.

Other forms of routine public behaviour are instrumental in the construction and mobilization of ethnic categories. Particular mention should be made of humour, verbal abuse and violence (all of which are, of course, important in the context of enduring relationships and in the private sphere). With respect to humour, the case of the 'ethnic joke' is well known (C. Davies 1990). Anthropological analyses of joking suggest that ethnic joking is likely to characterize situations where social restraints inhibit the overt expression of inter-ethnic hostility (Douglas 1975: 90–114). Ethnic jokes – and here one may legitimately stretch the concept of the joke to includes performances such as the Brer Rabbit tales of the American South, or the Anansi stories of the Caribbean – are a potent site of passive resistance to domination. They are equally effective in the categorization of ethnic subordinates. Jokes facilitate categorization where it may not be socially acceptable or explicitly possible; there's no such thing as *just* a joke, and ethnic jokes are no exception.

Inter-ethnic verbal abuse and violence do not require too much discussion here, except to suggest that humour, insult and violence shade into each other and are intimately connected. Verbal abuse and violence are concerned with the beating of ethnic boundaries through the enforcement of definitions of what the ethnic 'other' *is* or must *do*. Power is at the heart of the matter. However, for a variety of reasons, authoritative social control – legitimate according to local specifications – has provided political and legal anthropology with the bulk of its subject matter. Violence and its threat may, in the process, have been somewhat underestimated as a routine mechanism of control and a strategy for achieving goals. Violence to others, up to and including killing, may – in addition to all of its other dimensions – be the ultimate form of categorization. I will return to this in Chapter 7.

Power and control are also central to *sexual relationships*, which straddle the divide between the public and the private. The sensitivity of inter-ethnic sexual relationships has been documented in a wide variety of settings (e.g. Dollard 1957: 134–87; Okely 1983: 154–6; Pryce 1979: 80–94). It may be expressed in notions of group 'possession' of women and must in part, therefore, be considered as an aspect of patriarchy as well as ethnicity. In terms of ethnicity, what is typically at issue is the definition of which men may or may not have access to which women. The resolution of the issue is typically asymmetrical, in reflection of the power relationships between the groups in question, and between men and women. Access to another group's women may loom large in the ethnic identity of a dominant group, with lack of (male) control in this respect being a defining feature of subordinate categorization. When systematized racism enters the picture, a general prohibition of 'miscegenation' may – officially or legally, anyway – deny the men of a dominant group access to ethnically subordinate women.

Communal relationships, the more or less tightly knit networks which evolve over time in residentially shared localities, provide many opportunities for ethnic categorization. Most obviously, communities are often ethnically relatively homogeneous. Gossip may serve to mark the boundaries between one ethnic community and another and is one of the most effective ways of policing inter-ethnic sex and friendship relationships. All kinds of social interaction across communal boundaries are – following Barth and Anthony Cohen – important in boundary maintenance (hence the need for policing at times of changing boundaries). Local peer groups are particularly efficient at socializing their members into group identity, and dramatizing the articulation of ethnic categorization with respect to other ethnicities.

Membership of informal groups may be a dimension of everyday communal life. However, there are informal social groups which are not grounded in local communality but serve nonetheless as efficient contexts of ethnic exclusion and, through their tacit – or not so tacit – criteria of membership, of categorization. Mundane examples are to be found in ethnic peer groups within schools and in work organizations. There is also a spectrum of more formally constituted organizations – from the Ku Klux Klan to B'nai B'rith to immigrants' mutual aid associations – whose membership is ethnically specified and which pursue ethnically defined goals.

The domain of kinship relations – *marriage and the family* – is subject to a degree of public regulation. In many societies this regulation is formally embodied in law. There are few examples, however, of the formal categorization of permissible marriage partners in strictly ethnic terms, and where they can be found, as I have already observed, they typically involve organized racism in one form or another (laws prohibiting 'miscegenation' have been current in this century, *inter alia*, in some states of the American Union, Germany and, most recently, South Africa). The informal regulation of inter-ethnic sexual relations in the communal arena remains the most potent force maintaining ethnic exclusivity in marriage. Categorization generates a situation in which the operation of a courtship and marriage market, structured by individually internalized ethnic categories which are expressed consciously as preferences and unconsciously as encounters, will tend to reproduce the ethnic status quo without recourse to explicit regulation.

Another field of social life which is hierarchically structured in terms of power and formally regulated only to a limited extent is the domain of *market relationships*. Governed, on the face of things, by economic principles which emphasize the pursuit of either profit or relatively equitable exchange (notions of equity and acceptable profit being contextually defined), business and trading are nonetheless structured by ethnic categorization. This is so with respect to who can trade with whom, who can trade in what, and the price that different categories of people must pay for similar commodities or services. Ethnically organized market relationships can be found in contexts as diverse as the housing markets of Britain and the United States (Banton 1983: 336–65), the trading networks of northern Norway (Eidheim 1969) and the exchange relationships of 'primitive' New Guinea and northern Australia (Sahlins 1972: 277–314).

Employment is a particular kind of market relationship, characteristic of modern, industrialized societies. It may be informal or formal, but, for increasing swathes of the world's population, entry into the labour market represents – apart, perhaps, from limited eligibility to membership of a welfare system – their only possible relation to the means of production and, hence, their only source of livelihood. In ethnically heterogeneous labour markets – which are the rule rather than the exception – ethnic categorization is a powerful criterion governing the allocation of job-seekers to jobs by those who are authorized to make recruitment decisions. This is encouraged and reinforced inasmuch as recruitment to the positions of supervision and management which involve hiring and firing is, of course, also likely to be ethnically biased. In addition, the cumulative effect of ethnic categorization in housing markets and in access to education serves further to limit, systematically and disadvantageously, the labour-market options of particular groups.

A key moment during employment recruitment is the interview, no matter how perfunctory it may be. Although formalized diagnostic testing is becoming more influential in initial screening, interviewing and committee decision-making are central to processes of *administrative allocation* (Batley 1981). These formal and informal practices serve to allocate resources and penalties within and from public- and private-sector formal organizations. In addition to employment, these rewards and penalties include public housing (Flett 1979), welfare benefits (Howe 1985) and social work intervention of one kind or another (Hillyard and Percy-Smith 1988: 170–203; Liddiard and Hutson 1991). Interviewing and bureaucratized collective decision-making are important sources, alongside formal rules and certificated expertise or knowledge, of the institutional rationality which legitimizes the powers of delegated discretion exercised by officers in deciding individual cases. They are also the site of the creation of a distinctively modern and subordinated generic social category, that of the bureaucratic *client* (Collmann and Handelman 1981).

It is the discretionary nature of these gatekeeping encounters, within a permissive bureaucratic framework, which allows ethnic categorization its inevitable entry into the process – whether explicitly or implicitly (Erickson 1976; Grillo 1985; Karn 1983) – along with other ascriptive and stigmatizing categorizations (Lipsky 1980; Prottas 1979; Scott 1970). Administrative allocation processes have an increasing reach within modern states. Their significance in the social construction of patterns of disadvantage and of the everyday experience of being a member of a stigmatized social category, whether ethnic or not, should not be underestimated. Administrative allocation is a privileged context for the transformation of the nominal into the virtual (a distinction which was briefly introduced in

Chapter 4). Ethnic categorization in this context is likely to *count* in the lives of the categorized. It is authorized, offically legitimate categorization from which consequences flow.

Organized politics is the source of the statutes and regulations which underwrite the legitimacy of state and other bureaucracies. In states with histories of ethnic conflict, this conflict will be mirrored in the political system. In these situations, political parties and politicians may foster ethnic categorization through public rhetoric, legislative and administrative acts and the distribution of resources via networks of clientage. Official categorization of this kind can also, however, involve the *denial* of the existence of historically constituted ethnic groups, as in the Nazi state's refusal to acknowledge Sorbian identity in Lusatia (Burleigh and Wippermann 1991: 130–5).

Even in societies without an explicitly ethnically structured polity, similar trends may be observed, as and when the calculus of politics favours them. Rhetoric is in these cases perhaps more significant than legislation or administrative act. As moral entrepreneurs, politicians, in conjunction with newspaper proprietors, journalists and commentators, public officials and spokespersons for interest groups, may participate in the development and promotion of moral panic about ethnically constructed issues, such as immigration or black street crime (Hall *et al.* 1978). This is influential in the public constitution of a 'problem', in its identification with particular ethnic categories (or, rather, their identification with it), and eventually in the framing of legislative and administrative responses. Less subtly, politics has historically provided the platform for the expression and mobilization of overt ethnic chauvinism; moral panics about ethnic 'problems' shade into the incitement of inter-ethnic conflict and violence.

Looking at unintended consequences, welfare-oriented policy responses to perceived social problems may also contribute to the politics of ethnic categorization. The attempt to target resources and intervention at a section of the population which is perceived to have particularly urgent or specialized 'needs' may serve either to call into existence a new social category or to strengthen an existing categorization. This classification may emphasize the worthiness to receive resources of the category in question, as in the case of 'the elderly'. It may, however, identify members of the category in question as socially deficient or lacking in some fashion, and serve to label them further as 'undeserving' or 'troublesome', as in the construction and mobilization of the category of 'black youth' in British political discourse (Solomos 1988). It seems particularly likely that equal opportunity initiatives and other redistributive policies will have these effects.

Which brings me finally to *official classification*. An increasingly conventional understanding of the elaborate and pervasive schemes for classifying populations that characterize bureaucratic government, is that they mark a historical shift in state approaches to social control, from the public exercise of power over the body to the private disciplining of the mind

(Foucault 1979). However accurate this may in some senses be, it is also worth reminding ourselves that, as in Nazi Germany, the classification of persons may be a precursor to attacks on the body. Implicitly, this discussion has already touched upon aspects of official classificatory processes, in the context of administrative allocation and organized politics. The conjunction of power and knowledge that is embodied in legitimate social categorization has many facets. Suffice it to mention two here: one in principle benign, the other emphatically not.

The first is that indispensable adjunct to the planning processes of modern government, the census of population. In order to gather meaningful data, population categories must first be defined. Among these are ethnic (or 'racial') categories (Lee 1993). Thus they become established in official discourses, discourses which are powerfully constitutive of social reality through public rhetoric, the formulation of policy, the targeting of resources and social control measures, etc. The census categories may be used to collect and construct other statistics – on crime, unemployment, health – which also feed into policy formulation and implementation. The nature of these ethnic categories – or, indeed, the collection of the information at all – may, for a variety of reasons, be contested by the sections of the population to whom they are applied, and the state may use them to justify further policy in areas such as immigration control or internal policing (Bhat *et al.* 1988).

Census and other statistics are collective and reasonably anonymous; they do not directly categorize named *individuals* (although they may feed into administrative allocation). Indeed, not many states categorize their individual citizens in this fashion. Minor examples of such an approach include the compulsory categorization and recording, for purposes of affirmative action monitoring, of the ethnic identity of employees in many US Federal, state and private-sector organizations, or the identification of 'nationality' – denoting republic of origin – on the pre-1989 USSR internal passport. Other states, however, most notably Nazi Germany and the Republic of South Africa, having defined citizenship in terms of 'race' – a crucial escalatory move in ethnic categorization – have gone on, necessarily, to develop far-reaching systems of 'racial' categorization, governing every aspect of life (and death). The role of 'expert' knowledge in the construction of those systems, and their bureaucratized administration, are a grim reminder of the repressive possibilities inherent in administrative allocation (Bauman 1989; Burleigh and Wippermann 1991; Müller-Hill 1988).

There are many other contexts of ethnic – and indeed other – categorization to which research attention should be directed: friendship relations, education, religion, and institutionalized social control are only some of the possibilities. Some of the contexts I have discussed are themselves so broad – administrative allocation, for example – that they could usefully be disaggregated for the purposes of empirical research. A number of points should be remembered in any consideration of the research issues raised by this section.

First, although my own research background may have encouraged me to draw upon illustrative material from complex, urbanized societies (and disproportionately from Europe and North America at that), the schematization of 'contexts of ethnic categorization' at the beginning of this section is intended to have the widest possible applicability. Second, the different social contexts of categorization should not be understood as separate or hierarchical 'levels'. They overlap systematically in complex and interesting ways: routine public interaction, for example, takes place within a number of the other social contexts mentioned. A similar point could be made about informal social groups, which exist within (and contribute to the organization of) many different contexts. And so on. One research task is to problematize and examine this mutual reinforcement. The considerable potential for the mutual reinforcement of categorization in overlapping social contexts – what once we might have called over-determination – is of the greatest importance for our understanding of the power and resilience to intervention of, for example, racism. Third, the dialectical implication in each other of internal and external definition, group identification and categorization should not be forgotten. Although the discussion in this section has largely been about categorization, the social contexts identified are also significant in processes of internal definition. Given the interpenetration of the two, how could it be otherwise?

Categorization and power

Categorization contributes to group identity in various ways. There is, for example, something which might be referred to as 'internalization': the categorized group is exposed to the terms in which another group defines it and assimilates that categorization, in whole or in part, into its own identity. Put this baldly, however, the suggestion seems to beg more questions than it answers: *why* should the external definition be internalized, for example, and *how* does it happen? At least five possible scenarios suggest themselves.

First, the external categorization might be more or less the same as an aspect of existing group identity, in which case they will simply reinforce each other. It seems altogether plausible that some degree of external reinforcement or validation is crucial to the successful maintenance of internal (group) definitions. Similarly, categorization may be less likely to 'stick' where it is markedly at odds with existing boundaries and identifications.

Second, there is the incremental cultural change which is likely to be a product of any long-standing but relatively harmonious inter-ethnic contact. The ethnic boundary is osmotic, and not just in terms of personnel: languages and cultures may also interact, and in the process identities are likely to be affected. We, for example, may gradually and imperceptibly come to define ourselves somewhat differently in the light of how they appear to define us, and how they treat us (and, equally likely, vice versa).

Third, the external category might be produced by people who, in the eyes of the original group, have the legitimate authority to categorize them, by virtue of their superior ritual status, knowledge, or whatever. Such a situation implies greater social than cultural differentiation – if a distinction posed in terms as crude as this is admissible – inasmuch as legitimate authority necessarily requires at least a minimal degree of shared participation in values or cosmology.

Fourth, is a simpler case, or at least a cruder one: external categorization is imposed by the use of physical force or its threat, i.e. the exercise of power. The experience of violation may become integral to group identification. The categorized, without the physical capacity to resist the carrying of identity cards, the wearing of armbands, or whatever more subtle devices of identification and stigmatization might be deployed, may, in time, come to see themselves in the language and categories of the oppressor. They are certainly likely to behave in an appropriate manner.

Finally, there are the oppressed who do resist, who reject imposed boundaries and/or their content(s). However, the very act of defying categorization, of striving for an autonomy of self-identification, is, of course, an effect of being categorized in the first place. The rejected external definition *is* internalized, but paradoxically, as the focus of denial.

In these five possibilities, a distinction between power and legitimate authority is apparent. However, the contribution of categorization to group identity depends upon more than 'internalization'. The capacity of one group of people to effectively define or constitute the conditions of existence experienced by Others is enormously important in the internal–external dialectic of collective identification (something similar, at the individual level, has been discussed above, in the context of labelling). Categorization is consequential, and it is in the consequences that it may be most effective. This calls up the distinction which I have proposed between the *virtual* and *nominal* dimensions of ethnic identification, and emphasizes the virtual.

To revisit an example given earlier, the categorization of the Mapuche by the Spanish and white Chileans, in particular ways, must be expected to have influenced the behaviour of the Chileans towards the Mapuche: 'native policy' as Stuchlik puts it. The Chileans, like the Spanish before them, because of their eventual monopolization of violence within the local context and their consequent control of resources, were – and, indeed, still are – in a position to make their categorization of the Mapuche count disproportionately in the social construction of Mapuche life. And the internal–external dialectic can be seen at work: resistance to the Spanish was, for example, an important factor creating internal group identification in the shape of military alliances, and generating, between the sixteenth and nineteenth centuries, the wider collectivity of the Mapuche out of a network of small, mutually related kin groups (Stuchlik 1976: 15). In many senses, therefore, what it means to be a Mapuche is in part a consequence of what the Spanish or the Chileans have *made* it mean.

The effective categorization of a group of people by a more powerful 'other' is not, therefore, 'just' a matter of classification (if, indeed, there is any such thing). It is necessarily an intervention in that group's social world which will, to an extent and in ways that are a function of the specifics of the situation, alter that world and the experience of living in it. Just as the Chileans have the capacity to constitute, in part, the experience of 'being a Mapuche', so, for example, employment recruiters in Britain – who are typically white – contribute to the social constitution of the collective experience of growing up as a member of a black ethnic minority.

To return to Barth – and Weber – here one sees the unintended consequences of action at work. It is partly in the cumulative mutual reinforcement of these unintended consequences that the patterns of history, both in the present and as a framework of constraint and possibility for future generations, are produced. Since 'culture' is a matter of everyday life and its exigencies, the power of others to constitute the experience of daily living is a further important contribution of categorization to group identity. It is also powerful support for the view of ethnicity and identity, as everyday practice and historical process, that I have developed here.

One of my starting points is that ethnicity should be conceptualized within a theoretical framework which allows for its integration into the topic of 'social identity' in general. In its turn, however, social identity must be constructed as a proper subject for theorization in a manner that allows the inclusion of individual and collective identities within a unified analytical framework. Even the most private of identities is not imaginable as anything other than the product of a socialized consciousness and a social situation. Even the most collective of identities must, in some sense, exist in the awareness of individual actors.

Viewed in the abstract, identity – whether ethnic or otherwise – can be understood as two interacting but independent entailments: a name (the *nominal*) and an experience (the *virtual*). The latter is, in a sense, what the name *means*; this is primarily a matter of its *consequences* for those who bear it, and can change while the nominal identity remains the same (and vice versa). The nominal and the virtual unite in the ongoing production and reproduction of identity and its boundaries. The nominal–virtual distinction recognizes that ethnic identities – and, indeed, all social identities – are *practical accomplishments* rather than *static forms*. They are immanently, although not necessarily, variable. As a social form – in the constitution of a historically enduring ethnic group, for example – ethnicity is always potentially variable, nominally and virtually.

In the practical accomplishment of identity, two mutually interdependent but theoretically distinct social processes are at work: *internal definition* and *external definition*. These operate differently in the individual, interactional and institutional orders. Analyses of ethnicity – particularly within social anthropology – have, however, emphasized internal definition and *group identification* at the expense of external definition and *social categorization*. This is more than just a matter of empirical neglect. It is actually a lop-sided understanding. Identity is always the practical product of the interaction of ongoing processes of internal *and* external definition. One cannot be understood in isolation from the other.

A concern with external definition and categorization demands, finally, that analyses of ethnicity should focus on *power* as well as on *authority*, and on the manner in which different modes of domination are implicated in the social construction of ethnic and other identities. This is not an original observation. But if we do not do this, the result is likely to be a model of ethnicity that is as trivial as it is one-sided. Unless we can construct an understanding of ethnicity which addresses all of ethnicity's facets and manifestations – from the celebratory communality of belonging to the final awful moment of genocide – we will have failed not only ourselves, but also the people about whom we write.

6

Ideologies of Identification

In Chapter 4 I briefly introduced the arguments that ethnicity is a ubiquitous, general mode of social identification, and that homologous phenomena such as racism and nationalism can be understood as historically specific allotropes or versions of the wider principle of ethnic affiliation and classification. This chapter will begin to explore in greater detail what these arguments might mean and will critically examine some of our current conceptualizations of ethnicity, racism and nationalism, and the relationships between them.

'Race' is typically differentiated from ethnicity in terms of a contrast between physical and cultural differences (Banton 1988: 1–15). Whether explicit or implicit, and however formulated, this basic model underlies most social science discussions of the topic: 'racial' differentiation is something – the contentious issue is *what* – to do with physical differences between people. However, the 'physical differences' with which we are concerned in matters of 'race' are only differences which *make* a difference because they are culturally or socially signified as such. There is, therefore, nothing 'objective' about 'race'; hence the need felt by many of us to continue to hedge the word around with scare quotes.

Although it is possible to define these concepts in the above general manner, the *relationship* between 'race' and ethnicity is something about which there is little consensus and a good deal of touchiness. There may not even always be agreement that the distinction is, in itself, valid or important. For example, Sandra Wallman's argument (1986: 229) that phenotype or physical appearance – and this is what is generally meant by 'race' – is no more than 'one element in the repertoire of [ethnic] boundary markers', has already been mentioned. A perspective similar to Wallman's in many respects, although arrived at from a very different direction – 'a multiculturalist context that seeks to redress racial disadvantage by providing for ethnic difference' – is offered by Floya Anthias, who argues 'that "race" categories belong to the more encompassing category of ethnic collectivity' (1992: 421). 'Race,' she suggests, is simply one of the ways in which ethnic boundaries are constructed.

There is substantial merit in arguments which recognize a systematic relationship between ethnicity and 'race'; indeed, this book must be counted among them. However, in the form in which they are offered by Wallman or Anthias, they are unconvincing, for a number of reasons. To reiterate these, while 'ethnic' social relations are not *necessarily* hierarchical, exploitative and conflictual, 'race relations' would certainly appear to be. Although ethnic boundaries involve relations of power, and social categorization is inherent to the internal–external dialectic of ethnic identification, hierarchical difference is not *definitive* of ethnic relations. In other words it is possible to imagine and, in fact, to document ethnic inter-group relations in which the collectivities involved neither look *up to* nor *down on* each other. 'Race', however, unlike ethnicity, seems to be much *more* a matter of social categorization than of group identification (although still a matter of both). Furthermore, while ethnic identity is, of course, part of a structured or coherent body of knowledge about the social world – as an aspect of culture, how could it be otherwise? – 'racial' categorization appears to be both more explicit and more elaborated in its justification. Finally, and to repeat this chapter's point of departure, regardless of whether the comparative perspective is historical or cross-cultural, ethnicity seems to be a ubiquitous social phenomenon; those situations which we describe as 'race relations' are not.

The last two points – the role of explicit justificatory knowledge, and the greater or lesser ubiquity of each – raise slippery questions about the respective ontological statuses of ethnicity and 'race', questions which hide unacknowledged within many discussions of the problem. They are certainly questions begged by the physical–cultural distinction. Furthermore, if we allow a contrast between the physical and the cultural risks to sneak into our discussions through the back door, other, even more troublesome, conceptual oppositions, such as objective versus subjective, or material versus ideal, emerge. The result may be, at best, continued confusion and, at worst, continuing conflict about the nature of the topic under discussion.

In order to begin the work of clarification, I want to suggest that ethnic identity, although every bit (and only) a social and cultural construction, should be conceptualized as a basic or first-order dimension of human experience. There are three, rather different, aspects to this claim. The most general concerns the ubiquity of ethnic attachments. If we define ethnicity very broadly – as collective identification that is socially constructed with reference to putative cultural similarity and difference – then it seems uncontroversial to suggest that this has probably been around for as long as cultured humans have lived in social groups. This is, however, a point of view which demands considerable care in its articulation:

> Classifying the most diverse historical forms of social identity as 'ethnic' creates the scientifically questionable but politically useful impression that all ethnicities are basically the same and that ethnic identity is a natural trait of persons and social groups . . . This is not an argument which bears up to historical scrutiny. Rather, it is a nominalist operation intended to provide scholarly legitimation for ethno-nationalist ideologies. (Lentz 1995: 305)

This warning is important, timely, and well taken. There *is* a danger, in adopting too general a definition of ethnicity, of neutering the concept, while at the same time according it dubious extra-social potency. But to say that ethnicity seems to be one of the 'givens' of culture and human social life should *not* be misconstrued as saying that it is 'natural', other than in the sense that culture is a 'natural' propensity of humans (which is to say little beyond problematizing the value of the culture–nature distinction). To illustrate the point by analogy, sociality (Carrithers 1992) and the close care-taking of infants and children are ubiquitous in human experience. This doesn't mean – although it can easily be construed thus – that there are universal, and normative, patterns or forms of either.

In the same way, to argue that collective identifications and attachments based on perceived cultural differentiation seem to be historically ubiquitous, is *not* to justify ethnic or nationalist excesses, along the lines of 'they – or we – can do no other'. Such an argument *is* vulnerable to politicized misrepresentation, and a good example of how this happens is the way in which Geertz's original argument about 'primordial attachments' has been academically caricatured, as discussed in Chapter 4. But the danger of re-writing history by definitional fiat – and, in the process, lending support to arguments that are not only utterly repugnant but certainly untrue – while omnipresent, and necessitating vigilance, is not inevitable. Ethnic attachments are not necessarily malign; what matters is understanding the circumstances in which they become so.

And there is another, arguably worse, danger: of overlooking the consistency over time of the principles of collective identification and affiliation with which we are concerned and thus misunderstanding them. Ernest Gellner – whose hostility towards nationalism can scarcely be in doubt, and who knew what its costs were – recognized this in his discussion of the loyalty that people feel for the groups to which they belong and the fact that they identify with them:

> If one calls this factor, generically, 'patriotism', then . . . some measure of such patriotism is indeed a perennial part of human life . . . nationalism is a very distinct species of patriotism. (1983: 138)

If we do not acknowledge a very general, ideal-typical category of something that we can call 'ethnicity' – which, witness Barth's 'the social organization of culture difference', for example, will necessarily be imprecise – how are we in principle to distinguish ethnic attachments from kinship or organizational attachments (for example) and how, correspondingly, can we compare different 'ethnic' situations?

The second aspect of the claim that ethnicity should be understood as a basic dimension of social life alludes to taken-for-grantedness and embeddedness. Ask the question: what is it that constructs ethnic identification? At least part of the answer has got to be *culture*. While Hughes and Barth are absolutely correct to insist that cultural traits don't constitute ethnic difference, Handelman (1977) and, more recently, Cornell (1996) are equally correct to remind us that the cultural stuff is not irrelevant either. And *our* culture – language, non-verbals, dress, food, the structure of space, etc. – as we encounter it and live it during socialization and subsequently, is *for us* simply something that *is*. When identity is problematized during interaction across the boundary, we have to make explicit – to ourselves every bit as much as to Others – that which we have hitherto known without knowing *about*. This is what Bourdieu (1990: 53–97) calls 'habitus', the embodied and unreflexive everyday practical mastery of culture: unsystematic, the empire of habit, neither conscious nor unconscious. Nothing could be more basic and nothing more inextricably implicated in ethnicity (Bentley 1987).

In the third place, however, a great deal turns upon local histories, circumstances and situations. This, again, is to return to an earlier thread of my argument: ethnic attachments do not have the same salience and force everywhere. Experience, if nothing else, insists that this is the case. For many people(s), ethnicity is a background factor, part of the cultural furniture of everyday life, and consequently little attended to. But for many others, ethnicity is an integral and dynamic aspect of self-conscious self-hood and everyday discourse, rooted in early socialization and produced and reproduced in the ongoing concerns of the here-and-now. Ethnicity may have an individual psycho-social *reality*, which bestows upon it a particular immediacy and compelling urgency (and the word *may* is the most important word in this sentence). This capacity for ethnic identity to *really* matter – *when* it matters – is what Geertz was suggesting in his characterization of ethnicity as a primordial attachment. Geertz is talking about what people *feel*, as is Walker Connor in describing the 'ethno-national bond' as 'beyond reason' (1993). Similarly, John Rex has argued that ethnicity differs in this sense from group membership based on inter-personal obligation, cultural rules or shared interests (1991: 10–12). Ethnic identity may be imagined, but it is emphatically not imaginary; locally that imagining may be very powerful.

As I have argued in Chapter 4 and elsewhere, taking seriously the notion that ethnicity may be a primary – rather than a 'primordial' – social identity doesn't mean abandoning the social constructionist understanding of ethnicity or naturalizing it *à la* sociobiology (van den Berghe 1981, 1986). It does allow us, however, to appreciate one of the important differences between 'race' and ethnic identity. If ethnic identity is basic to the human condition, in the sense towards which I am feeling my way here, 'race' is not. And if ethnicity is arguably a basic, universal facet of the human cultural repertoire, ideas about 'race' are not. 'Racial' categories are second-order cultural creations or notions; they are abstractions, explicit bodies of knowledge that are very much more the children of specific historical circumstances, typically territorial expansion and attempted imperial or colonial domination. 'Racial' categorization has a shorter and more patchy history than ethnic identity.

Furthermore, and again in contrast to ethnicity, because of its genesis in systematic domination, and the specifically 'physical' referents which endow it with putative immutability, 'race' may be an aspect of identity which children acquire in strikingly different patterns of acceptance or rejection, depending upon whether they belong to 'racially' stigmatized categories or not (Milner 1975: 35–100; Troyna and Hatcher 1992: 19–23). Lest this last point be misunderstood as entailing some kind of deterministic inevitability – and remembering that 'race' is every bit as socially constructed as ethnicity – the internalization of a negative self-image or the rejection of 'racial' stigmatization also depend upon the contributions which schooling, familial socialization, and the politics of resistance can make to the production and promotion of countervailing positive images and experiences (Stone 1981: 44–89). The point here is that routine primary socialization within the context of ethnically signified cultural commonality will, as a matter of course and almost incidentally, provide a repertoire of positivity (embodied in language, religion, kinship institutions, etc.) with which, if appropriate, to resist subordination and denigration. The same is not necessarily true about 'race'.

None of this, of course, is to deny the possible significance that aspects of physical appearance (phenotype) can possess as ethnic boundary markers. However, phenotype and 'race' should not, as in the quotation below, be conflated:

> when 'race' is used in everyday discourse, it is usually to refer to or to signify the existence of phenotypical variation, that is, variations in skin colour, hair type, bone structure and so on . . . What exists is not 'race' but phenotypical variation: 'race' is a word used to describe or refer to such variation. (Miles 1982: 20)

The relationship between 'race' and phenotype cannot possibly be this neat. For example, socially signified and visible phenotypical differences – such as hair colour – may be invoked in processes of ethnic differentiation without ideas about 'race' being involved. On the other hand, putative 'racial' differentiation may be categorically asserted on the basis of physical differences which are either invisible to the unassisted naked eye (cranial indices are an obvious example here) or completely non-existent. Finally – and Miles seems, paradoxically, to recognize this himself when he says that one does not exist but the other does, that 'race' and phenotype are different orders of thing – phenotype is the material product of the interaction of genetic endowment (genotype) and environment, 'race' is a cultural fiction.

Other authors can sound just as confused. Thus Wade, criticizing 'the seemingly unexceptional approach' of Banton and Rex, argues that their work

> poses it [i.e. phenotype] as an obvious objective biological fact when in fact it is a highly socially constructed one. For it is not just *any* phenotypical variation that has become racialized (in any of the changing definitions of race), but a specific set of variations that have become salient in long-term colonial encounters. (Wade 1993: 21)

Phenotype cannot, on the one hand, be 'highly socially constructed' and, on the other, the range of variations – as implied by '*any* phenotypical variation' – out of which specific sets are historically selected for attention.

While I might not want to go all the way with Banton in arguing that, 'there is no distinctive class of social relations to be identified as racial relations' (1986: 49), his viewpoint resonates with that which I am suggesting here. To express that point of view in another way, ethnicity and 'race' are different kinds of concept, they do not actually constitute a true pair. To oppose the one to the other does not, therefore, seem to make much sense. The most that can be said is that, at certain times and in certain places, culturally specific conceptions of 'race' – or, more correctly, of 'racial' differentiation – have featured, sometimes very powerfully, in the repertoire of ethnic boundary-maintaining devices. In general agreement with Robert Miles (1989), it is racism – or racisms – to which we should be attending, rather than 'race'.

Does it matter, however, that we should agree on the nature of the difference between 'race' and ethnicity? Perhaps not, but it is certainly more than a 'quibble', and it is important to attempt to be clear about the matter. The issue has probably been responsible for even more confusion, and the generation of greater imbalance between heat and light, than the tussle between primordialists and situationalists. Consider, for example, the problem into which Anthias finds herself led when she argues that:

> racisms do not rely only on 'race' categorisation, but use the ethnic category more generally as their essential building block. The historical manifestations of racism, however, are linked to a diversity of economic and political projects and do not, therefore, emanate exclusively from ethnic processes . . . A group does not have to be depicted as a 'race', . . . to be subjected to racist practices or effects. My view is that all those exclusionary practices that are formulated on the basis of the categorisation of individuals into groups, whereby ethnic or 'racial' origin are criteria of access or selection, are endemically racist. (1992: 422, 433)

The basic project, of attempting to take the relationship between 'race' and ethnicity seriously without reifying either concept, is worthwhile, but words are here in danger of becoming too empty of meaning to have any continuing usefulness. However, this quotation does remind us of the importance of social categorization in matters of ethnic and 'racial' identity, and it is to this that I now return (with apologies for a small amount of inescapable repetition).

Group identification and social categorization (again . . .)

Barth's argument that ethnicity is transactional, and may be situational or changeable, does not necessarily – although it might seem to (Rex 1986: 26) – conflict with a view of ethnicity as a basic or first-order social identity, rooted in the fertile earth of early socialization. Just as ethnic identity may be more or less negotiable in some situations than in others, so specific ethnic identities, depending upon history and ongoing events, may be 'weaker' or 'stronger'. Sometimes ethnicity may take its place alongside the primary identities of humanness, gender and selfhood (Jenkins 1996); in other local contexts it will matter less. To argue that ethnic identity is a basic or first-order dimension of the cultural experience of being human, is not to deny either the likelihood of variation in the urgency and immediacy of its affect, or the possibility of its manipulation and negotiation.

As argued in detail in the previous chapter, the transactions during which ethnicity is produced and reproduced have two complementary characters. First, there is *internal definition*: actors, whether as individuals or in groups, define their own identity. Although conceptualized as internal, these processes are necessarily social and interactional because, even in the case of the introspection of the solitary individual, they are predicated upon the assumption of an audience, even if only 'at some point', and – otherwise we could not talk about ethnicity – draw upon a socially constructed cultural repertoire for their meaning. Second, there is *external definition*, the definition of the identity of other people. This may be as simple and straightforward as the validation of the others' internal definition(s) of themselves, and as complex and conflictual as the attempt by one actor or set of actors to impose an identity on another.

External definition cannot, even in theory, be a solitary act. For one thing, more than just an audience is involved: the others here are *object(s)*, and a meaningful acting *upon* their lives is implied. For another, the capacity to impose one's definition of the situation upon other people implies that one possesses sufficient power or authority to do so. We can only talk about power in the context of social relations; similarly, authority, by definition, can only be said to exist in its legitimation by others (Smith 1960: 15–33). Relations of power and authority provide one connection between ethnic identities, on the one hand, and social class and gender identities, on the other. Important principles of hierarchical social differentiation in most social contexts, gender and access to economic resources are likely to permit or obstruct the ability of one actor or set of actors to effectively categorize others.

The distinction between internal and external processes of identification is largely in the eye of the analytical beholder. In everyday social life internal and external definition are routinely and chronically implicated in each other in a dialectic of identification. Categorizing 'them' is part of defining 'us'; our identification of 'us' is entailed in and by a history of relationships with significant others (Hagendoorn 1993). To recognize this is, of course, to return to Barth's original argument, and to 'shift the focus of investigation from internal constitution and history of separate groups to ethnic boundaries and boundary maintenance' (Barth 1969a: 10).

In terms of collectivities, a group is internally defined and a category externally defined. People in their everyday social interaction systematically classify themselves and others. They distinguish, in doing so, between identities which are self-generated and those which are other-imposed. An example of the difference between social groups and social categories might be the transition from *Gemeinschaft* (the mechanical solidarity of community) to *Gesellschaft* (associational organic solidarity) identified by

Tonniës and Durkheim. This historical shift can be understood in two different ways, depending upon one's perspective on modernity and progress. From one point of view, it is a change from a society in which the primary loci of identification lay in ascribed, *categorical* identities of various kinds, to one in which relatively free association upon the basis of elective self-identification has assumed greater importance. From the other, we see a move away from the local intimacies of the communal *group*, to the anonymity of a mass society in which relationships between people are mediated by market relationships and self-interest.

So, while social groups define themselves, their name(s), their nature(s) and their boundary(ies), social categories are named, characterized and delineated by others. However, the plausibility of both interpretations of the transition from *Gemeinschaft* to *Gesellschaft* outlined above – and, once again, *pace* Barth – suggests that social collectivities are actually shaped, to greater or lesser degrees, by a combination of group identification and social categorization. Each is simultaneously implicated in the other; social identity is produced and reproduced in the dialectic of internal *and* external definition. Whether, in any particular case, one talks about a group or a category will depend upon an assessment of the *(im)balance* which has been struck between internal and external processes.

Ethnicity and 'race'

To return to the subtlety and awkwardness of the relationship between ethnic identity and 'racial' identity, perhaps the distinction between groups and categories can illuminate the problem further. Banton, for example, has argued that, 'Membership in an ethnic group is usually voluntary; membership in a racial group is not' (1983: 10). Ethnicity is thus about inclusion (*us*), while 'race' is about exclusion (*them*): group identification as opposed to social categorization.

This is a plausible way of looking at things, which makes sense of much of the difference between 'race' and ethnicity. However, at least two qualifications of Banton's argument are necessary. First, I have argued that processes of group identification and categorization are routinely and reciprocally implicated in each other. It may be possible to *characterize* this situation or that as one or the other, but it can never be more than a matter of emphasis. Defining 'them' in terms of 'race' may be an important dimension of our definition of 'us' (which will, accordingly, carry some 'racial' charge). Some groups may, therefore, identify themselves – 'us' – in positive 'racial' terms. Perhaps the most obvious historical example of this is the *Herrenvolk* ideology in Nazi Germany and its close cousin in Nationalist South Africa, but something similar also emerges, for example, in some strands of contemporary Israeli Jewish identity and in 'black nationalism' in the United States and elsewhere. As the latter cases suggest, group identification in terms of 'race' may represent the historical negation of a powerful negative 'racial' categorization, by reworking it as a positively valorized identity.

The second difficulty with Banton's formula is that many models of 'them' are hostile ethnic categorizations that do not appear to involve the ascription of 'racial' differentiation in any clear-cut sense. Here, however, it may be important to remember that, particularly in Europe and the United States, 'racial' rhetoric has been publicly disreputable since the Second World War. The 'ethnic cleansing' of the 1990s would probably have been described differently in 1940. Which, of course, is another reminder that 'racial' classifications are no less culturally signified and socially constructed than ethnic identities: 'race', in particular, is very much a product of the ebb and flow of history.

At this point, there is a further definitional question to be asked: what do we mean when we talk about racism? It is important to acknowledge that there is no consensus about the word's suitability or acceptability for the purposes of academic discourse. Even though I cannot agree with Banton in suggesting that 'It is possible to discuss the sociology of race relations without using the word "racism"' (1988: 28), he is correct in counselling caution about our use of the word (1983: 1–3). He argues, first, that the word's various political connotations and its epithetical status are apt to promote and conceal vague and unsystematic thinking. Second, he suggests that the use of one totalizing word overlooks what may be significant differences between different places and times: different phenomena may become lumped together under one, crude, rubric.

Banton's first point is well taken, although he does not suggest that the problem which he identifies is inevitable. His second reservation, however, is even more substantial. To rephrase his objection, the concept of racism reifies what may be a set of historically specific, albeit perhaps broadly similar, ideologies under the umbrella of a concept which is supposedly capable of consistent and rigorous definition and, consequently, application in all circumstances:

> Once people slip into the assumption that racism or capitalism or communism exist in the sense that, say, influenza exists, then they are led into one trap after another. One such error is to overlook differences between historical periods. (Banton 1983: 3)

This is partly right and partly wrong. It is right inasmuch as differences between times and places are significant and should not be overlooked. It is wrong inasmuch as the attempt to define a general ideal-typical model of racism does not necessarily depend upon the kind of crude positivism which the remark about influenza lampoons; it is, in fact, a necessary prerequisite for the successful comparative study of racism*s*. But how should such an ideal type be formulated?

There are – and, indeed, what else would one expect? – almost as many definitions of racism as there are people writing about it. At the risk of oversimplifying the matter, it is possible to identify a number of options (or, perhaps more accurately, issues; for good surveys, see Miles 1989: 41–68 and Rex 1986: 99–118):

- *either* (1) racism is a set of organized beliefs about 'racial' categories and their inferiority or superiority, which people consciously hold and can, to some degree, articulate; *or* (2) racism exists in institutional arrangements and practices which have systematically detrimental outcomes or consequences for 'racial' categories, rather than in consciously held beliefs, attitudes or values;
- and *either* (3) racism involves categorization on the basis of purported biological differences; *or* (4) racism involves categorization on the basis of any set of criteria which will allow difference to be asserted.

Adjudication among these options and their possible combinations is not straightforward. It may be possible to concede that they all have their uses. The one point about which I am definite concerns options (1) and (2), above (cf. Jenkins 1986a: 5–6). The *intention* to discriminate against or otherwise disadvantage 'racially' categorized others need not actually be present for racism to be identified (and not only because intentions are ultimately unknowable). A *consciousness* of 'racial' categorization – explicit classificatory and evaluative knowledge – and the differential *treatment* of those who are categorized thus, are surely, however, prerequisites of racism. The epistemological and other problems that are raised immediately by option (2) are enormous. To suggest that racism is not, somehow, at least a part of what people know and can talk about is to locate it *where* in the social world? If racism is not discursive, it is difficult – and thoroughly unrewarding – to imagine what its ontological status might be.

My argument is that racism(s) and categories of 'racial' classification and differentiation are most usefully conceptualized as historically specific allotropes of the general, ubiquitous, social phenomenon of ethnicity. They arise in the context of situations in which one ethnic group dominates, or attempts to dominate, another and, in the process, categorizes them in terms of notional immutable differences, often couched in terms of inherent inferiority and construed as rooted in different biological natures. The recognition that, as in the 'new racism' identified by Martin Barker (1981), the rhetoric of *inferiority* may in specific circumstances be downplayed or abandoned, in favour of apparently less malign notions of *difference*, is important. It is socially constructed *immutable difference* – and neither word is more important than the other here – which lies at the heart of the matter.

The usefulness of 'racial' categorization for the legitimation of colonial or imperial conquest and domination probably cannot be overemphasized. There are, however, other kinds of ethnic legitimation. One such is nationalism. Defined as a political philosophy, insisting that the combined rights to exclusive occupation of territory and freedom from alien rule are embodied in the existence of a distinctive national community of culture and, usually, language, it is understood by many commentators as a historically specific phenomenon, with its roots in the bourgeois revolutions of modern Europe (Anderson 1983; Gellner 1983; Hobsbawm 1990). Nationalism is about hegemony; the object of legitimation is, at least in part, the *internal* hierarchy of industrial society (i.e. class). An imagined community of national similarity and inclusion – based on cultural homogeneity – is created and invoked to justify or camouflage the exclusion by a new dominant bourgeoisie of another new class of urban, industrial workers.

However, this seems, to say the least, a little too straightforward. Anthony Smith is surely correct to insist (1986, 1994) that nationalism also has another set of roots, in the ethnic communality of the pre-modern world. Here a useful distinction might perhaps be drawn between *nationalism* and *national identity* (Smith 1991). It is in the urgency and immediacy of national identity, Gellner's 'patriotism', that one source of the power of nationalism to mobilize populations lies. It lies behind the conflicts that have, almost endemically it seems, resulted from post-colonial attempts at nation-building in the Third World – which brings us straight back to Geertz's primordiality – and which now threaten attempts to construct a viable geo-political framework for post-communist eastern Europe. It also contributes to an explanation of nationalism's obstinate potency in the modern world, despite the many confident declarations of its decline or imminent demise (e.g. Gellner 1983: 121; Hobsbawm 1990: 164–83).

Ideologies of identification

National identity and nationalism involve, almost by definition, group identification and social categorization: inclusion and exclusion. Whatever they may be, they are perhaps most usefully regarded, therefore, and in much the same way as 'race' and racism, as a historically specific manifestation of ethnicity. However, racism and nationalism have something else, which is both elusive and obvious, in common. They are both *-isms*: relatively coherent, if not necessarily explicitly organized or consistent, understandings of the world, which are integral aspects of specific social identities and which serve to identify individuals and groups and to locate them in the social world.

In a word, racism and nationalism are both *ideologies*. They are bodies of knowledge (a word that in this context denotes neither validity nor reliability) which make claims about the way the social world *is* and, crucially, about the way it *ought* to be. This knowledge is mobilized in the definition of criteria of group membership and principles of exclusion. It specifies the rights and duties which attach to membership, and the forms of treatment which it is appropriate to extend to non-members. These are bodies of *political* knowledge oriented towards the systematic constitution of the world in particular ways and the advancement of sectional interests.

Basis of identification	Ideology
Kinship	Familism
Co-residence	Communalism
Co-residence	Localism
Co-residence	Regionalism
Ethnicity	Ethnicism
Ethnicity/Nationality	Nationalism
Ethnicity/'Race'	Racism

Figure 6.1   *Identification and ideology*

The question arises of the relationship between ethnicity (including 'race' and national identity) and other forms of identification, with their attendant ideologies. A partial list of these – excluding (for reasons of space), class, gender, humanity, and doubtless others – is presented schematically in Figure 6.1. There is a hierarchical overlap between different 'levels' of identification and ideology. For example, kinship, because of the coincidence of descent and residence in many societies, may be associated with localism. Similarly, co-residence may generate both localism and regionalism; ethnicity may be bound up with regionalism, ethnicism *and* nationalism. Nationality, in its turn, may be as likely to find its ideological expression in racism as in nationalism.

As discussed in Chapter 4, the taxonomic logic of ethnic identity is basically hierarchical. My favourite metaphor for illustrating this is the Russian doll set: inside each doll nestles a smaller doll. Imagine each succeeding doll dressed in different national, ethnic and local costumes, as the focus of identification becomes more and more particularized. However, it can never really be anything like this simple: ethnicity overlaps with a hierarchy of other sources of identification, each with its own possibilities for inclusion and exclusion. How these relate to each other must in the first place be a matter for empirical exploration rather than theoretical specification.

Most of these ideologies of identification will be familiar in one form or another, in that they have accepted usages in the social science literature. The one exception to this is, interestingly enough, 'ethnicism'. In part, this reflects the fact that we use 'ethnicity' to refer to both a source or a kind of social identification *and* its attendant ideology. It may also, however, be the case that when faced with an ethnic ideology – an ethnicism – our response is to identify it as either nationalism or racism. Hence the coining of hybrid terms such as 'ethnic nationalism' (Smith 1991: 79–84) when, really, it is hard to imagine a nationalism which is not, in some sense, 'ethnic'. Similar conceptual redundancy is indicated by the notion of 'ethno-regionalism' (Hechter and Levi 1979).

A specific example of the kind of confusion produced by the absence of an ideological model of ethnicity is the argument about whether the Northern Ireland conflict is a 'race relations' situation (McKernan 1982;

Moore 1972; Nelson 1975) or a case of racism (Miles 1996). The most obvious problem here is the ethnic ideology of Protestant loyalism, which will be discussed in subsequent chapters. Loyalism is not obviously nationalist: that particular high ground has been claimed by its opponents, and loyalists themselves – for that reason – are, it seems, reluctant to identify themselves thus. Much depends here, of course, upon our definition of nationalism – Finlayson, for example, has argued (1996) that Northern Irish Protestant ideology is a nationalist discourse – and our preparedness to overlook local definitions of the situation, but loyalism cannot, by default, simply be removed to the other obviously available category, i.e. racism (which is not to deny that Ulster loyalists may *also* be racist). Ethnicity is so often celebrated as a positively 'good thing' – by obvious and explicit contrast with the evils of racism (there is more ambivalence about nationalism) – that there may be some reluctance to identify its ideological and conflictual possibilities, which are, as a consequence, easily interpretable as reflections of either racism or national identity.

A reconsideration of the relationships between ethnicism, nationalism and racism is overdue. If we conclude that 'ethnicism' does not hold much water as a working concept – perhaps because of its over-generality or lack of specificity – then the continued utility of the attendant concept of 'ethnicity' must perhaps also be regarded as problematic. More likely, however, is a solution to the problem which will encourage us to draw finer distinctions between ideologies of identification. Such an exercise will also involve the drawing of empirically grounded analytical distinctions between various ethnicism*s*, nationalism*s* and racism*s* (Balibar 1991). As matters stand at present, our conceptual categories may, in some cases – and racism as a generic term is the most obvious example here, since the word is constructed as much for purposes political as analytical – be too crude or monolithic to be of more than restricted utility, particularly for comparative analysis and research.

One last characteristic of ideology is also important. Ideology tells us how the world is, and how it ought to be. Let us concentrate on the last part of that definition. In part it tells us how *we* ought to be. In this sense our ideologies are burdensome to us. And this is, indeed, how many people experience nationalism, or ethnicism: as a constant social pressure, a collective impetus towards a degree of belonging or conformity with which they do not feel comfortable. But there is also the matter of how *they* ought to be. In this, the inherent categorizing and imperial potentialities of ideology reveal themselves most clearly. Ideology and categorization may be more than logically related.

In this chapter I have been working towards clarification, rather than aiming for definitive conclusions. Some areas of conceptual confusion have been identified and a beginning made on their disentanglement. I have suggested the usefulness to our thinking about ethnicity and 'race' of three theoretical moves.

The first is a reconciliation of the situationalist view of ethnicity, *à la* Barth, with the primordialist view attributed to Geertz. This prepares the ground for a possibly imprecise but nonetheless plausible distinction between ethnic identity and 'race' in terms of historical ubiquity and affective immediacy. By this token, ethnicity and 'race' do not, strictly speaking, appear to be the same order of social phenomena, in much the same way that diamond or graphite are not the same 'thing' as carbon.

The second move is the differentiation between internal processes of group identification and external processes of social categorization. Each is chronically and inextricably implicated in the other in the production and reproduction of identity. Although ethnic identity and 'race' both involve internal and external identification, the emphasis in each may fall on a different moment of the identificatory dialectic.

Last, there is the differentiation between social identities and their attendant ideologies of identification. This encourages the acknowledgement of a neglected area of concern: ethnic ideologies which are neither racist nor nationalist in their primary orientation. It also allows the adoption of a comparative and historical perspective – upon racisms rather than racism, nationalisms rather than nationalism, and ethnicisms rather than ethnicism – without sacrificing the small amount of general ideal-typical theoretical continuity which such comparisons demand.

Explorations

The chapters which follow are not, in any deliberate sense, intended to exemplify the arguments I have developed in the first part of the book. They present arguments in their own right and are certainly no less theoretical than Chapters 1 to 6. Chronologically, their original writing took place alongside – in and out – of the others, and they belong to the same flow of work. In contrast to those earlier chapters, however, they explore their arguments through engagement with the historical and ethnographic detail of actual places and settings. This creates a different feel – it is another way of writing altogether – and a different style. The two parts – the arguments and explorations of the subtitle – are complementary strategies for exploring the same issues.

The exploration of material about Northern Ireland, Wales and Denmark follows the evolution of my research interests over the last twenty years. That evolution has been at least as much governed by serendipity and biography as by an intellectual game plan. My interest in these places does have a bearing on one of my general arguments – that ethnicity is not to be restricted to 'them' or to the exotic Other – but this is not *why* I find them so interesting. It might be more accurate to suggest that my personal interest in Northern Ireland, Wales and Denmark is responsible for my appreciation of the everyday, non-Otherness of ethnicity and the issues it raises. Similarly, my interest in why and how ethnicity *matters* to people has emerged out of my experiences in these places, as have the comparative explorations of nationalism in Chapters 9 and 10.

Northern Ireland is not the easiest place in the world about which to write. The politics of writing – of naming, of identification, of categorization – are at least as sensitive there (here) as anywhere. In particular, I know that my consistent use of the geo-political expression 'Northern Ireland' – rather than its alternatives such as 'the six counties', 'the north of Ireland', 'Ulster', or whatever – will annoy at least some readers. This form of naming has, however, the merits of reflecting much everyday practice in the place itself, of being in accord with present international usage (which includes Dublin), and of indicating clearly the nature of the political beast about which I am talking.

One last difference between logical argument and the exploration of evidence is worth mentioning. More than any other kind of writing, exploration is provisional; the account always remains open. The chapters which follow were written, and are offered, in this spirit. It is also how I would like them to be read.

7

Majority Ethnicity

Ethnicity is not a peculiar attribute of minorities nor is it restricted to exotic Others. This chapter looks at a politically dominant and self-conscious ethnic *majority* – Northern Irish Protestants and, particularly, the Northern Irish Protestant élite – and how, during a long history of conflict, they have mobilized and manipulated their ethnicity and used ethnic communality to their advantage. During the modern history of Ireland, Protestants have been a numerical minority within the island's population, so this may appear to be an odd understanding of the situation.[1] There are, however, three senses in which Ulster Protestants can be seen as a majority. First, they are, and have been since the territory's creation, a majority within the six counties of Northern Ireland. Second, for most of the history of 'English' or 'British' Ireland they were a political majority, in the sense that they unambiguously held power. Third, within the overall context of the British Isles, they formed an organic part of the dominant, metropolitan Anglo-Saxon majority (Hechter 1975).

In looking at the mobilization and manipulation of ethnicity, I am drawing on that strand of the anthropological model which emphasizes that ethnicity is a social *resource*, to be drawn upon or exploited in varying contexts. However, inasmuch as most anthropological studies of ethnicity in urbanized or industrialized societies have looked at minority situations, they have tended to overlook the salience of other factors, such as class and the social construction of power relationships. At best, factors such as these have been treated as external 'structure', impinging upon the group in question as a more or less constraining factor in their lives (Davis 1975; Grillo 1980). To understand Northern Ireland, where state and economy were constructed by and in the social relationships between a dominant ethnic group and a subordinated ethnic group, and between the local majority and an external metropolitan power, a less abstract understanding of state and economy is necessary.

Another central focus of the anthropology of ethnicity has been its concern with the maintenance of *boundaries* between ethnic groups. This research orientation has led to many insights, not the least of which being that ethnicity is essentially relative, its nature shifting with the contexts of its mobilization. And this chapter will maintain that perspective: ethnicity is a function of inter-group relations; in the absence of such relations and their concomitant group boundaries ethnicity is unthinkable. But most of my attention here is on the mobilization of ethnicity as a resource by a dominant élite, in their strategies for the internal control of their own class-stratified ethnic group. Thus the focus of attention is to some extent shifted from *inter*-group to *intra*-group relationships. In terms of the themes which this book is exploring, this chapter is concerned with power relations, and with the interweaving of ethnicity with other principles of social identification, in this case, class.

The foundations of modern Ulster ethnicity: the Plantation

For our purposes, the history of the Northern Irish Protestant community may be traced back to the Ulster Plantation of the first decades of the seventeenth century. Although there had been some earlier colonization of the counties of Antrim and Down by Scottish settlers, the Plantation marks the beginning of the historical process which has resulted in the present 'troubles'; in the words of two recent commentators, here lie 'the colonial roots of antagonism' (O'Leary and McGarry 1993: 54–106). It was nothing less than an attempt at the wholesale de- and re-population of the north of Ireland. The established inhabitants – Gaelic in language and culture, Catholic in religion, and resistant to rule from London, or, indeed, Dublin – were to be replaced by 'planting' Anglophone, Protestant, loyal settlers in their stead.

Originally envisaged as an essentially military adventure, to secure the hitherto rebellious earldoms of Tyrconnel and Tyrone for the English crown, the scheme acquired a commercial orientation very early on. Following an agreement between the crown and the corporation of the City of London, the latter set up a joint-stock enterprise:

> to plant the country of Coleraine, and to rebuild and fortify its two main towns, Coleraine and Derry. In return, they were to receive extensive privileges, including the patronage of all churches within their territory, the fisheries of the Foyle and the Bann, and a long lease of the customs at a nominal rent. (Beckett 1966: 46)

The links of commerce thereby established between the province and the mainland were to set the pattern for much of Ulster's subsequent history. However, the relative geographical isolation caused by the Irish Sea, and the differences from the rest of Ireland which I shall discuss below, were also to set a pattern for the north-eastern counties. The history of the Protestants of the province since the Plantation is a curious mixture of insularity and backwardness contrasted with varying degrees of incorporation into the political, cultural and economic mainstreams of Britain.

Throughout the rest of Ulster, the Plantation took on a similar character to that described above, either directly initiated by the government in London or encouraged by them at one remove through 'undertakers' or agencies such as the London Company. In Antrim and Down, however, following a government-approved dismemberment of Con O'Neill's Clandeboye estates, the Plantation became more a matter for private adventurers. Here the Plantation acquired a distinctly Scottish character, in contrast to the strong English influences at work further west.

As a result of this colonization there developed a series of marked differences between Ulster and the rest of the island. There one saw the development of an essentially rural and agricultural society, based on commercially oriented tenant farmers, with an intensive subsistence peasantry on the western margins. In the north-east there eventually developed, by contrast, an urban and industrial society, based in the first place on smallholdings leased from the undertakers by the colonist yeomanry and small tenantry, many of whom had a background in the textile industry then emerging on the other side of the Irish Sea (Crotty 1966; Cullen 1969; Gibbon 1975: 9–12).

One of the original aims of the Plantation, and in this its military origins reveal themselves, was the physical removal of most of the native Irish population from the best, most fertile areas in the north. In this aim the Plantation failed, however, for at least two reasons. First, many of the colonists, in particular those holding large estates, were happy to find (Catholic Irish) tenants available on the spot and took advantage of their continued presence. Second, the Irish who were to be moved frequently resisted, as is witnessed by the planters' need for fortified houses or 'bawns'. The 'final solution' to the Ulster problem was not to work as well in practice as its architects in London had expected.

Nonetheless, although many or most of the former inhabitants remained, things had changed dramatically for them, and changed for the worse. Within twenty years, at the beginning of the seventeenth century, all of their customary rights to land and property vanished; in effect, they became aliens in their own country. A few, a very few, either retained their status or were granted new lands, but they constituted a tiny minority:

> The great mass of Ulster Irish remained on their former lands, but degraded to the status of tenants-at-will. As they became increasingly impoverished, economic pressure tended to drive them out of the more fertile and into the worst lands, where their descendants are still to be found. (Moody 1974: 5)

In 1641 the fruits of this policy towards the native Irish ripened into rebellion. Led by Sir Phelim O'Neill, and spurred on by fear of a Puritan-dominated House of Commons at Westminster, the Ulster Catholics rose up in revolt. Eight years later Oliver Cromwell arrived in Dublin and by 1652 the rebellion was over. The Irish were punished severely, by confiscation of most of their remaining land, and by deportation. The result of the 1641 rebellion was the consolidation of the original aims of the Plantation and the commercial domination of Ireland by the settlers, particularly in the north-east and the towns.

The end of the century saw further violence, most notably the siege of Derry in 1689 and King William III's defeat of the Jacobite army at the battle of the Boyne in 1690. The Treaty of Limerick in 1691 and the flight of the 'Wild Geese' to France signalled the final collapse of the Stuart cause. For Irish Catholics the major results of the Williamite wars were the Penal Laws of the early eighteenth century, which, although they were subsequently gradually relaxed, remained in force until Catholic emancipation was granted in 1829. In addition to the already severe restrictions on Irish trade, Catholics were excluded by the Penal Laws from the army, barred from politics at both local and national levels, and deprived of access to education. Protestant estates could not be sold to Catholics, Catholics were not allowed to lease land for more than thirty-one years and the inheritance laws encouraged the minute sub-division of Catholic-owned land. Nonconformist Protestants, those who refused to recognize the authority of the Established Church, also suffered to an extent, but in the north they were somewhat protected by the 'Ulster Custom', informal local land tenure arrangements which meant that tenants could sell their interest in a property and could not be evicted so long as they paid their rent.

The history of seventeenth- and early eighteenth-century Ulster has two important features for this discussion. In the first place, two contrasting ethnicities were established: native Catholic Irish, and Ulster Protestant settlers. The latter category was subdivided or segmented into the mainly Presbyterian Scots of the east of the province and the mainly Church of Ireland (i.e. Anglican) population of English descent of the western counties, although the nineteenth century did see a significant migration into Belfast of members of the Church of Ireland.[2] Although the communal or confessional distinction within the Protestant population remains important today, the ethnic cleavage has historically been – and remains – that between the native Irish and the settlers, with religion providing the main explicit boundary-maintaining mechanism. A shared Protestant ethnic identity emerged as differences between Anglicans and dissenters, English and Scots, were subsumed in the face of their more significant differences with and from the Catholic Irish.

One way to understand the salience of religion is as a consequence of the gradual decline of distinctive Gaelic Irish culture in the north. Taking such a view, religion eventually became all that was left as a cultural marker of difference between the populations. This interpretation may have some merit, but it is probably only applicable to very recent times, with the 'cultural convergence' produced by modernization, consumerism, and the penetration of external cultural influences. A more plausible explanation – because, in fact, northern Gaelic Irish culture survived better than one might have expected, arguably until the early twentieth century – is that religion became such a key constituent of the boundary because, within the north of Ireland, Protestants consistently *categorized* their ethnic Other thus, institutionally and interactionally. From the time of the Penal Laws onwards, religion *was* the nominal boundary, synonymous with political disloyalty, on the one hand, and fecklessness and unworthiness, on the other. This is recognized today, for example, in the local Northern Irish characterization of ethnic chauvinism as *sectarianism*.

The second point to note is that ethnicity in Ulster has been grounded in *consequences* – particularly economic consequences – since the earliest days of the Plantation. Catholics were first of all alienated from the land and eventually, via the Penal Laws, debarred from professional or political careers, further isolating them from the possibility of entrepreneurial economic activity. Thus were laid during the seventeenth and eighteenth centuries – built on the effective exclusion of Catholics from professional life, commerce and agricultural prosperity – the foundations of Protestant capital accumulation.

The consolidation of ethnic domination: the industrial revolution

The Protestant colonists came from areas of England and Scotland that had existing traditions of capitalist commodity farming and domestic textile industry. The potential for industrial development which this implied was given a further boost in 1698 by the arrival at Lisburn, Co. Antrim, of Louis Crommelin and his fellow Huguenots, refugees from religious persecution in Catholic France. Their sudden appearance is at least partly explained by the fact that Huguenots had been among William's best troops in the campaigns of ten years earlier. The significance of their immigration rests mainly in the fact that they brought to Ulster the craft of weaving damask, a very fine, patterned linen fabric; the manufacture of plain linen cloth was already well established in the province by the time of their arrival. Following the abolition by the British government, in 1696, of the tax on plain linens from Ireland,

> many English dealers began to buy Ulster cloth because it was cheaper than the Dutch and German linens. Since it continued to sell very well more weavers throughout Ulster began to weave for the London market and the industry spread to places as far apart as Strabane, Antrim and Monaghan before 1710. (Crawford 1972: 1)

Thus there were several reasons for the success of the textile industry in Ulster. First, there was the knowledge and skill of the settlers, both the original planters and the later Huguenot refugees. The importance of their craftsmanship, combined with some experience of small-scale capitalist production, cannot be overestimated.

Second, the economically privileged position of the Protestant settlers, particularly their secure land tenure system, mentioned earlier, encouraged the harnessing of this entrepreneurial potential. It supported modest capital accumulation, encouraging farmer-manufacturers to expand by either employing weavers, or 'putting out' extra work (Gill 1925). Finally, and perhaps of determinate importance, because – for political reasons which are obvious – their case had the ear of the London government, Ulster Protestants were in a position to petition for, and achieve, important economic concessions such as the withdrawal of the tax on plain linens in 1696:

The prosperity of the linen industry in Ulster was due to English demand for Irish linens . . . and to its duty-free entry into the English market. (Crawford and Trainor 1973: 33)

On these foundations, the technical know-how of the settlers, their secure relationship with the land, and their links with the mainland – based on what was, in the local context, a bond of shared politicized ethnicity – the Ulster textile industry was developed.

It was this industry, originally domestic in nature, that provided the necessary base from which industrial development gradually took off in north-east Ireland. The trend in the rest of the country, with some important exceptions in urban centres such as Dublin and Cork, was increasingly towards large-scale agriculture, with the emphasis on cattle. Until the famine years of the 1840s the western margins and the less fertile upland areas continued to be characterized by the smallholdings of the native Irish peasantry.

Once linen manufacture had been firmly established it became less reliant on the land tenure customs of Ulster and evolved into an independent industry in its own right. This had important consequences for the industrial and social future of the province:

the linen industry affected the character of Ulster society . . . It not only gave employment to manual workers; it produced a substantial middle class of bleachers and drapers, many of whom acquired considerable wealth . . . It also promoted urban development, for the towns were the natural centres for marketing the cloth woven by rural weavers; and at least in some areas, there was a tendency for weavers to concentrate in the vicinity of these market towns. (Beckett 1973: xii–xiii)

Thus in the wake of capitalist industrialization – on a modest scale at this time – we have the concomitant development and elaboration of class stratification within the Protestant ethnic community. Manufacturing, far from being a reflection of prosperity rooted in the land, was rapidly becoming a source of capital accumulation in itself.

Further economic stimulation came as a result of the agitation by the Volunteers for free trade and other reforms. In 1779 many of the remaining restrictions on the Irish export trade were lifted and in 1782, after a political meeting in Dungannon, Co. Tyrone, the Dublin parliament was largely emancipated from control by Westminster. In the years immediately following, the Dublin government of Grattan's parliament did much to stimulate grain production, brewing, woollen manufacture and the cotton industry. The north-east counties had a head start on the rest of Ireland and benefited disproportionately from these reforms.

The new parliament failed, however, to grasp the nettle of Catholic emancipation, a cause which was attracting some sympathy at this time from nonconformists. The organizational expression of this sympathy was Wolfe Tone's Society of United Irishmen, founded in Belfast in 1791. Once again, however, as so many times before and since, self-interest and ethnicity successfully undermined the movement's radical ideals. In County

Armagh, an area dominated by the textile industry and distinguished by an approximate demographic balance between Catholics and Protestants, a violent encounter occurred in 1795 which led to the formation of an Orange Society, which spread quickly in the countryside. With it came an increase in violent attacks on Catholic weavers, many of whom fled. There is considerable evidence of sympathy and support for the society among landlords and the magistracy; when a yeomanry was established to counter the United Irishmen's 1798 rebellion, the Orange Society provided many of its members. The Protestants may have been increasingly stratified along class lines; nonetheless, ethnicity remained the major axis of political mobilization (Senior 1966).

By the beginning of the nineteenth century Belfast had come to rival Dublin in importance as a mercantile and financial centre. In manufacturing, the north-east had established a predominance it has yet to lose. The expansion of the textile industry, new technological developments and the boom in cotton production stimulated by the Napoleonic Wars all combined to encourage systematic mechanization, both in yarn spinning and in weaving. By the 1830s factory production was rapidly becoming commonplace, with linen manufacturing eventually reasserting itself as the market for cotton became more competitive again in the conditions of peacetime.

The mechanization of the labour process in textiles led to the development of a local engineering industry, based in the first instance upon the market for machinery and repair services among the local mill owners. This development was heavily dependent upon the mainland, particularly for specialist expertise. However, despite the influx of entrepreneurs possessing such expertise, the enterprises set up during this period were local companies which were not accountable to external sources of control:

> Few of the early engineering works in the north of Ireland were established by local men; Joe Rider, John Hind, Stephen Cotton, George Horner and E.J. Harland came from England, James Combe and James Mackie from Scotland. From the middle of the nineteenth century, however, local men trained in the original works began to set up business for themselves or to take over the management of existing firms when founders retired or got into financial difficulties . . . It seems clear that the early entrepreneurs were attracted to the north of Ireland, not by the local market for small metal goods, but by the opportunity to exploit new techniques, such as iron founding, the making of steam engines and textile machinery, and the provision of a machinery repair service . . . the region was kept in touch with progress in industrial organisation in Britain not only by the political union of the two countries but also by periodic infusions of new blood from the British engineering industry. (Coe 1969: 193, 194, 196)

Business or other economic links with the mainland were not all one way, however. In addition to the inward flow of technology and entrepreneurial personnel, there was also a flow of investment capital, in particular – though not exclusively – a flow of local capital *out*, for investment in England and Scotland. Due to the restricted scale and scope of the local economy, the local economic élite's links with their fellow businessmen 'across the water' – sometimes the close links of family or marriage – provided a useful avenue for diversification and investment (Coe 1969: 190–2). From the middle of the nineteenth century onwards, Ulster rapidly became incorporated into the burgeoning industrial economy of the rest of the kingdom.

The increasing importance of large-scale manufacture, which required easy access to the sea for the import of raw materials and the export of its finished products, resulted in Belfast becoming the centre of industrial and commercial activity. The situation developed for three reasons. First, there was the city's centrality within the predominantly Protestant area east of the river Bann; second, its ease of communication, via the natural corridor of the valley of the river Lagan, with the smaller textile towns of the rest of the province; and third, its position as the major deep-water port on the north-eastern seaboard, providing ready access to the markets of the Empire and the rest of the world. Belfast's position was strengthened by the establishment of steamship services to Glasgow and Liverpool in the 1820s. In 1800 the city was smaller than either Limerick or Waterford; by 1891 Belfast had overtaken Dublin in both size and commercial importance.

Naturally enough, the industrial development of the Belfast area drew in many immigrants from the rest of the province. Although it was already happening before the Famine, rural distress in the 1840s and the subsequent flight from the land accelerated this population movement. Many of the new city-dwellers were Catholics from the southern and western districts of Ulster, attracted to Belfast by the availability of employment. They tended to take unskilled jobs in textile production or as navvies, building the new town. Skilled work, particularly in engineering, remained the preserve of the Protestant working man; industry and commerce were controlled by the Protestant bourgeoisie – either local or newly arrived – and hiring practices reflected the traditionally sanctioned hierarchy of Catholic and Protestant (cf. Reid 1980). Relations between an employer and his workforce were often paternalistic and a firm recognition of the relationship between employment and ethnicity structured the emergent labour market in the city, although this did not prevent the emergence, from the 1870s, of labourism and trade union organization (Patterson 1980). Historians of this period leave us in little doubt as to the systematic manipulation of ethnicity by the local elite, both in furtherance of their political ends – the maintenance of Protestant supremacy and the link with Britain – and, more indirectly, but no less definitely, their economic goals. The link between the political and the economic was clearly recognized by both workers and employers and formed the basis of the Unionist class alliance.

With the growing importance of shipbuilding and marine engineering from mid-century onwards, the industrial structure that was to characterize the local economy until the middle of the twentieth century and beyond, began to emerge. The development of the shipyards reflected the presence of a deep-water harbour, the large numbers of skilled men, such as boilermakers, in the local engineering industry (although many more were brought in from Clydeside), and the enthusiasm of the Harbour Commissioners in developing the Queen's Island site. As the nineteenth century drew to its close, the Belfast region became incorporated more and more into the wider United Kingdom economy, particularly that region of it which includes the other major Irish sea ports, Glasgow and Liverpool. Employers and men participated in national and regional industrial negotiations and disputes, and the commercial life of the city drew ever closer to Britain, much local capital continuing to be invested on the mainland (Coe 1969: 191; Lyons 1973: 270–86). By 1900 the economy was provincial no longer.

This account of the industrialization of Northern Ireland allows us to examine some of the local links between ethnicity and economic activity. During this period the linked processes of urbanization, industrialization and mechanization served to reinforce the economic and political dominance of the local Protestant bourgeoisie. Their economic position was made more secure, and their sphere of activities expanded, through the importation of technological resources from the mainland. Access to external investment markets when the local opportunities for capital accumulation became too limited further consolidated their economic base. These strategies were facilitated by their links of shared ethnicity – religious, political, and in terms of origins – with the English and Scottish bourgeoisie, who were a source of technologically innovative entrepreneurs and provided opportunities for Ulster Protestant businessmen to invest money in their enterprises. The economic and political interests of the local businessman – and the two are inextricably linked – were also well served by the stratification of the working class along ethnic lines. Class issues were never forgotten in local politics – the distinction between skilled and unskilled Protestant workers, although greatly undermined by restructuring, remains important today – but the increasing orchestration of ethnic solidarity by the Orange Order as the nineteenth century wore on ensured that, particularly following the Home Rule crisis of 1886, sectarian issues dominated the political arena. The important connection between ethnicity and access to work would probably have seen to that if nothing else did and this tendency was reinforced by the pre-eminence of élitist craft unions among organized labour.

Sectarian ethnicity was not the only factor, of course. It must not be forgotten that, from the point of view of Northern Protestants, the underdevelopment of the rest of Ireland was a powerful (with hindsight somewhat self-fulfilling) argument against Home Rule. A genuine and understandable fear of losing a relatively prosperous lifestyle informed politics and industrial relations. The outcome of these fears for the Ulster employer, occasional disputes notwithstanding, was the continuing control of his workforce and a high degree of industrial harmony. This was a subtle and ongoing process of negotiation and accommodation:

Ulster Unionism emerged as the product neither of a conspiracy of landed notables and industrialists to 'dupe the people' nor from the spontaneous convergence of a set of forces without prior political relations. (Gibbon 1975: 145).

Systematic connections between ethnicity, economic activity and politics in Ulster were socially constructed during the two centuries following the Plantation. These connections are neither accidental nor structurally determined. They were the result of the pursuit – not always consistent – of rational political and economic goals by the government in London and the Ulster Protestant establishment. They finally became systematized with the rise to importance of the Protestant industrial and commercial élite of Belfast in the second half of the nineteenth century. Their roots, however, lay much earlier.

Organized labour and the manipulation of ethnicity

So, the foundations of a hierarchical ethnic division of labour were laid in the military subjugation of the Ulster Irish and the subsequent Plantation. This division of labour was consolidated as the industrial revolution progressed in north-eastern Ireland. I shall conclude with some discussion of the subsequent development of the capitalist economy in Ulster, in particular during the life of the Northern Ireland state, between 1921 and the prorogation of the Stormont parliament in 1972.

Before the First World War, there had been some class-based political organization and industrial action, most notably Jim Larkin's organization of unskilled labour, both Protestant and Catholic, in Belfast in 1907 (Gray 1985). Industrial unrest rose to new heights, however, in the wake of the war, as it did throughout the United Kingdom:

> Industrial militancy was growing among Belfast workers. There had been a massive engineering strike at the beginning of 1919 which had brought Belfast industry to a halt for four weeks. Ominously for the Unionists the leader of the largely Protestant strikers had been a Catholic, Charles McKay. The workers' new class consciousness seemed to carry through to the local elections in January 1920, for twelve Labour councillors were elected to Belfast Corporation, one of them topping the poll in the Protestant stronghold of Shankill. (Farrell 1976: 27)

It might have been expected that, in the appalling social conditions of working-class areas of Belfast at the time, the labour movement would have taken seed and flourished. However, this was also a period of intense sectarian conflict, stemming from the pre-war Ulster Volunteer Force crisis and the Civil War in the rest of the island. The troubles of this period, combined with the blatant playing of the 'Orange Card' by local employers and, later, by the new Stormont government, had a substantial part in undermining inter-ethnic or cross-sectarian socialist activism. Listen, for example, to Sir Edward Carson, MP and Unionist leader, speaking at Finaghy in July 1920:

> these men who come forward posing as the friends of labour care no more about labour than does the man in the moon. Their real object . . . is that they mislead and bring about disunity *amongst our own people*; and in the end, before we know where we are, we may find ourselves in the same bondage and slavery as is the rest of Ireland in the South and West. (in Farrell 1976: 28; my emphasis)

During this period the identification of an equivalence between socialism and Irish nationalism, with respect to their perceived interests, was first formulated by Protestants; opposition to the latter generating rejection of the former. The Northern Ireland Labour Party struggled on under this electoral handicap until its eventual demise in the early 1980s.

The upshot of this during the years following the First World War was the wholesale expulsion of Catholic workers from many areas of Belfast industry, most notably the shipyards, a state of affairs encouraged by the fact that differences in skill levels between Catholics (a majority of whom were unskilled) and Protestants (a high proportion of whom were skilled) led, in some respects, to the reproduction of the ethnic division of labour among the trade unions. There was no General Strike in Belfast in 1926, and the unique events towards the end of 1932, when Catholic and Protestant workers marched together in Belfast to protest at their unemployment and destitution, were put down by the Royal Ulster Constabulary with rifles and armoured cars. But even though poverty dire beyond modern imagining was a fact of everyday life for urban working-class Protestants and Catholics, and in rural areas, throughout the 1930s (Bardon 1992: 529–34), sectarian ethnicity never ceased to matter:

> The extent of co-operation between the poor of both religions during the outdoor-relief riots of 1932 has been exaggerated and romanticized, and there is no evidence that intercommunal tensions were eased for more than a few days. (Bardon 1992: 539)

Sectarian violence returned in 1934 and, with a vengeance, in 1935. Although it was significant, it is possible to over-emphasize the role in these disturbances of the local Protestant establishment's manipulation of ethnicity:

> That politicians' sectarianism influenced public opinion is undeniable. However, that it alone was the cause of the riots is too far-fetched a conclusion. The strength of popular, everyday sectarianism cannot be underestimated. (Munck and Rolston 1987: 59)

To take the most measured view, 'while neither Craig [Viscount Craigavon, the Unionist Prime Minister] and his colleagues had created these divisions, they did little to assuage them' (Bardon 1992: 467). Nor, although in 1935 it was directly asked to by the Nationalist Party, did a Westminster government which had much in common with Northern Ireland Unionists – in terms of party politics, view of the world, and social networks and background – choose to intervene

After the Second World War, the Unionist government, newly incor- porated, with some reluctance, into the British Labour Party's welfare state, resolved to revitalize the Ulster economy, which was suffering now from the over-concentration upon textiles and heavy engineering of its formative phases. The main development strategy was the attraction of outside companies to the province by means of generous capital subsidies. Most of the new enterprises were sited in Protestant areas east of the river Bann and most of the new jobs correspondingly went to Protestants. This was particularly the case in engineering, which required skilled men. Furthermore, the new capitalism accepted quite readily the practices of the old. The toleration of local practices was a small price to pay for good industrial relations:

> A good many new businesses conformed without protest to the practices of old capital. In 1965, when new industry provided about 60,000 of 190,000 manufacturing jobs, the first Development Plan complained that only 10 per cent of new vacancies were being filled through labour exchanges. Evidently Orangeism was becoming absorbed into the new workplaces. (Bew *et al.* 1979: 189)

The relatively unproblematic nature of industrial relations in the Province at this time is well illustrated by a government survey, the Quigley Report (Department of Manpower Services 1974). Although there has been considerable controversy about this,[3] the basis of that industrial harmony seems to have been taken-for-granted, axiomatic discrimination in employment against Catholics. The outcome for the employer was the lowest unit labour costs in western Europe (Department of Manpower Services 1979: 20–1).

Thus organized labour was effectively split along ethnic lines, with the Protestant section bought off by the Unionist government and the local business elite, and inhibited from large-scale working-class identification and political action by its own industrial background and sectarian ethnicity. The arrival of the new multi-national enterprises served only to strengthen this state of affairs, since it was in their best interests – the maintenance of a relatively quiescent workforce and easy access to subsidies – not to resist it.

The management of this mobilization of ethnicity can only be understood if one appreciates the interpenetration of the political, legal and business spheres in Northern Ireland prior to the imposition of direct rule from Westminster in 1972. Between 1921 and 1972 the Northern Ireland state was the institutional embodiment of this interpenetration; perhaps the main integrating organization holding the system together was the Orange Institution (Bew *et al.* 1979; Buckland 1980; Harbinson 1973):

> The [Northern Irish] Prime Minister said in 1932: 'Ours is a Protestant Government and I am an Orangeman' . . . In the House of Commons the Prime Minister said: 'I am very proud indeed to be Grand Master of the Orange Institution of the Loyal County of Down. I have filled that office for many years and I prize that far more than I do being Prime Minister. I have always said I am an Orangeman first and a member of this Parliament afterwards. (Mansergh 1936: 240–1)

Unless it is appreciated how closely overlapping were ethnic attachment, economic interest and political power in Northern Ireland, coming together in the Orange Institution and the Unionist Party, the working of the informal network of political patronage, one of the linchpins in the maintenance of ethnic domination, cannot properly be understood (and it is interesting to note the similar predominance in politics in the Republic of Ireland of informal patronage networks: Bax 1976; Sacks 1976). The small scale of the local political and economic arena, and its relative autonomy prior to 1972, are vital to any explanation of the workings of this system of ethnic closure. The taken-for-granted coming together of the everyday workings of government, commerce and agriculture, in the hands of a small network of like-minded members of the same ethnic community, allowed influence to operate and manipulation to occur without too much need for conspiracy.

Since the suspension of Stormont in 1972, and the downgrading of local government in Northern Ireland in 1973, Northern Ireland has changed, and more than a little. In the first instance, it seems likely that incorporation into the British state did little to undermine the informal apparatus of Protestant control (O'Dowd *et al.* 1980). However, over the last fifteen years or so, a number of factors have transformed the situation: the local political dominance of Westminster, in the shape of the Northern Ireland Office, the development of a 'new' post-Unionist Northern Ireland Civil Service, the collapse of traditional Protestant skilled working-class employment, the impact upon local employment practices of UK legislation and European and North American influence, and the emergence of a local business elite which is dependent upon local consumers rather than labour and has reoriented itself away from an explicit emphasis upon ethnic communality. Whether or not discrimination against Catholics has diminished is a question for vituperative academic debate (Cormack and Osborne 1991; Smith and Chambers 1991). That issue aside, one arguable outcome of these changes has been a 'crisis of identity' for Protestants (Bruce 1994; Buckley 1989). Among other things,[4] this crisis reflects the loss by the local Protestant establishment of their central, controlling role in the management of the Province, and the changed economic circumstances of the Protestant working class, *vis-à-vis* Catholics.

But there is more to the Protestants' problem than this. One of the arguments I have been advancing in this chapter is that, historically, Ulster Protestant ethnicity has developed along two principal relational axes, involving complex interactions of similarity and difference: internally, with respect to Catholics, and externally with respect to the rest of Britain. Neither of these is unambiguously a relationship of similarity or difference, and each is implicated in the other. Put over-simply, Northern Irish Protestants have two significant Others; and each is, in different ways depending on the situational context – and to some extent only – *us* as well as *them*. While this can be as confusing for Ulster Prods as for anyone else, ambiguity *per se* is not the source of their present difficulty with respect to their sense of themselves, their sense of identity.

The problem lies in the undermining or, perhaps more accurately, the transformation of the British axis. The *categorizers* (of Catholics) now find themselves the *categorized* (by the British, and by the rest of the world). Those who have put Others in their place for centuries, are experiencing what it means to be put in their place. Those who have long looked down on Others, now find themselves looked down *as* the Other. Those who have, historically, constructed part of their identity out of and in the link with Britain – and an imagined footing of equality – are now having to face the hierarchy inherent in that relationship. Long implicit, it is now out in the open. The Protestant place in the imagined community of the United Kingdom looks increasingly marginal, if not altogether insecure. In the face of the distancing which began with Harold Wilson's televised accusation of 'scrounging' in 1974, a relation of kinship or alliance with 'across the water' can no longer easily be taken for granted – or even sustained – as one of the boundaries of Protestant ethnicity. And the alternative in that direction, independence, remains – in the absence of any renegotiation of relationships across the *other* boundary, with Northern Irish Catholics – largely unthinkable. The Anglo-Irish Agreement of 1985, and the subsequent prominence of the London–Dublin relationship in the wake of the local paramilitary cease-fires, has done nothing except dramatize the difficulty.

Culture and economic advantage?

Protestant ethnicity in Ulster was initially established and subsequently manipulated within the fields of military conquest and economics. The economic differences between Catholics and Protestants in Northern Ireland to which I have drawn attention remain important (the research evidence of which this paragraph and the next is a summary can be found in Cormack and Osborne 1983, 1991). Census and other official survey data indicate that, despite *some* narrowing of *some* gaps, and some mobility in managerial occupations, Catholics remain more likely to be unemployed than Protestants, more likely to be employed in the service sector than in manufacturing, and are over-represented in semi- or unskilled manual occupations. This ethnically skewed occupational distribution is likely to ameliorate only slowly, according to projections of future occupational and educational change.

The reasons for the persistence of ethnic economic advantage should be clear. It probably has little to do with different levels of cultural capital, as indicated – admittedly imperfectly – by formal educational achievement. In the past, Protestants consistently did 'better', educationally speaking. It is likely that, at least in part, this was a reflection of the different social class profiles of the two groups. However, this trend is changing – as are the social class profiles – although a bias of Catholic pupils away from vocational science-based and technological subjects remains marked. Historically, these educational patterns are probably best understood as a *result* of ethnic exclusion and closure, rather than one of its *causes*. Similarly, with respect to attitudes to work, recent research has discovered negligible differences between the two ethnic groups. There appears to be no ready-to-hand 'cultural' explanation for the striking differences in the pattern of employment between Protestants and Catholics.

The Protestant folk view of the situation is relatively straightforward: economic advantage has been their just reward for hard work, thrift and hard-headedness in business. Research into local ethnic stereotypes carried out in the early 1970s (O'Donnell 1977) discovered that 'industrious' was a major theme in Protestant self-descriptions. In this case, as in every case, group identification goes hand in glove with the categorization of Others. Here is a young Protestant man, himself unemployed, talking to the author in the late 1970s, threading some further themes into the categorization:

> you go down to the dole in Corporation Street and you'll see them in their thousands. I went down there one day and nearly never came back. That's another thing, they're nearly always on the brue [registered as unemployed] . . . claiming for everything, and doing the double [working illegally while on benefit]. Although maybe I shouldn't say that because there's a lot of Prods doing the double too. But I reckon there's hell of a lot more Catholics on the dole, claiming for everything off the Government. (Jenkins 1982: 31)

Nor is it only a matter of working-class stereotypes. Thomas Wilson, an Ulster Protestant and an economist, has eloquently exemplified this:

> As for business life, Presbyterians and Jews are probably endowed with more business acumen than Irish Catholics . . . For generations they were the underdogs, the despised 'croppies', the adherents of a persecuted religion, who were kept out of public life by the Protestant conquerors. They were made to feel inferior, and to make matters worse they often were inferior, if only in those personal qualities that make for success in competitive economic life. (Wilson 1955: 208–9)

Wilson appears to have moderated his views since, emphasizing (1989: 108) the importance of local *perceptions* that Protestants possessed a distinctive and superior work ethic. One could turn this round to say – and this is, to be fair, a plausible reading of the quotation above – that what mattered was the *categorization* of Catholics as idle, unreliable, shiftless, lacking in enterprise.

The notion that Protestantism – *qua* doctrine – encouraged economic enterprise in Ulster has found its way into other academic analyses (e.g. Baker 1973: 803), which is is not surprising in view of the continuing academic debate about Max Weber's argument linking the 'Puritan asceticism' of the Reformation with the development of capitalism. Whatever the merits of the Protestant Ethic thesis, however, there is a firm case for resisting the notion that Protestant economic supremacy in Northern Ireland has anything to do with the cultural norms – whether doctrinal or otherwise – of Protestantism. The economic advantage of Ulster Protestants must be traced back to the Plantation and the systematic dispossession of the indigenous Irish population. This act of initial domination, creating as it did two ethnicities in conflict – one advantaged, one disadvantaged – was consolidated during the industrial revolution and has yet to be undermined. The evidence of this chapter is that, historically and more recently, the opportunity structure for Catholics – itself the result of Protestant political domination – and the intimate relationship between Unionism and the local business élite are sufficient explanations for the ethnic division of labour in Northern Ireland.

This account of Ulster Protestant ethnicity and intra-group relations has at least one major weakness. The need to keep to a manageable length has encouraged a tighter argument than I would have wished. Consequently, the ins and outs of history have been smoothed over, if not ironed out altogether. Protestant workers were not, for example, as easily or comprehensively 'bought off' as I may at times seem to have suggested: witness the ongoing gulf between Unionism and paramilitary loyalism. That split also highlights another oversight: important differences between the urban bourgeoisie and rural Protestants would find a place in a more detailed discussion.

The mobilization of ethnicity as a resource in the pursuit of political dominance and capital accumulation may, if the Ulster situation is any guide, take many forms. In particular, during the period of industrialization and urbanization, that strand of Protestant ethnicity which of necessity 'faced outward' encouraged and facilitated – and was produced and reproduced by – the links with Britain through which technology was imported, capital exported for investment elsewhere, and political support mobilized. From the late nineteenth century, ethnic ties were increasingly – and apparently, at least to some degree self-consciously – part of the local Protestant bourgeoisie's strategy for dealing with the threat of organized labour. The 'management' of the class-stratified Protestant community was achieved in a number of complementary fashions, the two most important being the control of recruitment into employment – in a labour market which always had more job-seekers than jobs – and the creation of political unity, a class alliance against the external threat of Catholic nationalism. Protestant commercial and industrial supremacy in Ulster has been built upon these foundations.

Intra-group relations are not the whole story, of course: what about the boundary between Protestants and Catholics? The internal relations of the Protestant community have contributed, in no small way, to the categorization of Catholics. However, this isn't just a matter of *nominal* identification; the *virtualities* of categorization are also significant. Hence the emphasis in this chapter upon economic activity. For centuries, Ulster Protestants were disproportionately able to constitute what it meant – beginning with the most everyday matters of subsistence – to be Catholic. The specifics of that experience may have changed and shifted as circumstances shifted and changed, and there were doubtless local and individual exceptions and ameliorations, but the essential fact remained. Northern Catholic identity was to a significant degree – and for long enough for it to acquire a certain consistency, the solidity of history expressed in Barth's notion of the *universe of discourse* – a social construct emerging out of categorization (by Protestants) and out of the economic and other consequences of that categorization. The balance began to change in the 1960s, as external factors and developments within the Catholic community began to encourage a more vocal and successful assertion of Catholic group identification than had hitherto been possible. It has changed even more since, as Protestants have gradually seen their power to categorize slip away.

The economic sphere is, however, only one aspect of categorization and its consequences. As suggested in Chapter 5, violence – particularly killing – can be understood as the ultimate act of categorization.[5] Nominally, it forecloses on the possibility of a response or a redefinition; virtually, in terms of consequences, it is equally absolute. It really is 'putting them in their place' (and, as the republican hunger strike of the early 1980s demonstrated, it can work both ways: death can make the ultimate *claim* to identity and brand indelibly the Other in the process). Although there is no space to explore the matter in detail, the differences in the nature of Catholic and Protestant paramilitary violence can be interpreted within this framework. Summarized rather baldly, while Protestant paramilitaries have mainly focused their attacks on Catholic civilians, Catholic paramilitaries have largely taken the security forces to be their primary target (O'Leary and McGarry 1993: 34–40). As the Protestant power to categorize and define Catholics – a power upon which so much Protestant group identification has historically depended – has dwindled in other respects, violence has been one means of 'putting them in their place' that they have been able to retain.

As events in Drumcree, County Armagh, in July 1995 and 1996 illustrated, there are also other ways of doing this. The tenacity with which, in 1996, the 'traditional' claim of local Orangemen to parade down the Garvaghy Road was pressed home, the depth of Catholic dismay when the Royal Ulster Constabulary allowed the parade to proceed, and the damage done thereby to the fragile 'peace process', only make sense when it is realized that it was not the recognition of Orange 'cultural traditions' that was at stake. What *was* at stake was precisely the continued capacity of Protestants to put Catholics in their place, in this case by denying that they *had* an autonomous place, free from incursion. When all else fails, struggles over identity remain, and Ulster loyalists will seek ways to translate their imaginings of domination into social reality.

8

The Cultural Stuff

Barth, in a well-known passage in his 'Introduction' to *Ethnic Groups and Boundaries*, argued that the focus for the investigation of ethnicity should be 'the ethnic *boundary* that defines the group, not the cultural stuff that it encloses' (1969a: 15). By 'cultural stuff', he means language, religion, customs and laws, tradition, material culture, cuisine, etc. In arguing this he was, as outlined in Chapter 1, standing in a direct line of descent from Max Weber. It is an argument that must remain at the centre of our thinking. In insisting that there is no simple equation between the seamless tapestry of cultural *variation* and the discontinuities of ethnic *differentiation*, it prevents us from mistaking the morphological enumeration of cultural traits for the analysis of ethnicity. However, this argument might also be construed as suggesting that the cultural stuff out of which that differentiation is arbitrarily socially constructed is somehow irrelevant, and this surely cannot be true. For example, a situation in which the As and the Bs are distinguished, *inter alia*, by languages that are mutually intelligible for most everyday purposes – as with Danish and Norwegian – would seem to differ greatly from one in which the languages involved are, as with English and Welsh, utterly different.

A generally similar point was argued two decades ago by Handelman (1977: 190). He suggests – and for him category and group are synonymous – that the 'categorical corporate holdings of culture', far from being irrelevant, specify 'a corporate history in time and space'. They tell a story about 'why the category is substantial and legitimate', providing group members with 'the elements of a "social biography" which connects "culture" and behaviour, and the past to the present'. This aspect of the cultural stuff is, argues Handelman, important for distinguishing ethnicity from other kinds of membership category. Something similar is implied by Anthony Cohen's arguments (1985) about the 'symbolic construction of community'. More recently, in an attempt to understand the complexities of why some ethnic attachments are more contingent or flexible than others, Cornell (1996) has argued for a partial shift of analytic attention, at least, back to what goes on *within* the boundary – what co-members share as much as what differentiates them from Others – to the *content* of ethnicity; which includes the cultural stuff.

In this chapter I want to look at some of the cultural stuff of ethnicity in Northern Ireland. In particular, I am going to discuss the contribution made by the cultural *content* of ethnicity – specifically religion – to the nature of relations at and across the *boundary* between the groups involved. The nominal content of ethnicity in Northern Ireland is indeed religious; the opposition between Catholic and Protestant is its root classification. As the previous chapter argued, the historical and everyday *virtualities* of this, its consequences, can be traced in the economic field and, although this was not explored in detail, with respect to violence. But how does religion contribute to the situation apart from being a convenient marker of ethnic difference?

That the Northern Irish 'troubles' are about religion is an important facet of the image of the situation held by both the British public and external observers. It is an understanding of the situation that allows the violence to be explained away as an irrational anachronism, and the Northern Irish people to be dismissed as 'backwoodsmen' or 'ignorant peasants' who have yet to discover the modern era, let alone the twentieth century. This view has, probably inadvertently, been reinforced by analytical accounts with titles such as *Holy War in Belfast* (Boyd 1969) and 'Religious war in Northern Ireland' (Easthope, 1976). A strong version of the thesis that the 'troubles' in Northern Ireland are, indeed, a conflict of religion has been defended vigorously by John Fulton (1991); less adamant versions have been offered by John Hickey (1984) and Maurice Irvine (1991). The centrality of religion is also a thematic continuity in Steve Bruce's writings on Ulster Protestants (1986, 1994). In this chapter I will explore in what sense, if indeed any, it is correct to understand the Northern Ireland problem as a religious conflict.

Varieties of religious conflict

Before looking at the local detail of Northern Ireland, it may be useful to consider some general characteristics of situations of religious conflict, and how they relate to ethnicity. I am not, for example, concerned with the existence of doctrinal, ceremonial or cosmological differences between religions or sects. In the sense in which the word is used here, it is not religions as ideological systems which are in conflict, but their members. The very existence of different religions, sects, or communities of worship presupposes that there will be differences of opinion – which may be fundamental and total – between them, as bodies of belief, with respect to their corporate world-views, religious and moral doctrines, and ritual practices. They can, therefore, legitimately be said to be always 'in conflict' – in a weak sense – with respect to these issues.

The existence of conflicts of this kind doesn't *necessarily* lead to actual conflictual struggles – whether violent or non-violent – between individuals or groups who identify themselves as devotees of the doctrines concerned. It is with religious conflict in this latter, strong sense of the word that I am here concerned. What is it about a situation of conflict and struggle which distinguishes it as religious? We may begin by saying that such a situation is religious if a significant number of the parties to the conflict define it as being primarily about religion or religion-related matters. It is possible to tentatively identify five ideal-typical conflict situations which may be characterized as conflicts of religion in this sense.

The first may be described as a *missionary* conflict: members of one religious group seek to expand outside their own territory and proselytize non-members. This may involve force in the proselytizing or in the local response to it. Examples can be found ready to hand in both Christian and Islamic history. Some of the ethnocide reported from Amazonia in recent years appears, on the face of things, to fall into this category. However, it is also true to say, as this example illustrates, that missionary zeal often goes easily hand in hand with baser economic motives; it isn't easy to disentangle one from the other. In other words, missionary religion may also be an ideology of identification, no less useful for the legitimation and justification of dirty work, where appropriate, than racism or nationalism.

In the second place, there is the *holy war*: a dispute over territory or possessions which are regarded by at least one of the parties to the conflict as sacred or otherwise symbolically significant. Examples of this are once again all too easy to find: one only has to point to the long-standing disputes over the Holy Places of Palestine between Christians, Muslims and (more recently) Jews. In practice, of course, as in the case of the *jihad*, the distinction between missionary conflict and holy war may be more difficult to discern than is apparent from these definitions.

Third, a situation in which two or more religious groupings occupy the same territorial and social space, and the dominant grouping penalizes the religious practices of the subordinated grouping(s), may be described as *religious persecution*. Familiar examples of this kind of conflict are the Inquisition of medieval Europe or, if one accepts the characterization of Soviet state socialism as a secular religion (Lane 1981), the persecution of religious minorities in the Soviet Union. Similarly, one can point to many colonial situations in which a missionary conflict became, with the consolidation of conquest, religious persecution. Conflicts of this kind frequently also involve other broader, cultural issues, such as the right to use an indigenous language.

Fourth, *religious competition*, is characterized by two or more religious groupings – usually two – coexisting within the same space and struggling for dominance. Since there is a tendency for one or other of the parties to achieve that aim, such situations are often short-lived, in historical terms; an imperfect example may be found in the Catholic–Protestant conflicts in the Netherlands in the sixteenth and seventeenth centuries (Goudsblom 1967: 17–19). The resolution of a situation of religious competition may result in religious persecution in the period which follows.

Finally, there is a particular kind of situation of conflict which is about *religious politics*, that is to say, struggles for power and influence within religious institutions or groupings. Religious organizations are probably no more and no less vulnerable to conflicts of this kind than their secular counterparts. Schisms within modern Sikhism between the Akali Dal and the Nihang Buddha Dal factions – a conflict which was successfully manipulated to its own advantage in the Punjab during the 1980s by the Indian Congress Party – provide a recent example of religious politics. This highlights the possibilities that exist for religious politics to become implicated in secular politics, and vice versa.

How to distinguish between one type of situation and another in the real, as opposed to the ideal-typical, world, is not so straightforward. More than one of these types of conflict can be present at the same time, as in the early modern Netherlands, where it is possible to discern elements of a missionary conflict alongside religious competition. Similarly, a situation of one type may change rapidly into a situation more closely resembling another. In addition, as has already been mentioned, issues other than the religious may be implicated in religious conflicts. These distinctions and definitions are, therefore, nothing more than a potentially useful set of categories against which to set the description and analysis of particular situations.

An obvious question at this point is: how does religion interact with other principles of identification – such as class consciousness, economic interest, party solidarity or nationalism – which can make important contributions to the genesis and continuation of conflict? More generally, does it make sense to delineate a domain of the 'religious' which is distinct from these other factors? These questions are more easily asked than answered. However, it may prove possible to shed some light on the issues by returning to ethnicity, which can be either a *source* of conflict, or the cultural or ideological *idiom* in which conflict is pursued. Ethnicity is also, of course, a source of social *solidarity*. Difference and similarity, again.

A propos group identity, ethnicity is about the differences and similarities that are recognized as significant by their members. But which differences provide local models of ethnic identification with their content? Among others, the following are obvious possibilities: language, territorial occupation, religion, and a shared history (particularly, perhaps, a history of conflict with other ethnic groups). The important point to note is that religion may be – I might even want to put this more strongly, is *likely* to be – an important dimension of ethnic identity. This, of necessity almost, poses the further question: when are religious conflicts actually ethnic conflicts, and vice versa?

Framed thus, the question permits no clear-cut answer. However, some headway may be made by returning to the earlier definition of religious conflict: in this sense, a conflict is 'religious' if it is defined as such by a significant proportion of the parties to it. Without wishing to evoke disputes about false knowledge or ideology that have long since passed their sell-by date, the further question can, of course, be asked: what if the participants in a conflict *only think* it's about religious issues? What if it's *really* about ethnicity (or nationalism or class struggle or whatever)? Short of declaring, by epistemological fiat, that *our* analytical models of social reality are intrinsically more trustworthy than *their* folk models – in effect that the social scientist, like mother, knows best – there is no easy resolution of this difficulty. On the one hand, following authors such as Giddens (1979: 5), socially competent actors are reasonably knowledgeable about the meaning and consequences of their own practices and the practices of others. On the other, however, when the actors disagree about what's going on, the social scientist is arguably in a position to make at least *some* more sense of the situation than the immediate participants (Bauman 1990: 12–15; Jenkins 1983: 10). All one can do is to examine the specificities of each case and attempt to judge accordingly.

Religious differences and conflict in Northern Ireland

Since the late 1960s Northern Ireland has been the arena for a bitter and violently contested three-cornered conflict, involving the two major segments of its population and the British state. The current outbreak of political violence is the latest in a history of such conflicts in the island of Ireland taken as a whole; its genesis and subsequent progress must be understood in the context of that history, some of which has been outlined in the previous chapter. In what sense, therefore, can the present 'troubles' be thought of as a religious conflict?

If for no other reason, the Northern Irish conflict has a religious aspect because the two local protagonist groups identify themselves nominally as Catholics and Protestants. These are not, however, the only labels with which each community categorizes the other, or identifies itself. Depending on the context, 'British', 'Ulsterman', 'unionist', 'loyalist', or 'Orangeman', for example, may equate with Protestant, and 'Irish', 'fenian', 'taig', 'republican', or 'nationalist', with Catholic (O'Donnell 1977: 139–45). These bear witness that, in Northern Ireland, group identity is complex rather than simple, multiplex rather than single-stranded. In this particular case, it would appear to draw upon political, religious and ethnic-cultural themes as the source of its significance.

Nor is religion *just* a label. It is important to acknowledge that, taken solely at face value, Catholic and Protestant are, for many Northern Irish people, considerably more than nominal identifications. In an increasingly secular – although not actually disenchanted – north-western Europe, Northern Ireland (with the rest of Ireland) stands out in terms of belief and practical devotion. Survey evidence is clear that, with respect to both camps:

> People in Northern Ireland are not only far more likely than people in Britain to belong to a religious organisation, they are also more likely to attend church . . . In the ordinary senses of the word, the people of Northern Ireland are considerably more 'religious' than those of Britain. The churches in Northern Ireland are more conservative or orthodox in their theology than their British counterparts. (Bruce and Alderdice 1993: 6, 19)

Being a Protestant or being a Catholic makes an important everyday – and at least an every seventh day – difference to the Northern Irish. Religion has its own intrinsic virtualities; it is not just nominal, it is much more than just a label (although this isn't true for everyone: the survey evidence that Bruce and Alderdice summarize suggests that about a third of the population attend church 'rarely'). In terms of the meanings which frame everyday experience, it would be unwise to neglect religion. Although the labels Catholic and Protestant in Northern Ireland are indexical of many other differences, they also refer to authentic religious belief.

Apart from the names by which the opposing groups are identified, and identify themselves, in what other senses can religious differences *per se* be said to be part of the Northern Irish conflict? In the first place, doctrinal and theological differences between Catholicism and Protestantism are intimately bound up with the gulf which separates the two traditions with respect to the necessity and nature of mediation between God and mankind. In Northern Ireland this finds frequent expression in Protestant anti-papist fulminations and accusations of idolatry and authoritarianism. These, however, are conflicts in the weak sense of the word, and are not of major interest here: the same doctrinal differences exist between the two religious communities elsewhere without civil strife occurring. *A propos* religious differences of this kind, dissent between the various Protestant denominations and sects is also important. An extreme – and, in the local context, highly visible – example of this kind of disagreement is the hostility expressed by groups such as the Reverend Ian Paisley's Free Presbyterian Church towards the Ecumenical Movement and its local Protestant supporters. Once again, however, virulent Protestant denominationalism of this sort is not peculiar to Northern Ireland, nor is it – even in Northern Ireland – inevitably productive of violent conflict.

So what about the contribution of religion to conflict – in the strong sense – in Northern Ireland? One of the most apparent, and perhaps the most widely commented upon, religious dimensions of the situation lies in the field of education. Since the 1920s there have effectively been two education systems in Northern Ireland, one Protestant (controlled schools) and one Catholic (maintained schools), each insulated in all major respects from the other (Akenson 1973). The clergy are highly influential in both systems; indirectly in the Protestant, directly in the Catholic. Apart from the interactional segregation which such a situation reinforces, there is evidence of curricular differences between the two, particularly with respect to the teaching of Irish history, sport and, obviously perhaps, religious education.

However, it is no easy matter to assess the contribution made to the conflict in Northern Ireland by religiously segregated education. Although at the level of common sense one might expect it to have had some effect, Murray has argued that segregated education simply reflects the prejudice and social segregation of Northern Irish society in general and that the specific influence of education upon the local situation has been 'grossly exaggerated' (Murray 1983: 149). Be that as it may – and Murray's argument is persuasive – there can be little doubt that segregated schooling serves to reproduce, if not to create, the boundaries between the two ethnicities. This is particularly important, perhaps, with respect to the constitution and organization of infant and primary schools, the institutional social world within which primary socialization takes place, in ethnic terms and from ethnic points of view.

Religion also appears to contribute to conflict in Northern Ireland if we look at the regulation of sexual relations and marriage. One striking aspect of this problem concerns marriage between Catholic and Protestant (Lee 1981). In the wake of the papal *Ne Temere* decree of 1908, and the McCann case of 1911, intermarriage has been discouraged by the Catholic hierarchy and considerable pains may still be taken, both inside and outside the family, to ensure that the children of a 'mixed marriage' are brought up as Catholics. This is, what is more, an issue concerning which the Roman Catholic Church in Ireland appears to have recently adopted a firmer line than in other countries. Given the sensitive demography of Northern Ireland, the Church's policy in this respect is widely interpreted by Protestants – although this interpretation ignores the fact that the Church actively and publicly discourages intermarriage – as a stratagem designed to eventually tip the electoral balance in favour of the reunification of Ireland.

Nor does pressure against the mixed marriage come from only one side. Although there may not be the same kind of institutionalized barriers to intermarriage on the part of the Protestant churches, many Protestant clergy and lay members strongly disapprove of religious exogamy, possibly because, as a result of the local view of Roman Catholic policy discussed above, the traffic is largely seen to be one-way. Indeed, survey evidence suggests that, for precisely this reason, Protestant lay-people are actually more disapproving of mixed marriages than their Catholic counterparts (Gallagher and Dunn 1991: 12). The consequences are informal, although frequently effective, measures to discourage such unions (McFarlane 1979). However, ethnic closure – especially in the face of the emotions – can never, thank goodness, be absolute: of the 61 per cent of respondents who reported the religious composition of their own marriage to the 1991 Northern Ireland Social Attitudes Survey, 9 per cent were in a Catholic–Protestant 'mixed marriage', and this may be an underestimate of the global percentage of inter-ethnic unions (Bruce and Alderdice 1993: 14).

A third sense in which religion, or religious issues, can be said to influence the Northern Irish conflict is with respect to the relationship between church and state in the Republic of Ireland. As the 1978 Northern Ireland Attitude Survey found, 'a principal reason for unionist antipathy towards a united Ireland is the position of the Catholic Church in the Republic' (Moxon-Browne 1983: 39). This is a complex subject, of which Whyte (1980) and Clarke (1984) offer the best all-round, even if now somewhat dated, discussions (see also O'Reilly 1992). The problem is not whether the Roman Catholic Church in the Republic does in fact exercise an overweening, or even a significant, influence upon state policy and legislation with respect to matters such as divorce and contraception. Indeed, the fact that the availability of contraception, for example, has been significantly liberalized during the last decade – albeit in the face of a campaign of stiff opposition from the Church – suggests that this influence may be on the wane, and other indications of this trend could be suggested. The problem is, rather, that many Protestants in Northern Ireland persist in the belief that the Roman Catholic Church has considerable – or even total – sinister power in the Republic (Heskin 1980: 28–30). They fear for their civil and religious liberties accordingly.

Matters are not always clear-cut in these respects. For example, abortion – utterly illegal in the Republic, and for most practical purposes impossible in the north – is not an issue of major controversy between Catholics and Protestants in Northern Ireland (Porter 1996: 288–9). The mainstream of Northern Irish Protestant opinion opposes abortion, although perhaps with less collective consistency than their Catholic fellow travellers on this issue (Cairns 1992: 157). Ian Paisley has frequently publicly expressed his horror of abortion and roundly condemned the practice on the basis of scripture, and members of his Church – including his daughter – have shared public anti-abortion platforms with members of the Roman Catholic hierarchy. He, and many other Protestants, would support moves to restrict even further the minimal local availability of abortion, or prohibit it altogether as against the laws of God and nature. The security of conviction being what it is, however, such a position is not seen as either an unwarranted religious intrusion into the business of the secular state, or as a restriction on the freedoms of the individual citizen. At issue for many religiously enthusiastic Protestants, rather than the maintenance of some general constitutional separation between church and state, is opposition to any extension of the power or influence – as they perceive it – of the *Roman Catholic* Church.

So far, I have been discussing aspects of religion which, although they create social distance between Catholics and Protestants, or enhance Protestant fears of the reunification of Ireland, probably contribute only indirectly to the conflict as violent engagement. Religion is in this sense:

> a basis for segregating the population into two communities, largely ignorant of each other and susceptible therefore to prejudice and stereotyping. (Whyte 1990: 51)

Religion may, however, provide more immediate, and in their contribution to the 'troubles', more consequential factors. With respect to the informal regulation of routine public interaction, for example, religion-related items are an integral feature of the set of culturally specified markers by means of which actors 'tell the difference' or allocate ethnic identities to significant others (Burton 1978: 37–67; Jenkins 1982: 30–1). Without this repertoire of culturally signified differences certain kinds of violence – random assassination, for example (Dillon and Lehane 1973) – would be more difficult to pursue with any certainty of outcome. Among other things, the following signs or symbols are differences-which-make-a-difference for this purpose: religious or quasi-religious medallions or badges, knowledge of appropriate ritual forms – such as, for example, the Hail Mary – school attended, and Christian name, many Catholics bearing the names of saints. These are not the only, nor even necessarily the most important, ethnic markers; they are merely the obvious *religious* markers, and they are significant. 'Telling the difference' is an everyday cultural competence; here is the same Protestant young man who was quoted in the previous chapter:

> They wear crosses, fellas and all. A lot of our girls wear crosses but rarely the fellas. And they wear these white badges, here [*points to lapel*], the old men, I don't know what they are, it's like a flame in it. Priests wear them as well. I was told what they were one time . . . You can always tell by their names, Patrick and Seamus and Josephine. Nine times out of ten if it was Patrick he'd be Catholic . . . They're very strict about their religion. That wee girl I was going with, we were talking about religion and I asked would she change and that was as far as I got. (Jenkins 1982: 30–1)

More generally, the bare fact that the two political communities are of opposing religious persuasions is of considerable moment in providing each group with an everyday identity, recognized by themselves and by their opponents, which is to some extent capable of transcending and subsuming the internal differences of ideology, class, doctrine and political strategy, which perpetually threaten their fragile solidarity. In the case of the nationalist community this unity is given institutional form and cohesion by the Catholic Church itself. For the theologically less unified unionist community, such a service may be performed, as Rosemary Harris has suggested (1972: 156), by the Orange Order. While this institutional significance can be overplayed – the Catholic Church is ambiguous in its relation to the physical-force tradition of republicanism, and Orangeism doesn't command a majority of Protestants as members outside its limited rural strongholds – the point has some validity. There is, however, no symmetry across the boundary; in particular, the situation encourages Protestants to categorize Catholics as a monolithic ethnic bloc:

> the two communities are not mirror images of each other. The Protestant community is more fragmented than the Catholic. It is divided by denomination – a phenomenon which has no counterpart on the Catholic side. It is divided by theological preference: while among Catholics there are differences of emphasis between conservatives and progressives, there is nothing so sharp as the fundamentalist/liberal division in Protestantism . . . The Protestant community is more deeply divided by class then the Catholic community . . . We have here one reason for Protestant suspicions of the Catholic community. (Whyte 1990: 49, 50)

The centrality to religion of symbolism also contributes in an important and particular fashion to its role in the unification or collectivization of diversity. Anthony Cohen has argued convincingly (1985) that communal identities are, in his words, 'symbolically constructed': symbols can be shared without necessarily meaning the same thing to community members. This allows considerable diversity to shelter, and to knit together, behind a symbolic mask of collective religious identity. The supporter of physical-force republicanism and the pacifist can, for example, both be devout and practising Catholics and identify with each other accordingly in the practice of their faith. Furthermore, inasmuch as the Catholic Church is less fragmented, and Catholicism much more elaborately symbolized in terms of ritual and belief, it has a greater potential than the Protestant Churches to function – very visibly – as a 'communal umbrella'. Hence further impetus to the categorization of Catholicism as monolithic. To return to the theoretical point of departure, this is another indication of the importance of content – the cultural stuff – to relationships across ethnic boundaries.

The other sense in which religion is directly implicated in the conflict is perhaps more straightforward. Religion often concerns itself with issues that are apparently political, and politics may equally be self-consciously religious. An example of this elision of the two domains of discourse may be found in the Orange Order's Twelfth of July processions (Cecil 1993; Larsen 1982). An important feature of these events, the purpose of which is the commemoration of King William's victory over King James at the Battle of the Boyne in 1690, is the meeting at 'the field' at the end of the march; among other things, this is an opportunity for speechifying by local Unionist politicians and Protestant clergymen. A recurrent theme of such speeches is the need for vigilance in defence of the Protestant heritage of the Reformation, and the importance of the Orange Order and the Northern Ireland state to that defence. Similarly, a well-worn theme at the Reverend Ian Paisley's religious meetings, although he is an active Member of the European Parliament, is denunciation of the European Economic Community as a papist plot, foreseen, what is more, by the Book of Revelations in the New Testament. Returning to Handelman's point about 'social biographies', for Catholics as well as Protestants, religion and a religious reading of history contribute in no small manner to the weaving of oppositional mythical charters which legitimize the present impasse (Irvine 1991: 172–212). Religion also contributes in a similarly mythic way to the construction of the future, as a historicist teleology of collective destiny.

More generally, there is a long – and particularly Protestant – tradition of political clerics: many loyalist politicians have been ministers of religion, and clergymen have often found it useful to draw upon political rhetoric as part of their evangelizing. By the same token, politicians are capable of leavening their public message with religion. An apposite – if somewhat extreme – example from the early 1980s concerned Mr George Seabrook, a Northern Ireland Assemblyman, Belfast City Councillor and sometime member of Paisley's Democratic Unionist Party (DUP), who was charged, in July 1984, with using threatening or abusive language likely to cause a breach of the peace. His offence was to suggest, at a meeting of Belfast Education and Library Board, that the City Council should buy an incinerator to burn Catholics, whom he described as 'Fenian scum'. A self-confessed bigot, the specifically religious dimension of Mr Seabrook's remarks is betrayed by his suggestion that Catholic priests be burned, and his later statement that he would only apologize 'the day after the Pope marries'.[1]

It is tempting to dismiss this kind of venom as the extremism of a lunatic fringe. Before so doing, however, it must be pointed out that in response to Mr Seabrook's public utterances the DUP stopped short, in the first instance, of disowning him completely, being content to suspend him pending an apology. Such an apology not being forthcoming, his membership of the party eventually lapsed at the end of 1984, to the evident relief of his erstwhile leaders. Rhetoric of this sort is representative of a particular strain of Protestant political discourse in which are mingled Old Testament savagery, born-again fundamentalist piety, old-fashioned Empire Loyalism, and virulent ethnic chauvinism (Bruce 1986). To appropriate a local epithet, this is a tradition of 'bitter' Protestant politics. As such, it is the emotional and political bedrock upon which rests the phenomenon of Paisleyism:

> Although not all his political supporters would subscribe to his doctrinal view, there seems no doubt that Paisley's own brand of Protestantism provides an ideology that bears the same relation to the DUP's political tactics as Marxism does to a Communist party in Eastern Europe. The ideology serves to legitimize political actions, it serves as a unifying force, but it is flexible enough to be adapted to alternative policies in the pursuit of broadly similar goals. (Moxon-Browne 1983: 96)

In emphasizing this particular manifestation of the Protestant churches politically militant, one should not, of course, forget that an important body of Protestant opinion is politically moderate. It was, for example, Protestant clergymen who organized and participated in the Feakle talks with representatives of the Provisional Republican movement in December 1974; this is a strand of dialogue which has continued, on and off, up to the present, contributing to the negotiations which led to the cease-fires of 1994. However, it is probably true to say that this sort of centrist moderation is not representative of the majority of Northern Irish Protestants.

The relationship of the Catholic Church to politics is different again. Having no major role to play in the Northern Ireland state – apart from its importance in the sphere of education – it has tended to abstain from public or 'official' politics. Occasionally individual priests may involve themselves in local-level political issues or even more rarely, as in the case of Father Denis Faul, for example, in issues such as civil liberties, and senior members of the hierarchy do, from time to time, issue statements about specific incidents. This, however, is the sum of *public* political activity on the part of the Catholic Church. Recently individual Catholic churchmen have also played an ecumenical part in the informal and out-of-the-public-eye network of cross-community discussions that are, in a manner perhaps as yet not fully appreciated, part of the current 'peace process'.

The Catholic Church's relationship to republican politics, whether parliamentary or paramilitary, is ambiguous and equivocal. On the one hand, there is a necessary – and genuine – historical affinity with the goals and ideals of republicanism, broadly construed. On the other hand, however, the inherent conservatism of the Church prevents it from supporting either the violence which characterizes the campaign of the Provisional IRA, or the socialism of marginal groups such as the Workers' Party. The hierarchy's dilemma is effectively the same as that of successive Dublin governments: how should the Church support the Irish republican ideal in Northern Ireland without being seen to either condone political violence or encourage the radical politics that it regards as anathema? The contradictions and uncertainties which characterize local-level relationships between the Roman Catholic Church and militant republicanism – contradictions which came to a public head during the republican hunger strike protest at the Maze prison in 1980–81 – are well documented in ethnographic accounts of working-class Catholic neighbourhoods in Belfast (Burton 1978; Sluka 1989).

Thus there are at least four distinct strands of interconnection between religion and conflict in Northern Ireland. First, in terms of the signification of everyday cultural difference, religion is probably the most significant factor. Much else – nearly everything else – is shared: language, popular culture, consumerism, cooking, kind of housing – the list would have to be a long one. There *are* other cultural differences, reflecting in particular the modern reinvention of Gaelic tradition, north and south of the border, and the overt symbolization of politics (Loftus 1994; Rolston 1991, 1992), but religion – and all that goes with it – is perhaps the one that most touches most people. It makes a significant contribution to the ongoing social construction of the cultural content of the two different and mutually antagonistic ethnicities without which we would not be talking about this particular conflict.

Second – and this is so intimately related to the first point that the distinction may seem nit-picking – religious differences, as they are organized formally in the churches and in education, and less formally in families and social networks, structure the spatial and interactional pattern of much everyday social life in Northern Ireland. Formal and informal institutional factors, taken together with the authenticity of religious belief for many Northern Irish people, certainly don't make harmonious inter-ethnic relations 'on the ground' easier.

Third, some of the specific social doctrines and theological tenets of the Roman Catholic Church, combined with the political relationship between the Church and the Republic of Ireland state, contribute to a categorization or view of Irish politics, widely held by Protestants in Northern Ireland, which links the reunification of Ireland to authoritarian Catholicism and diminished civil and religious liberties.

Fourth, within the Protestant community, one finds a characteristic blend of politicized religion and sanctified politics which combines fundamentalism, anti-Catholicism, ethnic chauvinism, and anti-republicanism into a powerful, although not necessarily coherent, ideology that has as its focus the maintenance of Protestant control and 'culture' in Northern Ireland.

As a counterbalance, it should be remembered that some members of the various religious traditions in the Province see a role for religion in helping to resolve the conflict. Unfortunately, their efforts still appear to be more than outweighed by countervailing factors of one sort or another. And it must also be emphasized that although Northern Ireland has very high rates of church attendance, nominal membership of a religious grouping doesn't *necessarily* entail obedience to the dictates of faith or the pronouncements of the clergy. The pragmatics of birth control among Catholic women is as good an example of this as one might require. It is *not* correct to depict the Northern Irish populace as 'priest-ridden', and this may be a particularly inaccurate representation of those who are most directly involved in violent politics. Impressionistic evidence suggests that such people are often among the least devout of their co-religionists.

No claim is being made here, therefore, that the Northern Irish conflict is actually *about* religion, or that religion is the *cause* of the conflict. It would be very difficult to support convincingly such an interpretation of the situation, either currently or historically. Although a minority of participants may see it in these terms – and there can be little doubt that a particular strand of local Protestantism sees itself as still engaged in the business of defending, or even extending, the frontiers of the Reformation – the majority of Northern Irish people emphatically do not appear to see the 'troubles' as being *primarily* concerned with religion *per se* (Moxon-Browne 1983; Rose 1971). This is nicely encapsulated in a local joke:

> A gang of vigilantes patrolling the 'peace line' in west Belfast, came across an Asian door-to-door salesman. Since he wasn't local to the neighbourhood, they decided to interrogate him.
> 'Are you a Protestant or a Catholic?', the leader of the vigilantes asked him.
> 'I am a Hindu', the poor terrified man replied.
> 'We can see that', was the reply, 'but are you a Prod Hindu or a Fenian Hindu?'

But, if it isn't about religion, what is it about? The most important 'non-religious' dimensions of the Northern Ireland conflict are, in fact, well known. There is no need here to repeat the detailed discussion in the original paper from which this chapter is derived (Jenkins 1986b). To summarize, the major issues fomenting 'the troubles', each of which is a reflection of the other, are membership of the United Kingdom and the reunification of Ireland. This is a constitutional and nationalist conflict.

Intimately related to the major problems of national identity and government, however, other factors make important contributions to the persistence and virulence of conflict in Northern Ireland: religious differences, the particular economic and social disadvantage of Catholics, the relative privilege experienced by Protestants, the general and worsening economic deprivation of the province as a whole, the policies and practices of the British and Irish states in a variety of respects, and – not to be neglected – a long tradition of violent political action (this will be discussed in the next chapter). The significance of these factors cannot be understood without reference to the 'national question', the context within which they have arisen and from which they acquire their specific local meanings.

Ethnicity, politics and religion

To return to this chapter's original points of departure, it should, I think, be apparent that the Northern Irish conflict is not a religious conflict in terms of the definition that was advanced there. Although religion has a place – and indeed an important one – in the repertoire of conflict in Northern Ireland, the majority of participants see the situation as primarily concerned with matters of politics and nationalism, not religion. And there is no reason to disagree with them. Thus the central *nominal* content of local ethnicity – confessional difference – has to be set alongside a range of other things if we are adequately to understand the situation. Catholic and Protestant are ethnic identities which derive only part of their content from religion.

This is not to say, however, that the cultural stuff of religion is unimportant. Indeed, bearing in mind the five categories of religious conflict proposed at the start of this chapter, one can identify religious persecution during certain periods of Northern Ireland's history, and point to elements of religious competition and religious politics (particularly within, and between, the denominations of Protestantism) in the current situation. These are all present as sub-themes of the overarching conflict over national allegiances: religious issues and motifs provide actors with a vocabulary and institutional arena through the medium of which that conflict may be waged. On the other hand, however, the reality and undoubted force of confessional differences add fuel to the bonfires of nationalism and patriotism (and, of course, vice versa). It is possible to conclude, therefore, without any sense of contradiction, that although the Northern Ireland conflict is not *about* religion, it is, in fact, at every level bound up with religious differences. It is an ethnic conflict with a religious dimension.

So, although I don't want to go all the way with Fulton in arguing that 'the troubles' are about religion, I am disagreeing with an earlier position of my own that religion in Northern Ireland is 'mainly a convenient boundary marker' (Jenkins 1984: 260). I am now suggesting that religion is something more than that, a characterization of the local situation which seems, in some respects, to have been echoed recently by Buckley and Kenny (1995). I am also allowing religion a stronger role in the conflict than McAllister (1982), who argues that religious commitment – measured by ritual behaviour, devotion or self-definition, and belief in the supernatural – has little influence on the conflict. However, inasmuch as he is testing the hypothesis that 'the Northern Ireland conflict *centres* on religious values and behaviour' (1982: 343; my emphasis), he is only concerned with the strong model of religious conflict, as discussed earlier.

The situation in Northern Ireland is likely to have implications for our general understanding of conflicts which appear to have something to do with religion. An obvious point is that religious affiliation is not in any sense an 'uncontaminated' social identity in its own right, somehow isolated from or 'above' other categories or identities. To adopt such a view would be to fly in the face of the intuitions of decades of social anthropological comparative research and there is nothing in the contemporary Northern Irish situation to justify it. It is likely – if not inevitable – that religion will necessarily overlap and interact with other principles of affiliation and identification, particularly ethnicity, locality, nationality, class, and economic interest. It is, therefore, to be expected that a 'pure' religious conflict, untainted by any other considerations or issues, will be, to say the least, rare. This isn't to suggest that conflicts which are *primarily* about religion, and which hence fall within the scope of the definition of religious conflict proposed earlier, will not occur, but simply to insist that conflicts which are *only* about religion – or indeed only about *anything* – are unlikely. It is equally unlikely that conflicts will be solely ethnic, or solely class-based, for example, although these may well be their dominant themes.

Bearing in mind the polysemic and multiplex character of conflicts 'in the real world', and recognizing that group identity, the basis of recruitment for social conflict, is multi-dimensional, it seems sensible to identify a weaker form of religious conflict than that which we have hitherto used as a yardstick here. In other words, one can use the five ideal types of religious conflict outlined earlier to categorize the religious dimensions of a conflict that does not appear, in itself, to be primarily about religion. It is necessary to differentiate *religious conflicts* from *conflicts with a religious dimension*, in which religion is a sub-theme, an elaboration on the main issue underlying the conflict.

The conflict in Northern Ireland is primarily *about* nationalism and the politics of ethnic domination. However, since religious affiliation is effectively co-terminous with ethnicity in this instance, the situation may accurately be described as a conflict with a religious dimension. The various struggles in Northern Ireland are contributed to and coloured by religious themes, confessional differences providing the protagonists with an important medium through which to further their respective causes and a fundamental basis for group identification and social categorization. It would be a very different situation indeed without this repertoire of differentiation, historical contextualization, justification, and teleological imagination. It might certainly be less intractable. And, on the other hand, the troubled question of national allegiance is an important factor in the exacerbation of existing – and specifically religious – disputes between Catholics and Protestants.

To return, in closing, to the cultural stuff, the basic conclusion is that boundaries, and the interactions across them, are intimately and indissolubly bound up with the cultural contents of ethnicity. Although he has not developed it in detail, this is a conclusion towards which Barth himself has eventually been led. During a recent retrospect on *Ethnic Groups and Boundaries*, he acknowledged that:

> the issue of cultural content *versus* boundary, as it was formulated, unintentionally served to mislead. Yes, it is a question of analyzing boundary processes, not of enumerating the sum of content, as in an old-fashioned trait list. But . . . central and culturally valued institutions and activities in an ethnic group may be deeply involved in its boundary maintenance. (Barth 1994: 17, 18)

On a related tack, Stephen Cornell's argument (1996) is worth consideration: that patterns of ethnic persistence and change – the variable strength of ethnic attachments – depend upon the relativities of 'internal bases of ethnic attachment', namely shared interests, shared institutions, and shared culture. In his view, shared institutions and shared culture, rather than interests in common, are the keys to group stability and the persistence of ethnic attachments. Interests are, by definition, more likely to be a function of situation and circumstance, and hence more vulnerable to change, reinterpretation and manipulation. Although this argument has its problems – the extent to which interests arise out of shared culture and institutions, and are hence not easily separable out as an 'independent variable', is perhaps the most obvious – it encourages two interesting thoughts about Northern Ireland.

The first is that in religion the institutions and the cultural stuff come together in a most consequential manner. In Northern Ireland, taking into account the institutional segregation of schools and – something which hasn't much been alluded to – of locality and residence, alongside the authenticity for many locals of their religious faith and the segregation of much everyday life, they come together with a vengeance. In Cornell's terms, the stage is set for ethnic identities that are deep-seated and obstinately resistant to change. Which, it is hard to deny, is a reasonable characterization of Northern Ireland. Being a Catholic or a Protestant *really means something* to most Catholics and Protestants – although the range and variation in what it means to individuals might, following Cohen's argument (1985) about the 'symbolic construction of community', be moot – and ethnicity is, historically, an intransigent basis of group identification and social categorization. In my terms, as discussed in Chapter 5, the ethnically organized conjunction of the institutional and the cultural during the earliest years of socialization (in school, residential space, church) establishes the potential for ethnic identity to be entered into as a *primary identity*.

To go beyond Cornell's argument, there is something specific about the cultural stuff in this case anyway. Religion is distinctive in its particular ritual and symbolic content. It is arguable (Jenkins 1996) that the ritual symbolization of identity – as in *rites de passage*, but in many other forms too – is an effective procedure for making collective identities matter to individuals, affectively and cognitively. Through participation in ritual, people may come to identify themselves in a manner and with a degree of commitment and enthusiasm that amounts to something altogether greater than the sum of its parts. This is likely to be another factor contributing to the strength of ethnic affiliation in Northern Ireland.

The second interesting, and much more tentative, thought is about the implications of all this for the future likelihood of a political settlement in Northern Ireland. Local 'interests' – the collective desires for an end to violence, for an acceptable solution to the national question, and for an equalization of economic disadvantage, which have become so apparent recently – may to some extent be hostages to the ongoing potential of institutions and culture to generate continued ethnic difference, distance and enmity. Just because the cultural stuff is imagined, doesn't mean that is imaginary. Far from it. And that the 'troubles' are not *about* religion, doesn't mean that they don't, in part, hinge upon religious differences.

9

Violence, Language and Politics

In this chapter I want to revisit, from a rather different direction, the matter of different 'levels' of identification and analysis first raised in Chapter 4. Ethnicity is one of the most significant of social identities with respect to the relationship between localities and their regional or national arenas and institutions. In the contemporary world, one of the most important ideological manifestations of ethnicity is nationalism, conventionally defined as the expression and organization of political claims to territory *and* self-determination. I am going to focus on the question of how to understand the differences between nationalism in two regions – Northern Ireland and Wales, one a 'Province', the other a 'Principality' – of the same nation-state, the United Kingdom. In doing so, I will take another oblique look at one of the themes raised in the previous couple of chapters, the matter of the cultural stuff, in this case language and the local use of violence rather than religion.

Northern Ireland and Wales

The two territories have some things in common. Culturally, they are part of the 'Celtic fringe' of the United Kingdom. Each is small enough to be a locality and big enough to be a region, and each has a relatively low population density. They have mixed urban-industrial and rural-agricultural economies, although the industrial area of south Wales is larger and more populous than the equivalent greater Belfast area of Northern Ireland. Northern Ireland is also significantly more economically disadvantaged than Wales; the unemployment rate in Northern Ireland, the highest of any UK region, is approximately twice that of Wales.

The most obvious difference between them is that, although Wales is part of the British 'mainland', sharing a land border with England, Northern Ireland is separated from the bigger island by sea, sharing a land border with the Republic of Ireland. This is not simply a geographical difference, it symbolizes a significant political reality. Wales forms a political unity with England. England and Wales – one sometimes feels that this ought to be capable of expression as one word – constitute, with Scotland, the (relatively) ancient kingdom of Great Britain. Northern Ireland, however, as a consequence of the political settlement of the 'Irish problem' in 1921, lies outside this structure; with Great Britain, it constitutes the United Kingdom of Great Britain and Northern Ireland. While Wales participates fully and securely in British parliamentary democracy, Northern Ireland's constitutional position is more ambiguous in at least two respects. First, although successive British governments have reiterated their support for the Province's place within the UK, this support is explicitly conditional upon a majority of the Northern Ireland population wishing to maintain this status quo. Second, the Anglo-Irish Agreement of 1985 allows the government of the Republic of Ireland a formal consultative role in the internal affairs and administration of the Province. Northern Ireland is, therefore, more loosely incorporated into the federal United Kingdom state than Wales.

The two territories differ in the way that their populations are structured in terms of ethnicity. Northern Ireland is shared by two relatively clear-cut and mutually antagonistic ethnic populations, Catholics and Protestants, in a violently conflictual situation, the origins of which go back four centuries to English subjugation of the native northern Irish and the colonization of their lands. In Wales, the situation is more complex and less conflictual. In terms of recent history, major immigration began in the nineteenth century as a consequence of the industrialization of the south Wales coal valleys. As discussed in Chapter 3, labour was drawn in from elsewhere in Britain, from Ireland, and from as far afield as the Mediterranean. Partly because many people from rural Wales shared in the experience of migration to the Valleys, partly because of the role of the organized labour movement in forging a new, distinctly working-class, communal life in south Wales, and partly because the new migrants had to assimilate culturally in order to work underground and in the metal works (many, for example, learned to speak Welsh), sharp and conflictual ethnic differentiation did not occur – although the resultant distance between North and South Walians should not be underestimated. Over successive generations, an authentically Welsh population of sorts – more about this later – now lives in south Wales, albeit a population with a diversity of antecedents. The most recent wave of immigration has occurred in the last two decades or so, an influx of relatively affluent outsiders – typically monoglot English speakers – into rural, Welsh-speaking areas of north and west Wales (Day 1989; Symonds 1990). Although this has sown the seeds of conflict, something to which I shall return, it is unlikely to produce anything resembling the Northern Irish situation in terms of substantial, mutually hostile ethnic blocs.

The final difference between the two territories is in the history and nature of their nationalist political movements. As someone who grew up in Northern Ireland and who moved, eventually, to south Wales, one of the first differences that I noticed was in the rhetorical and actual politics of nationalism. Putting to one side, for the moment, Finlayson's argument (1996) that the Ulster Protestant cause is a nationalist ideology, and accepting the more limited definition of the situation held by most – if not all – local actors, in Northern Ireland, the nationalist objective is the reunification of the island. Since the late 1960s, and intermittently before that, the most important means to this end – a situation which the current peace process has yet to change – has been guerilla violence. In Wales, by contrast, the defence and promotion of Welsh culture – symbolized most sharply by the Welsh language – is the dominant item on the nationalist agenda, with some form of devolved self-government coming a poor second. The legitimate tactics for achieving these goals in Wales are constitutional democratic politics and a limited degree of direct action and protest. Since means and ends are never easily distinguishable in politics – and this is perhaps peculiarly the case with nationalism – these differences lead me to question the degree to which the two nationalist movements, in Northern Ireland and in Wales, can be regarded as even varieties of the same phenomenon.

The violence of politics

At the level of the strikingly obvious, Northern Ireland differs from Wales in that it has, for approaching thirty years, been the site of a complex and bloody struggle among various armed ethnically organized political movements and the British state. That armed struggle has been one of the defining realities of nationalist politics in Northern Ireland does not, however, mean that the use of violence is a consensual strategy, embraced and supported by all those who might identify themselves as nationalists.

Among the Catholic public élite in Northern Ireland there is a broad spectrum of opinion concerning the role and acceptability of violence. The hierarchy of the Roman Catholic Church, the confessional community of the nationalist section of the population, has been unequivocal in its condemnation and rejection of political violence, a stance which was underlined by the appointment in 1990 of Bishop Cahal Daly, a vociferous critic of paramilitary organizations, as Primate of All Ireland. The public pronouncements of individual priests with republican or nationalist sympathies may complicate this generalization, as does the issue of whether or not the sacraments or a religious funeral should be available to unrepentant 'terrorists', but the overall picture is consistent.

A similar stance with respect to violence is adopted by the (overwhelmingly Catholic) Social Democratic and Labour Party (SDLP). As the political voice of constitutional nationalism, advocating the reunification of Ireland via democratic process – presumably when either the Catholic population becomes a majority in Northern Ireland, enough of the Protestants change their mind, the British parliament has a change of heart, or, more recently, the ongoing process of European unification renders the problem solved through irrelevance – the SDLP has no choice. It must oppose violence, although it has a long association with various forms of non-violent extra-parliamentary action. In purely political terms it also has little choice. To embrace violence would be to render itself indistinguishable in many respects from its main rival for Catholic votes, the republican Sinn Féin.

The other major 'collective actor' at this level is the republican movement (a historical identification, deriving from its past advocacy of a
particular kind of government in what was then the Irish Free State),
specifically the Provisional Republican movement: Sinn Féin – which may
be translated from the Irish as 'Ourselves' – a political party, and the
Provisional IRA (Irish Republican Army), a well-armed, illegal and highly
successful paramilitary organization. This dual-pronged strategy is publicly
represented as 'the ballot box and the Armalite', the latter being a useful
American assault rifle. The Provisional movement is clear in its advocacy
of violence as a legitimate means of forcing British withdrawal from the
Province and as a defensive strategy for protecting the Catholic population
from the security forces and from the attacks of Protestant paramilitary
organizations.

Public political debate within the nationalist community, is, therefore,
characterized by the interplay of a range of opinions about the legitimacy
of violence. What, however, of the ordinary members of that community,
the constituency to which nationalist politicians must appeal? In the north
Belfast Catholic enclave studied by Frank Burton in the early 1970s
(Burton 1978), support from the community for the use of violence by the
Provisionals was shifting, situational and conditional. The defensive role –
at a time of vicious interpersonal sectarian attacks in this part of Belfast, in
effect an organized campaign of civilian assassination on the part of loyalist
paramilitaries – was seen as legitimate. Offensive violence was seen as
considerably more problematic, however. Within the area there was considerable public tension between the Catholic Church and the republican
movement. By the early 1980s, when Jeff Sluka undertook field research in
Divis Flats, a Catholic area of west Belfast, this tension had increased
considerably (Sluka 1989). Public support in the area for the 'armed
struggle' as the means of securing a united Ireland was substantial; more
than half the people surveyed by Sluka expressed views of this kind. The
urban nationalist community's experience of the Northern Irish 'troubles',
in particular specific episodes such as the H-Blocks hunger strike, appears
to have led to increased, consolidated and less equivocal support for
violence as a political option (although it must also be remembered that
many people in these same communities are still led by their religious faith
to a rejection of violence). The situation in urban Catholic neighbourhoods
at the time of writing – in the middle of a fragile peace initiative and with
the experience of more than eighteen months relatively free of serious
violence – can only be guessed at. The large vote for Sinn Féin in Catholic
west Belfast in the 'peace process' elections held at the end of May 1996,
can be interpreted in at least two ways: as an endorsement of negotiation or
as support for the IRA.

In rural communities, the research literature – which is typically social
anthropological – suggests a rather different picture: of Catholics and
Protestants continuing to interact as well as possible despite the 'troubles',
of an implicit rejection of violence, of a degree of harmony and coexistence

(e.g. Buckley 1982; Bufwack 1982; Donnan and McFarlane 1983; Glassie 1982). Given that some of the most violent areas of the Province are rural – near the border with the Republic – and that the IRA for a long time now has been waging an intermittent campaign in rural areas against part-time members of the security forces (who are, almost by definition, Protestant and who live 'in the community'), this may seem somewhat surprising. It is in part a reflection of the locations chosen for anthropological field studies; in part a reflection of the period during which most of them were undertaken, relatively early on in 'the troubles'; in part the product of face-to-face fieldwork, which, perhaps, overexposes the researcher to the civilities of everyday life; and in part a testimony to the enduring residual power of a consensual model of the social world in much anthropological thinking.

It is also, of course, in part an accurate reflection of a dimension of rural life in Northern Ireland. My concern here is not to deny that there is an important truth in this comforting picture of country folk living their everyday lives as uneventfully as they can manage. But it does seems likely that the picture – particularly in the current climate – is more complex. Certainly, recent research in County Tyrone, in a community near the border (Hamilton *et al.* 1990: 39–56), suggests a situation closer to that which exists in Belfast or Derry: conditional support among Catholics for the Provisional IRA's campaign and conflict between this support and Catholicism and 'moderate' constitutional nationalism.

Finally, with respect to nationalist opinion in both urban and rural areas of Northern Ireland it cannot be emphasized too strongly that support for, or rejection of, the methods of the Provisional IRA (or, indeed, other smaller republican groups such as INLA, the Irish National Liberation Army) is related to enthusiasm for Irish unity in complex ways that shortage of space precludes me from exploring here. Nationalism does *not* necessarily translate into either acceptance of, or support for, violence (in much the same way that support for the union with Britain does not necessarily translate into sectarianism). Nor should it be forgotten that the context within which Catholic support for violence must be understood is the violence of the state security forces and Protestant paramilitary organizations. With the benefit of hindsight, the present conflict in Northern Ireland has its immediate historical roots in the violent and inept repression of the (largely Catholic) Civil Rights Movement by the (Protestant) Stormont regime in the late 1960s. And one popular image of the subsequent 'troubles' which must be rejected is that of the British Army as a disinterested mediator or referee, standing between two 'tribal' factions: for many years now it has been a three-cornered struggle, with an ambiguous relationship existing between the British state and Protestant loyalists.

Moving across the water to Wales, one of the most obvious features of Welsh nationalism is the more or less complete rejection of violence against persons. There is a sporadic history of extra-parliamentary activity in support of the nationalist political agenda, particularly by Mudiad

Amddiffyn Cymru (MAC, Movement for the Defence of Wales) and the Free Wales Army in the 1960s (Clews 1980), and there were three deaths as a result of explosions at the time of the Investiture of the Prince of Wales in 1969. However, violence against English people or their representatives – as opposed to their property – does not seem to form a current part of this dimension of nationalist activity. The tradition of direct action has been continued in the 1980s by Meibion Glyndŵr (The Sons of Glyndŵr), with their incendiary campaign focused on absentee-owned second homes and the estate agents who sell them. Once again, the focus is upon attacks on property. Within this framework of direct action, public debate has been caused, for example, by the remarks of the Anglican cleric and poet R.S. Thomas, to a meeting of Cyfamodwyr y Cymru Rhydd (The Covenanters of the Free Welsh), calling for a campaign of 'non-violent night attacks' upon the homes of English people in Welsh-speaking districts.[1] The constant quest seems to be for a rhetoric and a method which will legitimize direct action.

Organizations such as these represent, in terms of the numbers of people involved, a tiny element of Welsh nationalism. Nor are they representative of a wider strand of opinion, although there can be little doubt that the issue of second homes is one about which many people hold strong views, leading to ambiguity about the Meibion Glyndŵr campaign. Although both have a history of resort to extra-parliamentary direct action, Plaid Cymru (the parliamentary political party of Welsh nationalism) and Cymdeithas yr Iaith Gymraeg (the Welsh Language Society), the two main institutional expressions of Welsh nationalism, are unequivocal in their rejection of the use of violence of any kind. In a recent anthropological study of nationalism in North Wales, the absence of any debate about the legitimacy of violence is striking (C.A. Davies 1989).

Nor is it just that violence hardly represents an option. It is explicitly rejected both on pragmatic grounds, as a likely obstruction to the movement's goals, and on moral grounds, in reflection of the strong thread of Christian pacifism which has always existed within Welsh nationalism (Evans 1973; Rees 1975). The furore aroused by R.S. Thomas's advocacy of non-violent direct action is a good indication of the depth of feeling on the issue. The majority of the nationalist political constituency in Wales do not regard violence, particularly where life and limb are concerned, as either a sensible or a proper means to achieve their goals. It is not – certainly not *yet* – an 'armed struggle'. And it probably isn't going to become one. However, as already mentioned, there is considerable ambiguity about the 'second homes' arson campaign. This reflects a perceived increasing shortage of homes for local young people due to distortions in the housing market caused by affluent – and non-Welsh – absentee home owners. I will return to this in more detail below. It is relevant here because there is some evidence to suggest that, due to the 'second homes' issue and concern about demographic threats to rural Welsh culture, opinion in Welsh-speaking areas may be becoming more equivocal about the use of increasingly violent forms of direct action.[2] Although violence has always been on the margins, one can perhaps no longer take for granted the 'natural pacifism' of nationalism in Wales (N. Thomas 1991: 18).

The politics of language

The previous section offers a clue about where to begin any comparison of the relationship between nationalism and language in Wales and Ireland. Most of the nationalist organizations in Wales have Welsh names; this is not the case in Northern Ireland, where only Sinn Féin adopts an Irish name (and even that derives from an earlier, all-Ireland historical context). The plain fact is that, whereas in Wales the Welsh language, despite a long-term trend of decline, remains the first language of daily use for a substantial proportion of the population, in Northern Ireland Irish is, effectively, dead (and it couldn't be called healthy in the Republic).

To look at Wales first, a number of indicators can be used to illustrate the contemporary status of the language (Coupland and Ball 1989). Census figures, for example, suggest a decline in the number of Welsh speakers from about 930,000 in 1901 (50 per cent of the total population of Wales) to a little over half a million (19 per cent of the population) in 1981. Since the 1970s, as a result of the work of language activists and the impact of the 1967 Welsh Language Act, Welsh as an everyday presence in the public domain – in official and other documents, on television and radio, and on public displays and signs of various kinds – has, however, increased in salience. All routine public interaction in Wales now takes place in an environment in which Welsh is to some extent – and no matter how superficially – obviously and unavoidably here-and-now. In terms of its distribution, while the language remains more important in everyday conversational use in *y fro Gymraeg* – the rural heartland of the north and west – in absolute numbers the majority of Welsh speakers now live in the industrial areas of south Wales (C.A. Davies 1990; C.H. Williams 1989). And in the south there is also everyday use: in a town like Swansea, for example, if you keep your ears open in the market on a Saturday morning you will hear Welsh spoken. It is anything but exotic.

It is not possible to produce properly comparable figures for Northern Ireland, since use or knowledge of Irish is not enumerated by the census (which is telling enough in itself). The last native Irish speakers passed away during the 1960s and the language now survives solely by dint of formal education and activism. Surveying the available statistics and research, the most recent and comprehensive account has concluded that:

> the death of native Irish in its last refuges in Northern Ireland in Rathlin, the Glens of Antrim and the Sperrin Mountains has not been balanced by any substantial accretion of effective second-language learners who have proved their ability to transmit Irish naturally or semi-naturally to their own offspring. (Hindley 1990: 40)

Elsewhere (1990: 155–6) the same author cites research which suggests that less than one per cent of the population in Northern Ireland has any 'complex' knowledge of Irish, with hardly anyone using it as the language of daily life in the home. More Catholic school children know French than know Irish, which serves only to emphasize the degree to which the promotion of Irish speaking in Northern Ireland has become a lost cause. Something similar, if less emphatic, would have to be said about the status of Irish in the Republic (1990: 159–60).

The contrast is complete. Welsh, although in decline during the twentieth century, remains an important language of everyday life and there may be some grounds for qualified optimism about its future. Irish in Northern Ireland – and throughout the rest of Ireland – is a dead or dying language, for which the best that can be hoped is probably a degree of embalming. The roots of the different trajectories of these two Celtic languages lie in earlier history, but one of the important points to recognize is that *if* there are grounds for guarded optimism with respect to Welsh, this is in a large part due to long-standing campaigns of activism in the present century and, indeed, earlier (Jones 1973). This activism is an integral part of the nationalist movement in Wales. It would not be overemphasizing its importance to suggest that the language issue is in fact the central, uniting theme of Welsh nationalism. Cymdeithas yr Iaith Gymraeg, the Welsh Language Society, is one of the key institutional expressions of nationalist sentiments and ambitions (C. Davies 1973). It is not insignificant that the two major nationalist political achievements in Wales have been the Welsh Language Act, the result in 1967 of a sustained and controversial campaign of non-violent direct action and disruption, and the establishment of the Welsh-language television station, S4C, Sianel Pedwar Cymru or Channel Four Wales, the latter in the face of public opposition from no less a person than the then Prime Minister, Margaret Thatcher (C.A. Davies 1989: 37–58).

To underline the centrality of culture and language to the politics of nationalism in Wales, one has only to consider the issues which are salient in the 1990s. The first of these is the 'second homes' problem, which has been an issue for some time (Bollom 1978). The concern here is that people living outside rural, Welsh-speaking areas are buying up properties in these areas for use as occasional holiday homes, at what are for them low prices but which are unaffordable for many local people. The nationalist objection to this trend derives from the shortage of affordable rural housing. The price distortions which are produced in local housing markets in *y fro Gymraeg* mean that local young people have nowhere to live in their home areas. This, together with rural unemployment, produces emigration and a loss to the area of Welsh speakers. Second homes, and the estate agents who sell them, have thus been the main targets of Meibion Glyndŵr's campaign of arson.

Migration and housing are at the heart of a second focus of concern: the immigration into *y fro Gymraeg* of non-Welsh-speaking people, whether they be young families seeking a rural idyll and the 'good life', or retired people who have sold a house in a more expensive area of the UK and bought a cheap retirement home in rural Wales (Day 1989; Symonds 1990). The arrival of relatively affluent, house-buying newcomers is a further constraint on local housing markets and the ability of locals to maintain an active presence in them. The demographic structure of whole areas also alters, with the presence of many more elderly people putting pressure on health and social provision. The younger immigrants and their children alter the character of school populations (and these kinds of problems are not peculiar to Wales; for a discussion of the Scottish situation, see Jedrej and Nuttall 1996).

It is this which has produced the third issue of current importance: Welsh-language education policies. With the shift during the 1980s in the balance of rural school populations in north and west Wales from mainly Welsh-speaking to, in some areas, mainly English-speaking, the issue of whether education should be in the medium of Welsh has provoked conflict between parents, community members and cultures. In Dyfed, for example, this has, in part, found expression in conflict within local government between the Labour Party and Plaid Cymru.

All three issues – holiday homes, immigration, and education – are manifestations of the same problem: the perceived threat to Welsh culture, and its most visible and important manifestation, the language. How, argue nationalists, is Welsh culture to be maintained, let alone promoted, if the only arbiter of policy is the market, whether for labour or for houses? This is the central essence of the current nationalist political agenda and, incidentally, goes to the heart of one aspect of the difficult relationship which exists between nationalism and the Welsh labour movement: there is still much work to be done in constructing a satisfactory image of 'real' Welshness which admits the majority who do not speak Welsh (Bowie 1993; Giles and Taylor 1978). Nor is cultural differentiation quite as simple as this anyway. A recent ethnography has looked at different *kinds* of 'Welshness', focusing upon the 'Valley Welshness' of the ex-mining and steel-producing communities of the valleys of south Wales, as distinct from from the 'British Welshness' of the borders and the southern coastal margin, and the 'Welsh Welshness' of the north and west (Roberts 1994). Here we return to Barth's point about 'the cultural stuff'. It may not be stretching the point to suggest that the sharing of a common ethnic boundary – with and against the English – is among the most important factors constitutive of Welshness.

Language and culture are not the only items on the nationalist agenda, and self-government or devolved government remains a distant goal, despite the defeat of the 1979 referendum on the issue (Drucker and Brown 1980). The way forward for nationalists in this respect is now seen to lie within Europe, as the overall framework within which some degree of local political autonomy can be achieved (Rees 1990). These limited aspirations aside, however, the language, and its defence, remains the unifying framework of Welsh nationalist political discourse and strategy.

In Northern Ireland, by complete contrast, the language is hardly an issue. It serves some symbolic purpose – it may be heard, for example, from the platform at the annual conference, the *Árd Fheis*, of the Provisional movement, and there have been minor struggles to rename some Belfast streets in Irish (there are many anecdotes concerning the Provisional IRA's use of Irish in radio traffic to confuse the security forces). There is also small-scale language activism (Hindley 1990: 156–9). However, the defence and promotion of the Irish language is peripheral – at best – to the central demands of nationalism in Northern Ireland. Irish unity, self-government and freedom from Britain are of overwhelming significance and non-negotiable.

This is not to say that culture and language are irrelevant within Irish nationalism. They clearly have a place; there is, if nothing else, too much symbolic capital and mileage in the issues for the republican movement for it to be otherwise. There is also a long history of 'cultural nationalism' in Ireland (Hutchinson 1987); with its centre of gravity in Dublin, however, this slipped down the order of priorities once the Irish nation-state – minus the six northern counties – was established in 1921. While Irish-Gaelic culture continues to do useful service rhetorically, it is no longer central to nationalist objectives, whether they derive from north or south of the border. With the development of tourism and international economic links, and the ongoing Europeanization and globalization of social life in the Republic, Irish culture has perhaps become more of a marketing phenomenon than a matter for struggle.

Some explanatory options

I have compared two constituent territories of the United Kingdom, each part of the 'Celtic fringe', each institutionally integrated into the UK in different ways and to different degrees, and each possessing well-defined and supported nationalist movements. In Northern Ireland, violence is part of the 'rules of engagement' with the British state; in Wales, this is emphatically not the case. Wales is relatively uncontroversially part of the UK state, and the most important political issues, which serve to unify the competing strands of nationalist opinion, are culture and language. In Northern Ireland, by contrast, 'cultural' issues are relatively insignificant when compared to the central nationalist objective: freedom from British rule.

How are we to understand these differences? The burgeoning social science literature on nationalism seems an obvious place to turn for inspiration. One of the most celebrated and influential contributions to the debate has been Ernest Gellner's *Nations and Nationalism* (1983). In his account, nationalism, as a self-conscious political ideology concerned with the self-determination of 'nations', is a product of the nineteenth-century rise of industrial society, with its linked requirements of cultural-linguistic homogeneity and a workforce generically educated for participation in a modern economy. Here the stress is upon the relationship between an industrial system and a literate, national 'high' culture. Benedict Anderson, in his discussion of the 'imagined political communities' which are nations (1983), adopts a perspective that is in important respects similar to Gellner's, although the emphasis is upon industrial *capitalism*, rather than the more general 'industrial society', and upon the homogenizing potential of print technologies in the creation of national self-consciousness.

One of the few authors to have examined comparatively the situation in Wales and Ireland is Michael Hechter, in *Internal Colonialism* (1975). In that book, and more clearly in a subsequent paper on 'ethnoregionalism' (Hechter and Levi 1979), Hechter relates the development of different kinds of ethnoregional – in this context, nationalist – movements to different configurations of ethnically structured divisions of labour. In other words, what matters is how different ethnic or national groups are incorporated into the economy and into the stratification system, producing either a *hierarchical* or a *segmented* cultural division of labour (an analysis which has much in common with the notion of *ranked* and *unranked* systems of ethnic stratification: Horowitz 1985). Within the economistic framework that he proposes, Hechter also acknowledges the role of cultural differentiation and the behaviour of the state in producing nationalistic political movements.

Gellner, Hechter and Anderson all offer analyses in which economic factors are, in one way or another, central. Anthony Smith, by way of contrast, puts forward a model in which cultural or symbolic factors are most important (Smith 1981, 1986, 1991). Smith's emphasis is on group identification as a complex bundle of cultural processes – in fact, ethnicity – preceding nationalism as a modern ideology and, paradoxically perhaps, encouraging its continued vitality when, according to other authors (Gellner 1983: 110–22; Hobsbawm 1990: 163–83), its vision and seductive attraction ought to be on the wane. Kedourie's argument (1985) is even more idealistic than Smith's: for him, nationalism is a political philosophy in its own right – not 'a reflection of anything else' (be it economic or cultural) – with its power rooted in nineteenth-century political history.[3]

Thus, on the one hand, there are models of nationalism that are rooted in economic factors while, on the other, culture, ideology and/or values are emphasized. There are some authors who synthesize elements of each side of the debate (e.g. Breuilly 1985). With the limited exception of Hechter, whose arguments are, for my purposes, disappointingly non-specific, they do not, however, contribute much to an understanding of the differences between nationalisms in Wales and Northern Ireland. In particular, issues such as the role of violence and the significance of language and culture seem to be poorly accounted for. Since these are, as I have suggested, important for our understanding of those differences, this is a major shortcoming. The other shortcoming of much of this literature – and there are, once again, limited exceptions to this generalization (e.g. Breuilly,

Hechter) – is the somewhat surprising de-emphasis of the state and political action.

Returning to the relationship between localities and their regional or national institutional contexts, I want to suggest that, in addition to economic and cultural factors – and as the arguments of the previous chapters should have made quite clear, these are *extremely* important for our understanding of, for example, Northern Ireland – politics and the state, especially long-term processes of state formation, must be placed at the centre of models of nationalism. In particular, drawing on Max Weber's classic discussion of the rise and nature of the nation-state (1978: 54–6, 901–26) and Anthony Giddens's more recent discussion of the importance of 'internal pacification' in state formation (1985: 172–97), I propose to look at two linked historical processes that are central to any understanding of why nationalism in Northern Ireland is so different from nationalism in Wales. These are the incorporation of each territory into the United Kingdom state, and the attempt by that central state to monopolize violence in each territory (and, correspondingly, the degree to which violence has been removed from the political domain).

Northern Ireland and Wales compared (again . . .)

To look first at processes of state integration, Wales was finally politically united with England in 1536, by the 'Act of Union'. Before that, integration, built upon the accession of the Welsh Tudor dynasty to the English throne, following Henry Tudor's victory at the battle of Bosworth Field in 1485, had been effective rather than constitutionally formalized. Before that again, the last major Welsh rebel against Anglo-Norman suzerainty, Owain Glyndŵr, had been defeated in 1408, and before that again, by 1283 Edward I had subdued the kingdoms of Gwynedd and Deheubarth. Not only is the political unity of England and Wales long-standing, it is legitimized by the role of the Tudors in the establishment of the modern English state and by their contribution to modern images of the continuity and the role of the English monarchy. The use of the title Prince of Wales for the male heir to the throne is indicative of the perceived stability of the Union.

There have, it is true, been some changes in the twentieth century. A range of specifically Welsh public and governmental agencies have come into being, the most important being the Welsh Office, created in 1964 and run by the Secretary of State for Wales, a ministerial post of cabinet rank. Barry Jones (1988) has argued, however, that the degree of autonomy from London which these institutions possess is often limited, as is the extent to which they have penetrated and established a legitimate reationship with Welsh civil society. Despite some degree of local institutional specialization, the unity of England and Wales remains the established and taken-for-granted political order for most Welsh people.

Northern Ireland, however, is a wholly different case. Apart from the period between 1800 and 1921, Ireland has never been an institutionally integral part of the British polity. Irish history since the arrival of the Normans in 1169 has been a history of more or less violent attempts to impose or maintain British control, and more or less violent, resistance to that control. The north of the island proved particularly obdurate and remained the heart of Gaelic Irish culture; so much so that, as we saw in Chapter 7, in the sixteenth century the English adopted a policy of dispossessing the indigenous Catholic Irish population by force, replacing them with immigrant Protestant Scots and English settlers. This settlement – the Plantation – is the reason why there are in Northern Ireland today two mutually antagonistic ethnic populations, and the reason why they are nominally identified in religious terms as Catholic and Protestant.

The province of Northern Ireland was established as part of the United Kingdom in 1921, in reflection of the, often violently expressed, determination of the Protestant population not to join the rest of Ireland in its newly won freedom from British rule. Many Catholics in the north, perhaps the majority, did not accept the legitimacy of the partition of the island. Between 1921 and 1972 the province was a semi-independent member of the federal United Kingdom, with its own parliament, governing its internal affairs largely in the interests of Protestants. Following the *force majeure* imposition in 1972 of direct rule from London – the result of renewed serious violence, the perceived inability of the local administration to deal with it (let alone deal with it even-handedly), and the likelihood of ever-increasing British military involvement – the province remained substantially apart from the rest of the UK. It is legislatively distinct, it has completely different systems of local government and public service administration, and its membership of the UK is constitutionally strictly conditional upon the continued assent to the status quo of a numerical majority of the population. There is nothing conditional about the unity of the rest of the Kingdom. Furthermore, since the Anglo-Irish Agreement of 1985, the government of the Republic of Ireland has a formally defined – although locally contentious – consultative role in the Province's affairs.

In terms of state integration, therefore, Wales is strongly and securely a part of the United Kingdom, firmly tied in to the legislative and administrative order. Nor are the law and the institutions of government the only relevant considerations here. Drawing on Linda Colley's analysis (1992), Wales and the Welsh are able to maintain their distinctiveness in the context of an overarching and relatively recently constructed *British* identity, the authentic creation of which must be counted among the great successes of the state-building project which followed the 1707 Act of Union. Northern Ireland, by contrast, is a peripheral and weakly integrated member of the UK; part of the greatest failure of that project and perhaps its greatest victim:

British state-penetration of Ireland was therefore, at best, formally accomplished no earlier than 1801. Yet it remained incomplete and persistently illegitimate. Ireland was never treated as if it were just like England or the rest of Britain . . . the programme of plantations meant that the ethnic politics of the island could not develop on the model of the English, Welsh or Scots: cultural autonomy within a wider political union . . . the processes which encouraged ethnic integration and nation-building elsewhere in early modern Europe were mostly absent from the relationships between the two largest islands of the nineteenth-century UK. (O'Leary and McGarry 1993: 73, 75)

The unity of the Kingdom, when viewed from this point of view, begins to appear as imagined, as it of course is. However, with respect to Tom Nairn's celebrated argument about the 'break-up' of Britain (1981), for example, the account offered here suggests two things: the 'twilight of the British state' that he first diagnosed decades ago looks these days more like an obstinate northern midsummer glow than a prelude to pitch darkness, and the origins of the crisis, such as it is, are to be sought farther back in time than he looked, in the oldest origins of the state itself.

The strength or weakness of political integration is, as one might expect, relevant to the issue of the state's monopolization of violence. In Wales, following Glyndŵr's defeat in 1408, the state monopolization of violence has been more or less total. Such major interruptions of the state's capacity to guarantee public order as there were – the Civil War, for example – were conflicts within the state of England and Wales, the legitimacy of which was not in doubt. In the nineteenth century there was violent class-based conflict and disorder – the Rebecca Riots of 1842–3 and the earlier Chartist rising in Newport, for example – but this was largely similar to contemporary events in England. There was no peculiarly Welsh problem of public order. From the mid-nineteenth century onwards, the domain of political activity in Wales has been governed in the main by rules which do not allow for violence. The military has long since withdrawn from politics, in Wales as in England.

Northern Ireland, once again, is different. In Ireland violence has never been – and is not yet, north or south of the border – successfully monopolized by the state. Every century since the first arrival of the Normans has been marked by uprisings against the English or British state. More to the point, the state has been ethnically partisan. After 1921 it only managed to achieve a partial monopolization of violence in Northern Ireland by authorizing informal Protestant violence in the shape of a local, paramilitary police force. For fifty years, the state in Northern Ireland was, effectively, the Protestant population, and its rule was based on direct coercion or its promise.

Violence remains, therefore, a key item in the repertoire of political options in Northern Ireland; it is an integral part of the rules of the political game. The current peace process notwithstanding, at least three of the major parties to the current situation – Protestants, Catholics, and the British state – depend upon violence, whether explicitly or implicitly, as the means to their particular ends.

Which brings us, once again following Max Weber, to an important distinction, between *power* and *authority* (see Smith 1960: 15–33). Power is basically the capacity to make other people do what one wants them to do, most typically through the use of coercion. Authority is the legitimate and delegated right to command obedience. Power is rooted, ultimately, in the use of force; authority in law and custom. In Wales, for a very long time now, the state has been legitimate and so has its authority. Most of the spectrum of nationalist politics operates within the framework of this overall legitimacy. In Northern Ireland, however, the legitimacy of the state is problematic for the Catholic nationalist population (and since 1972 and direct rule, this has also been true for many Protestants). Politics in Northern Ireland is thus a matter of power rather than authority, at least with respect to the basic questions of the nature, form and functions of the state, and violence is one of the accepted possibilities with respect to political action.

But what about the issues of culture and language? Once again, the key to understanding the situation seems to be the history of territorial integration into the state. The Welsh gave up armed struggle against England very early on in the history of its incorporation into Britain. As a consequence, it was subject to a less direct and repressive form of control and government than either Ireland or Scotland. This arguably created the social and economic space within which Welsh language and culture – not being sufficiently dangerous, perhaps – could survive. Whereas in Ireland and Scotland, indigenous culture and the Gaelic languages become identified with Catholicism,[4] and with political rebellion in post-Reformation geo-political struggles, in Wales the language eventually became identified with Protestant nonconformity. This may have been a threat to the established Church, but it wasn't a threat to the state (the campaign to disestablish the Anglican Church in Wales eventually succeeded in 1919). During the nineteenth century, and this once again is a reflection of the two countries' differing relationships to the central state, there was the Great Famine in Ireland – which, with the benefit of hindsight was the biggest single blow to Gaelic Irish culture – and massive industrialization in south Wales, which brought a late flowering of Welsh culture to the coal valleys. Just as the Famine would have been unthinkable in Wales, so industrialization was out of the question for the south and west of Ireland.

The north of Ireland was, by the nineteenth century, if not altogether Anglicized, culturally distinct in its local mixture and cross-fertilization of Gaelic Irish, Anglo-Irish, English and Scottish cultures. The Plantation, two centuries earlier, had seen to that. Throughout Ireland, the state's control was more repressive and more severe than anywhere on the British mainland. In the north, where industrialization did occur – although not on anything like the scale of south Wales – it was largely in Belfast and its hinterland. The Irish language did not survive the migration to the eastern seaboard in search of employment. There was neither the social nor the economic space available to facilitate any late recovery for a language and a culture which had been marginalized – at best – by the Plantation, undermined by the Penal Laws during the eighteenth century, and dealt a final blow by famine and rural social dislocation in the nineteenth century.

The suggestion is, therefore, that the conditions which facilitate the survival of a minority language are bound up with the way in which the linguistic homeland becomes integrated into a central state. Further, part of the structure of integration will be mechanisms and institutions of social control, and some of these may be specifically aimed at discouraging the indigenous language and culture. This latter occurred more severely in Ireland than in Wales.

Comparing the nationalist movements of Wales and Northern Ireland, it is clear that the differences between them with respect to their capacity for the use of violence and their emphasis upon language and culture are, in large part, a reflection of the history of each territory's integration into the British state.[5] Where the language of a peripheral territory has survived it is, *ipso facto* perhaps, likely to be a substantial item on the political agenda of any nationalist movement; where it has not survived in any major way, it is unlikely to be a focus for popular support. So much at least seems obvious. Similarly, where the process of internal pacification, which Giddens has characterized as a central aspect of modern nation-state formation, has been successfully extended to the periphery, violence is unlikely to form part of the nationalist struggle. Where violence remains one of the array of local political possibilities, it will, necessarily almost, be used.

A number of things can be said in closing. It appears, for example, that organized nationalist *movements* cannot be looked at in isolation. Their character and development, whether they be the ideological expression of the aspirations of peripheral minority peoples or dominant metropolitan populations, are inextricably bound up with historical processes of modern nation-state formation. In discussions of local-level identities and movements which are, in whatever sense, definable as nationalist, it is, therefore, not possible to limit the scope of analysis to that local level. The local has to be understood alongside, and analytically integrated into, the regional, the national and, these days, the supra-national (even the global). Nor is it possible to ignore an often substantial history of contact and state integration. Nationalist movements are not things unto themselves, and their history is shared with other peoples and places within a context of metropolitan expansion, power and the struggle for control.

Restoring the historical politics of state formation to its properly central place in our understanding of nationalism, should not, of course, be at the expense of attending to economic and cultural factors. As I hope this comparison of Northern Ireland and Wales suggests – and it is also the implication of the previous discussions of Northern Ireland – this cannot possibly be the case. I am suggesting a middle-of-the-road argument – which is in considerable sympathy, for example, with the framework recently put forward by Llobera (1994) – that any analysis of nationalism must take account, within an appropriately historical framework, of political, cultural and economic factors. Anything else will be partial (probably in both senses of that word). As an example of a properly three-dimensional analysis of nationalism, the reader should perhaps look at O'Sullivan See's discussion of Northern Ireland and Quebec (1986).

Reviewing the comparative case studies, the question may be asked: to what extent are we actually talking about the same phenomenon in Wales and Northern Ireland? Here the issue of the legitimacy of the central state is central. The fact that each 'nationalist' movement has recourse to essentially nineteenth-century rhetorics of self-determination does not make them the same thing (and much the same could, I suspect, be said about the various nationalisms which have reappeared in eastern and central Europe and the Balkans). In Wales the struggle is over culture and language and the state is, for the overwhelming majority of the nationalist population, a legitimate institution albeit one whose reform they seek. In Northern Ireland, the struggle, for most nationalists, is *about* the state. Their minimum goal is its transformation; at most they seek its dissolution into an authentically Irish state (and, what is more, a kind of state somewhat different from the existing Republic of Ireland).

The state's legitimacy – which is, after all, at the heart of whatever generic political philosophy of nationalism it is possible to identify – is wholly different in Wales and Northern Ireland. How then can it be sensible to continue to subsume them under the same conceptual umbrella? Is it perhaps time to unpack – one might even say deconstruct – the notion of 'nationalism'? The fact that so many academic writers on the subject have confidently predicted its demise, only to be contradicted by the unravelling of the geo-political framework of the Cold War in Europe, is a further argument in favour of this approach. Nationalism is dead, long live nationalisms? This is the question which I will explore in the final chapter.

Before going on to that, a few more words about ethnicity and the cultural stuff. Elsewhere in this book I have raised the question of how to differentiate ethnicity from one of its most reactive allotropes, nationalism. The answer – to which I will also return, and in detail, in the closing chapter – seems to definitively implicate processes of nation-state formation in nationalism. But those processes are also involved in the construction of differences *between* nationalisms. Nationalism in this sense might be thought to have its own array of allotropes. And these differences reflect not only the negotiation, exchange and imposition involved in political processes (of state-creation, or whatever) across the boundaries between groups; they also reflect differences of culture.

Culture and political processes are reciprocally entailed in each other. If we accept, for example, that collective propensities to use violence are 'cultural' – inasmuch as they involve hierarchies of moral judgement and ideology – then they are, in part at least, emergent aspects of the histories of state-integration that I have been discussing (cf. Brown 1975). The choice of political strategy – whether to resort to violence or not, for example – is not only defined by interests, circumstance and situation. Nor are interests in any straightforward sense 'culture-free' (whatever that might mean). Northern Ireland's long-standing political history, in which violence – employed by the state and by allies and opponents of the state – has been a locally legitimate or accepted means to whatever end is in sight, is also a political culture, with respect to the specification of those means and ends. To say this is *not* to characterize the Northern Irish and their present difficulties as a 'culture of violence', and to dismiss or blame them accordingly. It *is* to insist that the local cultural content of ideologies of ethnic identification. such as nationalism or ethnicism, is not independent of either ongoing political processes – at local, regional and national 'level' – or the history of relationships with Others.

Finally, it has been suggested that a nationalism whose primary objectives are couched in terms of 'culture', and a nationalism that has self-government in its sights, are rather different phenomena (cf. Hutchinson 1994). Fair enough. But it is not quite that simple. What do they have in common? Is each not, after all, a matter of culture? And don't nationalists in Northern Ireland and Wales face a similar problem: how to create a sense of shared collective identity in populations that, for historical reasons, can see their differences *from* each other more clearly than their similarities *with* each other? How, in the first instance, are nationalists themselves to create that sense of shared identity in their own breasts? How to create, if you like, a new and authentic national ethnic identity out of two (or more) old ones, whose authenticity is sanctioned by shared history and the consequential oppositional realities of everyday life? Aren't these political problems about culture? In this sense, the distinction between the cultural-ideological *content* of ethnic identity and the political processes that produce its *boundaries* is a distraction from the reality that each feeds off the other in an ongoing internal–external dialectic of collective identification. Ends and means are never easy to disentangle.

10

Nations, Nationalisms

One of the notes on which the previous chapter ended was the suggestion that it may be time to move towards more open models of nationalism. Some other recent discussions of nationalism have argued for something similar, a move to relativize our approach: 'no single, universal theory of nationalism is possible. As the historical record is diverse, so too must be our concepts' (Hall 1993: 1). Or, in Anthony Smith's words, 'the complexity of the empirical issues . . . rules out the possibility of uncovering law-like regularities or sweeping generalisations in this field' (1994: 392). This doesn't, however, mean that we should abandon model-building and theorizing. Nor can we – or should we – relativize the notion of nationalism altogether. If the concept is to retain any analytical value, the varieties of whatever it is that we persist in calling nationalism must also have something in common. Although probably not the only common thread – political membership conceived as *citizenship* might be another (Verdery 1993: 38) – ethnicity, individual and collective identification which draws upon a repertoire of perceived cultural differences, is the most ubiquitous and plausible, and the most widely recognized (cf. Connor 1978; B. Williams 1989).

Nationalism in this view is historically and locally variable, and bound up with ethnicity. Taking these propositions together, the basic anthropological model of ethnicity may have more to offer historical and sociological accounts of nationalism than has, perhaps, been appreciated. This is particularly true if we emphasize the social constructionist aspects of the model: that ethnicity is perpetually defined and redefined by social actors in the course of interaction, and that the membership of ethnic groups, their boundaries and the cultural stuff upon which they draw, are all, to some considerable extent, variable. This Barthian transactional approach starts from the point of view of actors themselves and emphasizes the situational contingency of ethnic identity. While Barth's more recent discussions of ethnic diversity and pluralism (1984, 1989) still focus on interaction and negotiability, something else also emerges: ongoing 'streams of tradition' or 'universes of discourse' in which individual actors differentially participate, and which – despite the use of imagery which suggests movement and practice – possess a degree of stability over time. History combines with the give-and-take of the moment in the social construction of ethnic boundaries and identities. To paraphrase someone else – from a different tradition – actors may make their own identities, but they do not do so in circumstances of their own choosing.

Ethnicity and nationalism

It is a tribute to the solidity of intellectual boundaries that 'The remarkable congruence between theories of nationalism and anthropological theories of ethnicity' has been overlooked to the extent that, 'the two bodies of theory have largely developed independently of each other' (Eriksen 1993a: 100). In Chapter 6 I argued that one way to understand nationalism, and other -*isms* such as localism, communalism, regionalism and racism, is to regard them as ideologies of ethnic identification. They are more or less structured bodies of knowledge which make claims about how the social world *is*, and how it *ought to be*, organized along ethnic lines. Allotropes of the general phenomenon of ethnicity (or, to be more exact, of ethnicism), they are historically and locally specific. There is thus no equation of nationalism with ethnicity: first, not all things ethnic are ideological, and second, nationalism differs from other ethnic ideologies and is defined by the specific historical conditions of its emergence.

As a relatively recent reflection of the gradual move of human societies into self-reflexive history which is a concomitant of literacy (Goody 1977), nationalism is an aspect of the growth of ever more complex political units, based, to some degree, on notions of ethnic and cultural commonality (however much, *pace* Benedict Anderson, imagined). As an ethnic identification which, more than most, is explicitly socially constructed and orchestrated as a historical project, 'the nation' is actually a fine example of Barthian transaction and negotiation at work: 'nationalism can be thought of as a specimen of the big family of *we-talks*' (Bauman 1992: 678). Similarly, Smith suggests that ethnicity offers 'a potent model for human association which has been adapted and transformed, but not obliterated, in the formation of modern nations' (A.D. Smith 1986: x; see also 1994: 382), and Llobera argues that to make a bid for nationhood, 'the first thing you must have is a reservoir of ethnic potential' (1994: 214). Nationalism is rooted in, and is one expression of, ethnic attachments, albeit, perhaps, at a high level of collective abstraction. The 'nation' and 'national identity' or 'nationality' are, respectively, varieties of ethnic collectivity and ethnicity, and are likely to be historically contingent, context-derived, and defined and redefined in negotiation and transaction. This proposition applies as much to symbolic or ideological content (nationalism) as it does to group boundaries and membership (national identity, nationality, citizenship).

Not everyone agrees with this. Hobsbawm, for example, argues that nationalism and ethnicity are 'different, and indeed non-comparable, concepts' (1992: 4): in this view nationalism is a recent and programmatic political philosophy, while ethnicity expresses authentic or primordial group identity, rooted in the distinction between insider and outsider. Ethnicity may be 'one way of filling the empty containers of nationalism', but, for Hobsbawm, there is no necessary relationship between the two (see also 1990: 63ff.). Although Anderson (1983) and Gellner (1983) each recognizes a connection between ethnicity and nationalism, they also share, with each other and with Hobsbawm, an understanding of political modernization as the triumph of the nation-state and of nationalism as a specific philosophy of political legitimacy with eighteenth- and nineteenth-century roots in the cultural homogenization produced by industrialization and the bureaucratic state. Thus, nationalism is the product of industrialization and bureaucratic government (Gellner); of the convergence of capitalism and the information technology of printing (Anderson); of all these things *plus* the French Revolution's recasting of political membership as citizenship (Hobsbawm). Viewed in this light, nationalism is the modern new broom that sweeps ethnicity clean out the door of the nation-state.

Many more authors could be cited to make the same point. To differing degrees, they offer a similarly functionalist argument: nationalism provided an ideological means, following the collapse of feudalism and absolutism, for the modern incorporation of élites and masses into the same political space, the nation-state. However much it may incorporate a sense of *we-ness*, nationalism for these authors marks a distinctively modern break with a traditional past characterized by ethnic fragmentation and small-scale communalism. It is both a consequence of and a cure for the disenchantment produced by the rationalization of modern industrial society.

The functionalism of this argument is not, however, its main weakness. The model of nationalism as a modern replacement for, or supersession of, ethnicity, appropriate to the demands of the industrialized social world of nation-states, depends upon definitions of nationalism and ethnicity which are more constraining than may be defensible. The definition of ethnicity which is implied is certainly more limited and more limiting than Barth's broad notion of 'the social organization of culture differences' (which, if it *is* what we mean by ethnicity, must include nationalism within its scope). Nor is the difficulty simply definitional: ethnicity is conceptualized, even if only implicitly, as historically and culturally 'Other', creating in the process two problems. Historically, the argument tends towards tautology: nationalism is what supersedes ethnicity, which is what precedes nationalism. Culturally, we are left with no authentic place within modern nation-states for ethnicity, other than as axiomatic homogeneity, on the one hand, or as an immigrant or peripheral presence, on the Other.

A further criticism is that this school of thought takes modernity's view of itself – as radically discontinuous with what went before – too much at face value, overemphasizing the centrality to nationalism of the *modern* (nation-)state. If we accept the *absolute* modernity of nationalism, what are we to make, for example, of the argument (Runciman 1958: 280–1) that the 'nascent spirit of nationalism' was encouraged by the attempts of the late thirteenth-century Papacy to undermine the power of the Hohenstaufen Emperors? Or Moore's characterization (1987: 136) of European rulers of the same period as a 'new order', proclaiming a 'moral fervour' which found an expression in the emergence of a number of nation-states? Reynolds has, perhaps, articulated the question most clearly:

> The fundamental premise of nationalist ideas is that nations are objective realities, existing through history . . . It seems normally to be taken for granted that the nation-states of today are the true nations of history and that only they can ever have inspired loyalties which deserve to be called nationalist . . . The trouble about all of this for the medieval historian is not that the idea of the permanent and objectively real nation is foreign to the middle ages, as so many historians of nationalism assume, but that it closely resembles the medieval idea of the kingdom as comprising a people with a similarly permanent and objective reality. Not all the kingdoms of the middle ages, however, were destined to become modern states, and if we start from nationalist assumptions we are in danger of prejudging the relative solidarity of those which did and those which did not. (Reynolds 1984: 251–2)

This critique is supported by Llobera's recent suggestion (1994) that the beginnings of European nationalism emerged in the early Middle Ages, only to be stalled by the rise of absolutism. Furthermore, to the European examples one can add Duara's argument (1993) that the concepts of 'nation' and 'nationalism' are applicable to the study of pre-modern China.

It is, nonetheless, impossible to dissent completely from the view that 'nationalism, as ideology and movement, is a wholly modern phenomenon' (A.D. Smith 1986: 18). One should certainly beware of the anachronistic use of words such as 'nation' and 'nationalism', that did not, apparently, achieve common currency in their *modern* usages until the late nineteenth century (Østergård 1992a: 17). However, that nationalism is a *wholly* modern phenomenon is not self-evident. There is a *prima facie* case for arguing that ideologies and politics which are recognizably nationalist, and identities which can be described as national, predate the rise of 'classical' nationalism from the late eighteenth century onwards (cf. also A.D. Smith 1986, 1994). If so, this has implications for the study of modern nationalism.

If nationalism is an ideology of ethnic identification, and therefore approachable via the basic anthropological model of ethnicity, we should be as much concerned with how nationalisms and nationalists define themselves – and how they are defined by other actors – as with how we as social scientists should define them. This avoids substituting 'the reality of the model' for 'the model of reality' (Bourdieu 1977: 29) and offers a flexible approach which, instead of fixing the notion too firmly in the post-Enlightenment political landscape of western Europe – as one might socialism, for example – is catholic in its recognition of ethnic identifications as national(ist) and their ideological and symbolic expressions as nationalism(s). The boundary between 'ethnicism' and 'nationalism' thus becomes indeterminate, lying somewhere along a continuum of gradual change within historically evolving traditions or universes of discourse.

This argument, that nationalism may be less definitively modern than is commonly accepted,[1] differs from Anthony Smith's thesis about the ethnic origins of nations (1986) in that I do not wish to draw too sharp a line between ethnicism and nationalism. I disagree with other aspects of his work too, such as the distinction he draws between 'ethnic nationalism' and 'territorial nationalism' (1991: 82). From my perspective, *all* nationalisms are, in some sense, 'ethnic'. I appreciate the point he is trying to make and its importance, but I would prefer to distinguish between nationalisms which claim territory on the basis of putative common ethnicity and those which attempt to construct ethnic commonality within an already-occupied territory. These points aside, however, my argument owes much to Smith. There are two reasons for emphasizing the possibility of pre-modern nationalisms. First, I want to loosen the entailment of nationalism in the nation-state. To define a phenomenon wholly in terms of what may, at least arguably, be its historical consequence seems to risk a misunderstanding. Second, following from this, I want to explore the possibility that the goals of nationalism are not exhausted by the project of the ethnically exclusive or culturally homogeneous nation-state (cf. Hutchinson 1994).

The first move in this argument is to offer a minimal heuristic definition of nationalism. Thus nationalism is an ideology of ethnic identification which:

- is historically and situationally contingent;
- is characteristic of the politics of complex societies (states but not necessarily nation-states);
- is concerned with culture and ethnicity as criteria of membership in the polity; and
- claims a collective historical destiny for the polity and/or its ethnically defined members.

This model may appear not only too complex, but also unhelpfully vague – which destiny? historical according to whom? how and by whom are such claims defined and pursued? etc. – but I hope that its utility will become more apparent in the comparative discussion of cases which follows.

The full spectrum of nationalist possibilities is not, therefore, likely to be captured by a definition of nationalism such as Gellner's (1983: 1):

> a theory of political legitimacy, which requires that ethnic boundaries should not cut across political ones and, in particular, that ethnic boundaries within a given state . . . should not separate the power-holders from the rest.

There are phenomena which are either rhetorically constructed as 'nationalism', or which an observer can ostensibly identify as such, which do not fall within such a model.

The second move is, instead of talking about nationalism – in anything other than the most abstract or general of senses – to talk about nationalism*s*. This is not, of course, a very novel suggestion. Other authors have typologized nationalisms (e.g. Alter 1989; Breuilly 1985; Hall 1993; Smith 1991), typically within a framework which distinguishes, whether explicitly or implicitly, between *nationalism in general* and specific historical instances of *nationalist movements* (Smith 1991: 79–80). The latter are usually the objects of classification. My proposal is different, its definition of nationalism-in-general is looser, covering a wider range of phenomena. It is as much concerned with *similarities* between nationalisms and other social phenomena as with *differences* between them. Nor are the historical instances which I am interested in examining and comparing necessarily organized *movements*.

Nationalism in three countries

This chapter continues the comparative project begun by the discussion of nationalisms in Northern Ireland and Wales in Chapter 9. That chapter focused upon language, violence and the history of the integration of each region into the United Kingdom state. In Northern Ireland the objectives of contemporary nationalisms are the reunification of Ireland and the removal of British government. In Wales, by contrast, secession is an insignificant nationalist project compared to the protection and promotion of Welsh culture – particularly the Welsh language – and the economic and social development of the areas in which that culture retains its vigour.

Northern Ireland and Wales also differ with respect to the kinds of political action which are perceived as legitimate by nationalists. In each place a gulf separates constitutional nationalists, who pursue their goals through electoral means, from those who advocate the use of force. In Northern Ireland, however, armed struggle has considerable legitimacy in the eyes of a large number of nationalists, whereas for the great majority of Welsh nationalists even modestly violent direct action is bitterly controversial. These different nationalist discourses reflect different regional histories and experiences of incorporation into the British state. As a consequence, it is possible to argue that the nationalisms of each region are, in some senses, qualitatively different phenomena (although both can legitimately claim to be nationalist).

I will return to these issues. For the moment they provide the context for the argument that follows, and indicate its antecedents. In this chapter the scope of comparison has been extended to include Denmark as well as Northern Ireland and Wales. The choice of cases reflects my own experience of these countries, rather than any extrinsic logic of comparison. It also reflects my scepticism about existing theories of nationalism: in their different ways, Wales, Northern Ireland and Denmark did not seem to 'fit' the analytical models to which I first turned in order to understand them.

But as case studies they are particularly appropriate for this discussion. They are integral, if peripheral, elements of modern European industrialized society, the conventionally recognized birthplace of nationalism. Northern Ireland and Wales are each part of a nation-state political system, while Denmark constitutes one in its own right. All have long histories of political change available for inspection. If, therefore, their nationalisms can be shown to differ significantly from each other and from the 'state modernization and industrialization' model, that will be telling support for my argument. In the context of these comparative intentions, I want to pose an apparently simple question: what is the nature of nationalism in each of these countries? This entails a further, deceptively simple, question – does nationalism exist in each of these countries? – which requires us to remember the definitional criteria of nationalism outlined above. Moving from the more to the less straightforward, I will begin with Wales.

Wales

Wales has been an integral part of the British – and before that the English – state since the so-called Act of Union of 1536. But it remains culturally and politically distinct. Having been spared the depopulation of the Highland Clearances or the Irish Great Famine, Wales is linguistically the most 'Celtic' strand in the United Kingdom's 'Celtic fringe', with approximately 20 per cent of its population still speaking Welsh. Although representing a history of decline, this is significantly higher than the equivalent figures for speakers of Scots Gaelic or Irish. From the late eighteenth century Wales, like other European cultural peripheries, experienced a romanticist 'revival' of 'folk' culture, sponsored and invented by an urban elite brought into being by industrialization (Morgan 1983). Under the aegis of nonconformist Liberalism, the seeds of nationalism were sown. Medieval classics such as the *Mabinogion* found a new audience as the *eisteddfod* movement campaigned to create a publicly respectable voice for a language which still, at that time, dominated rural and working-class life. Today, despite centuries of in-migration the Principality retains a cultural identity which, elusive as its definition might be, can legitimately be called 'Welsh'.

Economically, Wales – particularly south Wales – is part of the metropolitan British economy. Its first industrial revolution, beginning in the eighteenth century, was characterized by the interdependence of coal mining and metal manufacture in the southern valleys. Here there developed a locally specific working-class communal life: culturally and linguistically Welsh, nonconformist in religion and politically socialist. This economic strength eventually turned – with mass unemployment in the 1930s, post-1945 restructuring, and the return of recession in the 1970s – to decline, only partially arrested by inward investment and by UK and European subsidies.

Due to the antiquity and nature of its incorporation into the British state, Wales is institutionally less autonomous or distinct than, for example, Scotland. It has political distinctiveness, however, in terms of the politics of party. Wales has been characterized for the last century and a half by movements with strong links to religious nonconformity: first Liberalism and then, from the early 1900s, the socialism of 'the Labour Ascendancy' (Morgan 1981: 272–303). As much as anything, Wales differs from England politically in that Conservatism has always been a minority affiliation.

Although nationalism in Wales can be traced back – in the agitation for the disestablishment of the Anglican state Church – into the nineteenth century, not until the twentieth was there a nationalist *movement*. The Welsh Nationalist Party was founded in 1925, and was renamed Plaid Cymru in 1945. It won its first seat in the British parliament in 1966. At the time of writing it returns four members to Westminster. Its support remains strongest in *y fro Gymraeg*, the Welsh-speaking rural west and north. From its beginnings, the *Blaid* has emphasized cultural issues (language and education), economic development, and political devolution within the United Kingdom as the best way to represent Welsh interests. Secession or independence have always been marginal to the party's platform. Its commitment to non-violent electoral politics increasingly emphasizes Europe as the most significant political arena in the 1990s.

Although the dominant political voice of Welsh nationalism, Plaid Cymru remains a minority party in Wales electorally. Its oppositional vision of the political future of Wales has always competed with the articulation of class conflict and communitarianism offered by the Labour Party. It also competes with the other major voice of nationalism in Wales, Cymdeithas yr Iaith Gymraeg (the Welsh Language Society), founded in 1962. Using non-violent direct protest, in judicious combination with lobbying, the latter's achievements include state funding for Welsh language education and the statutory definition of Welsh as having 'equal validity' in Wales.

Welsh is everywhere: road signs, toilets, train timetables, in the bank, and so on. There is the Welsh language television station, Sianel Pedwar Cymru (S4C), and a modest but locally significant Welsh-medium cultural production industry. During the 1990s Cymdeithas has been at the forefront of protests about new Welsh language legislation and the continued reluctance of government to grant Welsh full official status. Demographically, the decline in the number of Welsh speakers may have been arrested. Reflecting the impact of education and job opportunities, the future of the language appears to lie not in *y fro Gymraeg*, but in the industrialized and urbanized south-east (C.A. Davies 1990).

Although there is no room for an account of the gains and losses of Welsh nationalism (see C.A. Davies 1989), there are some things to add. First, not all nationalism is non-violent, as discussed in Chapter 9. There is also the prospect of an anti-nationalist backlash. There have been (to date unsuccessful) cases in north Wales in which individuals have had recourse to the 1976 Race Relations Act in response to their rejection under local authority Welsh-language hiring policies. In Dyfed, national legislation permitting schools to opt out of the state education system has facilitated a campaign by English-speaking parents, many of whom are recent in-migrants, against the County Council's Welsh-language schooling policies. In reflection of this kind of conflict, and the undoubted existence of a strand of authoritarian and exclusionary linguistic-nationalist rhetoric, academic analyses have appeared which characterize Welsh nationalism as racist (Borland *et al.* 1992; Denney *et al.* 1991; for a critique, see Williams 1994).

Hostility to nationalism is not, however, confined to 'non-Welsh' immigrants. Many Welsh people feel excluded, patronized and devalued by the language movement. This is compounded by class antagonisms: in the south-east, Welsh has become identified with middle-class speakers, often working in the public sector. As discussed in the previous chapter, there is a serious problem – for Welsh nationalists not least of all – with respect to the relationship between the language and authentic Welsh identity. Plaid Cymru consistently attempts to construct a vision of Welshness which while inclusive of English speakers is sufficiently exclusive to serve as a model of national identity (and attract votes). Its recent electoral alliance in Ceredigion with the Green Party is an example of this in practice. Such a vision of the creative interplay that is possible between similarity and difference is vital, if only because a nationalism which is wholly identified with Welsh – and remember that it is with respect to the language that nationalism has had its greatest impact – is, in modern Wales, doomed to minority status:

> The issue of language has . . . given rise from the early part of this century down to the present to a crisis in identity . . . English-speaking Welshmen spiritedly and justifiably counter that . . . they too are a distinctively 'Welsh' people. (Howell and Baber 1990: 354)

There is thus an everyday problem to do with 'national identity' and the 'nation'. What qualifies people for membership in the nation and an authentic Welsh national identity? And who licenses authenticity? Howell and Baber go on to list the attributes, other than the Welsh language, which distinguish the Welsh: 'their separate history, instinctive radicalism in religion and politics, contempt for social pretentiousness, personal warmth and exuberance, sociability, love of music and near obsession with rugby . . .' Leaving aside the gendered nature of this particular construction of Welshness, only one item on the list has any analytic potential: the idea of a separate history. But this history is an 'invented tradition' (Hobsbawm and Ranger 1983), a 'myth to live by' (Samuel and Thompson 1990). That invention is still under way and still evolving.

Even as a social construct, a separate history is, for Wales, problematic. There cannot be *one* history (although see Davies 1993). And separate from what? The answer, of course, is England. But Wales has never been isolated. As discussed in Chapter 3, its history, even as a nationalist mythical charter, is one of engagement with its neighbours and participation in a variety of streams of tradition and universes of discourse. Wales is, and has probably always been, a 'plural society', characterized internally by diversity and, in its external relations, by its open and much-trampled cultural boundaries. The question for nationalism is how to integrate this plurality of voices into a Welsh national identity.

As I also argued in Chapter 3, to describe Wales as a plural society is not actually to say very much. Europe – as most of the rest of the world – has always been a tangled thicket of cultural pluralism. This is one of the things which nationalisms, in their imagination and invention of consistency, often seek to deny. The irony for Welsh nationalism is that such a denial is only possible at the cost of political success. The public articulation of a narrowly definitive Welsh identity is not only the pursuit of a chimera, it is politically unwise. If, as a consequence, Plaid Cymru is attempting to define Welshness in terms of common territorial location, shared economic and social problems, a sense of difference that is not exclusively linguistic, and a 'European future',[2] that need not disqualify it as nationalism.

Northern Ireland

Nationalism in Northern Ireland must, first, be seen within the all-Ireland framework. It claims that context for itself, and it is part of a longer history than the seventy-year life of the six-county northern state. But the history of Ireland is also the history of its relations with England. Irish nationalism evolved as resistance to English rule, and was in the first instance inspired by an English political tradition (Boyce 1991: 388).

The relationship with 'across the water' has changed many times. From the twelfth to the early seventeenth centuries, Ireland was an insecurely possessed English colony, with large areas remaining under Irish control. Subsequently, Ireland in the seventeenth century was a frontier (part colony, part periphery), in the eighteenth century a separate kingdom within a federal polity, and in the nineteenth superficially integrated into the British state. The Anglo-Irish Treaty of 1921 partitioned the island into the Irish Free State and Northern Ireland. The northern state was an uneasy product of the refusal of Ulster Protestants to accept government by a Catholic majority. Its membership of the United Kingdom remains insecure, contingent upon the consent of its electorate.

And as the relationship with Britain has changed, so too nationalism in Ireland has appeared in different guises: the 'embryonic ethnic nationalism' of Gaelic Ireland at the end of the Tudor period; an Anglo-Irish 'national identity based on religion and love of the *patria*', developing into 'intimations of nationalism' by the seventeenth century; nationalism as 'a fully formed and articulated sentiment in the Ireland of the Protestant ascendancy in the last quarter of the eighteenth century'; the revived Catholic national identity of the nineteenth century, forged out of a 'nationalism of the Catholic democracy' and 'the resurgence of Gaelic ethnic nationalism' (Boyce 1991: 19). Although Boyce's view might be contested by historians of a more nationalist bent, it supports my argument about the historical contingency of nationalisms. *A propos* the modernity of nationalism, one can point to the late seventeenth- and early eighteenth-century debate about the nature of the Irish nation – although the term found only rare use – and who belonged to it (Connolly 1992: 114–24). As significant as the contested identities to which this debate attests is the fact that, at a relatively early period, it took place at all.

The twentieth century has seen more change. The Republic of Ireland won its independence by violence; the northern Protestants vetoed their inclusion in that independence by the same means. In the south, nationalism is the political common ground: *all* politicians in the Republic are, in some sense, nationalists, and the Irish Constitution – pending the fruition of recent developments – still formally claims the six counties of the north. Nationalism is also an embarrassing irrelevance: there is little evidence that politicians or voters in the south *want* the six counties 'back'. The 1985 Anglo-Irish Agreement, and the recent 'peace process', can in part be read as an attempt to forestall that scenario with some kind of joint sovereignty. In most respects, 'normal politics' is the order of the day in the contemporary Republic of Ireland.

In Northern Ireland, partition had deep roots in violent conflict between the British (before that the English) state, the Catholic Irish and a population – settled in Ireland for many centuries – identifying itself variously as Ulster Protestant, British, or Scots-Irish. Cultural and political differences between the Irish and the descendants of the settlers found, and still find, powerful expression in religion. As I suggested in Chapter 8, although essentially political, the Northern Irish conflict is symbolized and reinforced by an important religious dimension.

Partition reinforced a further ethnic identification, with the new state of Northern Ireland. This Ulster identity, although claiming an ancient Gaelic province as its own,[3] was Protestant, new – rooted in the north's development as the industrialized region of Ireland and northern anti-Home Rule agitation during the previous thirty years – and distanced from both the Irish and the English. The latter distance increased over subsequent decades, as successive British governments allowed the internal affairs of the Province to slip ever further beyond their oversight and Ulster Unionists were happy to let them.

For most of the period between partition and the present 'troubles',[4] northern nationalists were torn between refusing to recognize the new state and striving to improve the Catholic lot (Phoenix 1994). Nationalist political participation was discouraged by the stance of Unionism, the Protestant party of government in Northern Ireland for an unbroken fifty years. Northern Catholic politicians had to choose between a dangerous and uncertain military strategy (which would attract little Catholic support but would invite a repressive response from the state), remaining aloof from the Unionist state and waiting for history to deliver the millennium of Irish unity, or attempting, under unfavourable conditions, to improve the socio-economic position of the minority.

These options reflect two political traditions: gradualist constitutional 'nationalism' and physical-force 'republicanism' (Ruane and Todd 1992: 189). In Northern Ireland, republican nationalism was represented by Sinn Féin, allied to the Irish Republican Army (IRA), and constitutional nationalism first by the Nationalist Party – until 1969 – and subsequently by the Social Democratic and Labour Party (SDLP). In reflection of the old conflicts of the post-independence Civil War, the same distinctions can be observed in the politics of the Republic of Ireland, although the official legitimacy of nationalism there makes for more complexity. The poles of republican and constitutional nationalism are represented by Sinn Féin and Fine Gael, respectively, with Fianna Fáil occupying a shifting position which is usually towards the constitutional end of the spectrum.

The differences between modern nationalisms re-emerged in the early 1960s in the campaign to redress the electoral, social and economic grievances of Catholics. The Civil Rights Movement, and Protestant reaction to it, led to escalating violence, the introduction of the British Army, the dissolution of the local parliament and the assumption of direct rule from London in 1972. In 1969 resurgent nationalist violence split republicanism into the Official and Provisional movements, reflecting a shift in the centre of gravity of republicanism to the north, a retreat from the socialism which had been influential within the movement, and a return to physical force and identification with a Gaelic cultural tradition. These developments were associated with a new, working-class militant republicanism in Belfast and elsewhere. The Provisional movement – in its IRA and Sinn Féin branches – is now the authentic voice of a large constituency of northern Catholics. Constitutional nationalism reorganized into the SDLP, absorbed some of the civil rights activists, and has forged a new strategy under the auspices of the Anglo-Irish Agreement of 1985, relating directly to Dublin and London. Although it aspires to Irish unity, the SDLP's nationalism is compromised these days by its relationship with establishment politics in Dublin.

This account suggests some observations. Irish history, first, is a history of nationalisms – both Irish and British – rather than nationalism. Nor – as I suggested in Chapter 9 – is it easily shoehorned into the frameworks proposed by Anderson, Gellner or Hobsbawm. The problem, for example, with Coakley's argument (1990) that Irish nationalism in some senses conforms to the European norm and is in some senses deviant, is its presumption of both *an* Irish nationalism and a *typical* European model. Furthermore, nationalism of various hues is of considerable antiquity in Ireland. There are few reasons to confine our recognition of Irish nationalism to the nineteenth century and since.

Which brings me to 'streams of tradition', *pace* Barth. Notions of shared history require caution: history is both the circumstances in which men and women make themselves (and make more history), and the myths and inventions by which they live. Too little can be made of history, and too much. If there are today *two* nationalist traditions in Northern Ireland then we must explain them with reference to more than history (unless one regards what happened every yesterday as history, in which case all social science is history). It was despite the mutual enmities of the past and the present that the leaders of Sinn Féin and the SDLP, calculating the odds about the future, held the private talks which produced a joint submission to the Dublin government, which made a major contribution to the Anglo-Irish Downing Street Declaration of December 1993, the paramilitary cease-fires of 1994 and the subsequent 'peace process'.

History, tradition and current politics combine, in Northern Ireland as in Wales, in questions of identity. Are Protestants, for example, Irish? Leaving aside the nationalist rhetoric which insists that they are, the answer is complex. Survey evidence suggests that there has been a change in identification. In 1968 three identities were important in Northern Ireland: 'British', 'Irish' and 'Ulster'. By 1978 this had polarized into 'British' (most Protestants) and 'Irish' (most Catholics), a state of affairs that has apparently changed little since (Moxon-Browne 1991: 29). However, as Moxon-Browne says, Protestants know what they're *not* better than what they *are*. It depends upon with whom they are contrasted. Ulster Protestants, to return to the dicussion of Chapter 7, have two Others. Do they feel quite as British as the British? How do they identify themselves as against the English? And how do the *other* British identify them? Nor do we know what the difference is between middle-class Unionism and working-class loyalism (analogues of constitutional and republican nationalism). As social anthropology insists, 'it's not as simple as that', particularly in rural districts (McFarlane 1986). Nor is it clear that 'Irishness' is the same in the north as in the south. Etcetera.

It is, however, quite clear that Northern Irish Catholics and Protestants have no consensual common national identity, and that Protestant identity is ambiguous. Some aspects of this ambiguity – this 'crisis of identity' – have been discussed in Chapter 7. There is, however, more that can be said. Witness, for example, the attempts by the Ulster Defence Association – a now-illegal Protestant paramilitary organization – and others to invent a new history and mythology of and for the Ulster Irish (Bruce 1992: 233–6; Buckley 1989). Witness the social science disagreement about whether Protestant ethnic chauvinism is racism (Miles 1996; Nelson 1975). And if not racism, what? Nationalism? Ethnicism? Does a Protestant nationalism make sense? It made sense, after all, in eighteenth-century Ireland. But if it were to make sense, in what terms – given the locally definitive Catholic appropriation of nationalist rhetoric – would Protestants make their case?

Although they might see themselves as *British* nationalists, Protestant Ulster nationalism is at the moment an unlikely prospect, despite Finlayson's recent insistence to the contrary (1996). His argument requires us to overlook the self-identification of most Ulster Protestants *and* to substantially redefine nationalism. This is surely is too much to expect. At the heart of the problem is the nature of the Protestant claim to a 'historical destiny'. In denying themselves an Irish future in 1921, and accepting a reluctant and conditional incorporation by Britain, they arguably wrote themselves out of history for fifty years. When they re-emerged in the late 1960s, as oppressors of the Catholic minority and an embarrassment to the rest of the United Kingdom, their moment had passed. It shows no sign of returning. They remain, neither fully Irish nor fully British, seeking a destiny as well as an identity.

Denmark

On the face of it, there is no nationalism in Denmark. A lack of nationalist movements has, in fact, been identified as a general characteristic of Nordic societies (Elklit and Tonsgaard 1992). Although this absence may reflect their own tight definition of nationalist movements,[5] for Elklit and Tonsgaard it indicates the solution through other kinds of politics of ethnonational grievances which could otherwise foment movements of this kind. Not everyone, of course, takes this view. Eriksen, for example, suggests (1993a: 102–4) that weak nationalism has been influential in the history of the Nordic peoples, and a similar thesis runs through the contributions to Tägil's collection on nation-building (1995).

The absence or weakness of nationalist movements is part of a Nordic political style that emphasizes conflict avoidance and the promotion of consensus. The most cursory look at Denmark illustrates the point: it is difficult to find anything that would identify itself, or might be identified by others, as a nationalist political party *per se*. The tiny parties of the right which campaign about immigration and similar issues – Den danske Forening, Nationalpartiet Danmark and De national-liberale – are perceived as neo-fascist or racist rather than specifically nationalist. Yet this is despite Denmark's progressive loss of once substantial peripheral territories (Borish 1991: 28–37). It is despite invasion and occupation by Germany three times between 1848 and 1945. It is despite incorporation into a European Union of which many Danes, perhaps the majority, are deeply suspicious and fearful. It is despite increased unemployment. It is despite recent immigration from southern Europe and further afield and increased ethnic intolerance (Enoch 1994). And it is despite a contemporary European political climate in which nationalism has regained much of its potency. Any one of these might provide the catalyst for a nationalist political party. But there is none.

Understanding nationalism's apparent absence, no less than its presence, demands recourse to history. The development in Denmark of a characteristically Nordic political style is only part of the explanation (and something which itself requires explanation). Three other themes in recent history are significant (Jones 1986: 59–151; Østergård 1992b: 63–83). First, contraction and international decline produced a political territory which, with the notable and complicated exception of the southern border region, is a linguistic and cultural unit. Second, the reaction to contraction was a rapid and non-violent process of modernization, taking Denmark from late absolutism in the early nineteenth century to the foundation of a precocious social-democratic welfare state by the early twentieth. Finally, this process does not seem to have been underwritten by industrialization – Denmark remains among the least industrialized of northern European states – but by land reform, the modernization of agriculture and a corporatist political strategy based on egalitarianism.

Hvad udad tabes, det skal indad vindes – 'What is lost outwards, shall be won inwards' – was the motto of the Danish Heath Society, which in the nineteenth century promoted the cultivation of hitherto infertile land. It is paradigmatic of an acceptance of constraints, and a resolve to overcome them, which was central to modern Danish nation-building. Inward looking and reconstructive, within a culturally homogeneous polity, that process is crucial to understanding why there are no nationalist movements in Denmark today.

But the detail of everyday life suggests a different picture. Take, for example, the white cross on the red field of *Dannebrog*, the Danish flag. Many Danish houses have a flagpole in the garden, from which the flag is flown to mark the whole range of domestic festivals and rites of passage. Those households lacking a flagstaff may display instead a small portable version on a wooden base. At Christmas, miniature paper *Dannebrog*, which are sold in every supermarket, adorn the tree, and a birthday cake is incomplete without at least one. 'Flying the flag' is central to the symbolization of Danish national and civic culture; in the process, family celebrations become more than simply domestic.

A comparative perspective brings this into focus. In Northern Ireland, flags – on the one hand the Union Flag or the Ulster flag, on the other the Republic's tricolour – are part of ethnic boundary maintenance and a recognized element in the rituals of confrontation of the annual 'marching season' (Bryson and McCartney 1994). In Britain, a private citizen flying the Union Flag would be diagnosed as eccentric, at best, or racist and fascist, at worst. The latter is certainly what is symbolized by the Union Jack T-shirt of the English football fan abroad.

Dannebrog painted on the face of a Danish football supporter, however, symbolizes something different; certainly not the xenophobia which informs much British political discourse, even in the mainstream, and from which the English football fan draws a sense of his place in history. But what *does* it signify? And what does it mean when Danes tell you, with unself-conscious pride, that Queen Margrethe II's line of descent extends back more than a millennium to Gorm the Old, the oldest royal line in Europe? Or, to return to the flag, what about its myth of origin, which has it dropping from heaven as a gift to King Valdemar II during a battle in 1219? Although Danes acknowledge the invention of this particular tradition, 'even so it is considered the oldest of present-day European flags' (Jacobsen 1986: 23). Here it is possible to have one's traditional national cake and eat it.

The recipe for that cake is the usual *bricolage* of contradiction and affinity. Insofar as one can generalize, Danes are ferociously understated in their national pride, modesty and restraint being important components of a relatively consensual model of 'proper' Danishness. They celebrate the fact that Denmark is a small country, *et lille land*. Østergård, a perceptive local commentator, calls this 'lilliput-chauvinism' (1992b: 56) or 'humble assertiveness': 'We know we are the best, therefore we don't have to brag about it' (1992c: 170). And there is also defensiveness. Although it is 'bad form' to be a nationalist, 'intrinsic nationalism surfaces immediately foreigners start criticizing anything Danish' (Østergård 1992c: 169). Thus, if it is not too much of a conundrum, a defining feature of Danish nationalism may be a refusal to acknowledge itself as nationalism.

If there *is* something which can be called Danish nationalism what are its other distinguishing features? Much depends on context: the Danes are, if nothing else, abundantly supplied with a classificatory hierarchy and choice of Others. In the Scandinavian or Nordic context a distancing rhetoric comes into play: ethnic jokes and stereotypes are common, touching upon the most mundane areas of daily life (Linde-Laursen 1993). These only make sense, however, within a commonly recognized cultural, linguistic and political affinity, particularly with Sweden and Norway. Important as national-ethnic boundaries and identities are, a shared *Scandinavian* identity (Gerholm and Gerholm 1990; Gullestad 1989) is a resource which can be drawn upon to make sense of similarity and difference. Greater differences of language and culture, and more distant histories, suggest that a shared *Nordic* identity remains an as yet unrealized project.

The broader European context is more ambiguous. The distinction between Scandinavia and Europe is one of the fault lines which structures that ambiguity: is Denmark European or Scandinavian? The conventional answer to this question, 'something of each', leaves unbroached the even more interesting question of why Scandinavia might not be considered part of Europe. Nor has the admission of Sweden to the EU clarified the matter; Norway remains outside. This ambiguity came to a recent head in the prolonged political struggle within Denmark over ratification of the Maastricht Treaty and European economic and political unification (Heurlin 1994; Skovgaard-Petersen 1994). After two referenda, and only by a narrow margin, the Danish political establishment achieved the 'yes' vote that it wanted. Of the reasons which informed the uncertain and the opposed, two stand out: a local distrust of centralization *per se*, and a desire to preserve the Danish welfare state. These come together in a fear of reduced sovereignty (Lyck 1992; Sørensen and Væver 1992) which must be understood in the historical context outlined above. There is also a cultural context, in which the perception of Denmark as *et lille land*, vulnerable to cultural and linguistic domination, plays a part (cf. Christensen 1994).

There is, however, another European context. Europe begins in Germany. Denmark has been invaded by Germany three times in modern history; the last time is a living memory. Influential in the modern construction of Danish identity was the question of Slesvig and Holstein, resolved by plebiscite in 1920 after a campaign in which Danes and Germans used stereotypes of the other to define themselves (Adriansen 1992). And here the contrast between Northern Ireland and Denmark becomes most obvious. The 1920 campaign about partition in southern Denmark was fought with posters and speeches; in Ireland in 1920 the matter was settled by guns and bloodshed. Today in the south of Denmark, a substantial minority of *hjemme tyskere* ('home Germans'), Danish citizens who are linguistically German, ensures the continuing vitality of the issue, as does the presence of a linguistically Danish minority in Germany (Østergård 1995). The differences between the two countries in terms of size and affluence further feeds Danish distrust. If Danish nationalism exists, it is for many Danes, depending perhaps upon generation and geography, articulated as much in opposition to Germany as anything else.[6]

And there are many other things against which it can be defined: immigrants, Americanization, etc. One of the things that is most striking is the level of recent collective scrutiny within Denmark of the nature of *danskhed* (Danishness). A range of issues have problematized what has previously been taken for granted if not consensual (Harbsmeier 1986; Østergård 1992d). Among the most interesting epiphenomena of this debate are specifications of the qualities of Danish national character, whether by Danes – 'individualism, solidarity, faith in authority and discipline' (Østergård 1992b: 21) – or, more controversially within Denmark, by outsiders: privatized, individualized, suppressed and collectivized, according to Reddy (1993: 130–56).

As well as EU referenda campaigns and local perceptions of the residential presence of 'foreigners', this debate reflects other issues. The most important concerns the future of *den danske vej*, the 'Danish way' (Østergård 1992b: 63), the social experiment which since the mid-nineteenth century has attempted to blend capitalism with equality into a historical destiny which Denmark has chosen for its own: the nation as 'a social laboratory' (Manniche 1969). Rooted within an agrarian populist political tradition which is both egalitarian and libertarian, 'This is the ultimate Danish discourse: Everyone is in the same boat' (Østergård 1992e: 14). As this core component of national identity has come under pressure, not least from consumerism, affluence and increasing social stratification within Denmark, so too has *danskhed* come into question.

Among the reasons I began to look systematically at the Danish case was the fact that conventional wisdom in the social science literature about nationalism didn't help me to understand the place. I was fairly convinced, as an intermittent anthropological tourist, that there was *some* kind of nationalism going on – people cannot, after all, spend as much time waving and flying their flag as Danes do without being, in some sense, nationalists – but I was unsure how best to make sense of it. Now, after the more systematic look, there remain questions to be asked about Danish nationalism. Is it *really* nationalism? And, if so, what are my reasons for identifying it as such?

In the first place – which is not quite as trivial as it might sound – what I have described is, in some respects, identified as nationalism by Danes. It is a contested description in Denmark, but it can be found sufficiently often to be credible. In the second, it is possible to offer a plausible definition of nationalism that is sufficiently broad to include the Danish case, but sufficiently focused to exclude cognate ideologies of ethnic identification. By this definition, the conditions for, and components of, nationalism are an ideology of ethnic identification (*danskhed*), ethnic criteria of political membership (Danish citizenship, contested for immigrants), a state context (Danmark), and a claim to a collective historical destiny (*den danske vej*).

The notion of ideology implies structure and organization as a body of knowledge of how the world *is* and how it *should be*. This is the '-ism' in nationalism. Is what I have been talking about sufficiently organized to qualify? The answer is 'yes' and 'no'. 'No', in the relative absence of nationalist *movements* or *parties*. 'Yes', in the existence of a universe of discourse, a stream of tradition, which identifies, and identifies *with*, Denmark in terms of national character and historical destiny. This is the weak ideology of Danish nationalism, and it is showing signs of weakening further. The debate about *danskhed*, and the concern about threats to *den danske vej*, reveal a dissensus about how the world is and how it should be which is antagonistic to the certainties of nationalism. In the resolution of this uncertainty, Danish nationalism will be redefined.

Identity, ideology and the everyday

Danish nationalism, as I have described it, is an everyday and very ordinary matter, rather than a structured nationalist movement. The recent literature offers some suggestively homologous notions which may help us further understand the Danish situation. Emphasizing the everyday, Linde-Laursen talks about the 'nationalization of trivialities' (1993), the way in which national communities that are culturally very close in many respects, Danes and Swedes in this case, 'do' everyday life – washing the dishes, for example – differently, and use these distinctions as boundary markers denoting much larger imagined differences of hygiene and proper behaviour. In similar terms, Wilk contrasts:

> official, planned, government policies of nationalism and unofficial, unplanned, nonpolitical ideas and practices of nationalism which are outside the power, reach or interest of the state. (1993: 296)

A broadly homologous distinction has been drawn by Eriksen (1993b) between 'formal nationalisms', ideologies of ethnic identification that are part of the institutional and political organization of the modern nation-state, and 'informal nationalisms', that are rooted in the daily round of civil society. Both exist within the context of the nation-state and may complement or oppose each other. When Duara (1993: 14) contrasts the 'discursive meaning' of the nation, located in ideology and rhetoric, with its 'symbolic meaning' – to be found in 'cultural practices . . . such as rituals, festivals, kinship forms, and culinary habits' – he appears to address the same issues. More recently again, Michael Billig has explored in some depth a notion of 'banal nationalism' – as opposed to 'hot nationalism' – that speaks to a similar set of concerns:

> the ideological habits which enable the established nations of the West to be reproduced . . . these habits are not removed from everyday life, as some observers have supposed. Daily, the nation is indicated, or 'flagged' in the lives of its citizenry. Nationalism, far from being an intermittent mood in established nations, is the endemic condition. (Billig 1995: 6)

Not the least important thing about these converging arguments and models is that they underline the ethnic character of nationalisms, and the importance of the cultural stuff in their everyday social construction.

In this context, the distinction between *nationalism* and *national identity* (e.g. Smith 1991, 1994) may be helpful: the latter is the ethnicity to which nationalist ideological identification refers. Borneman, writing about Berlin, makes a similar point when he differentiates *nationalism*, as a public ideology of identification with the state, from *nationness,* which is an implicit sense of being the kind of person, or living the kind of life, appropriate to membership in that state: a 'praxis of belonging' and 'a subjectivity . . . derived from lived experience within a state' (Borneman 1992: 338, 352). This is another allusion to everyday civil society and the symbolic meaning of the nation.

National identity or nationness can exist in the absence of nationalism (and Ulster Protestants may be a case in point); nationalism without some kind of national identity is unthinkable. In Northern Ireland and in Wales, for example, the politics of authentic national identity are at the heart of organized nationalism and its ideologies and also distinct from it, threaded in and out of the banal routines of living in cultural stuff such as religion and language. It is from the everyday and the banal that Billig's 'hot nationalism' draws its sustenance. To take these ideas further, national identity is to nationalism, as unofficial, informal, everyday nationalism is to the official and the formal. Informal, unofficial nationalism and national identity, if this argument is correct, are similar, although not actually the same thing. And the existence of formal, organized national-ism does not mean the absence of the informal, the unofficial, or the banal. Quite the reverse.

Nor should it be thought that everyday life is somehow free from ideology. Here we return to the cultural stuff again. Everyday life is fundamentally ideological: in religion, in discourses about the various yardsticks of deviance – normality, respectability, propriety, morality (Jenkins, forthcoming) – in child-rearing wisdom, in folk history, in models of gender and sexuality, in the building-block categories of language. And, which is what interests me here, in discourses about ethnic identity and its allotropes: locality, community, region, nation, 'race'. These are all bodies of knowledge which make claims about the way the social world *is* and about the way it *ought* to be. Everyday ideology may not be formally structured and organized, but it has pattern and it matters in people's lives.

If Eriksen and Wilk, in particular, are correct in locating distinctions of this kind within the broader relationship between the state and civil society, then much will depend upon the nature and history of that relationship in any specific case. In Denmark, for example, where a strong state and civil society have evolved side by side along *den danske vej*, informal (or unofficial or banal) nationalism draws the formal symbols of the state – because, as Østergård reminds us, *Dannebrog*, despite its domestication, 'actually symbolizes the power of the monarchy and the state' (1992a: 22) – into the intimate settings of daily life. In the process it becomes difficult to know where state and civil society begin and end in Denmark, and informal nationalism to some extent fills the space created by the relative absence of official state nationalism.

These distinctions – between formal-official and informal-unofficial nationalism, between the discursive and the symbolic meanings of the nation, between hot and banal nationalism, between state and civil society – are further support for the arguments advanced in this chapter. As a convergent set of ideas produced by different authors, writing about different places, from different points of view, they offer the beginnings of a useful new framework for understanding different nationalisms and the differences between them. They also remind us of the importance of maintaining a historical perspective. The relationship between state and civil society is, in any given case, the product of history. Nationalisms, ideologies of ethnic identification of a particular kind, are streams of tradition, universes of political discourse located within history. And as local political narratives, they are also social productions, by means of which people make sense of and live in a complex and changing contemporary world.

These case studies suggest that there is more to nationalism than is allowed by the 'state modernization and industrialization' model. Although comparison of this kind cannot 'prove' or 'disprove' anything, it supports the view that we should move beyond that relatively unitary model, towards a more flexible theoretical framework which is concerned with nationalism*s* rather than nationalism. Of course, the reader may doubt whether the case studies actually represent comparable phenomena. Certainly, they document very different histories and situations. In part, this is precisely my point. While each can legitimately be described as referring to 'nationalism', the differences between them are sufficiently significant to suggest that nationalism is a broad church with many mansions under its roof.

In Wales the nationalist tradition is recent and more or less unified, focusing upon culture and language within a pragmatic acceptance of an existing constitutional status quo. Although it has its roots in nineteenth-century Romanticism, Wales during that period was already an integral part of a centralized state. Processes of economic or political modernization do not seem to have been central to the formation of Welsh nationalism.

In Northern Ireland, by contrast, constitutional and republican national-isms, divided against themselves, are aspects of a tradition of resistance to rule from and by Britain which extends back to the early modern period and beyond. That tradition, however, has been discontinuous, adopted by different groups at different times in the pursuit of different ends. Taking account of the various historical expressions in Ireland of British nationalisms complicates the situation even further.

Danish nationalism is different again: implicit and elusive, a low-key ideology of everyday discourse rather than a matter of organized politics. Existing in a social and political context which in many senses refuses to legitimize nationalist *movements*, it reflects Denmark's history of relation-ships with its neighbours and is an expression of faith in the Danish experiment in welfare state capitalism and social democracy. The com-plexities of the Danish case stem not only from the variability of nationalism but also from its subtleties and relationships to other locally dominant political ideologies (social democracy and welfarism, for example).

Yet, allowing for these differences – in degree of organization, strength or weakness of ideology, political goals and objectives, and practical strategies and tactics – these are all nationalisms. But in what senses? First, they are all, in some respect, identified as nationalism by the relevant locals. This is one of the reasons why a degree of scepticism about the possibility of Ulster Protestant nationalism is indicated. Second, it is possible to formulate a definition of nationalism broad enough to include them all, but capable of differentiating nationalism from racism, ethnicism, or regionalism, for example (although the boundaries between such things will always be continua of degrees of differentiation and distance). In each case it is possible to identify the conditions for and components of nationalism which I defined earlier: an *ideology or ideologies of ethnic identification, historical contingency and variation*, a *state context, ethnic criteria of political membership* and a claim to a *collective historical destiny*.

Historical destiny may seem an odd notion – even dated or anachronistic – to introduce into the argument (and perhaps Eriksen's 'future orientation' [1993c] might sound less worrying). To some, mindful of the terrible ends to which notions of history and destiny can be bent, its use may appear irresponsible. But it is crucial. One distinguishing feature of nationalisms is their appeal to the past – an ethnic-national history embodied in such things as myths of origin, royal genealogies or cultural romanticism – in the construction of a collective project for the future. This is the inspiration for Benedict Anderson's evocation (1983: 147) of Walter Benjamin's imagery of the 'angel of history': looking back, in nostalgia and anger, but irresistibly propelled forward at the mercy of progress. Nationalism differs from Benjamin's angel, however, in that it does not present its back to the future in futile resistance to change. It is, rather, actively in the business of moving forward, in the pursuit of the historical destiny that it claims for itself. Perhaps a more appropriate image is Anderson's other description of nationalism, as Janus-headed (1983: 144), simultaneously looking ahead and behind.[7]

The future towards which nationalism looks is not, however, as tightly circumscribed as some commentators argue. The collective project need not be independence, secession, or any of the other political goals that may come to mind most readily under the sign of nationalism. It may be cultural preservation and promotion, as in Wales, or the creation of a particular kind of society, as in Denmark. And, as in both cases and in Northern Ireland, there may be important subsidiary concerns too. If literacy gave people, in history, a different kind of past, it also created for them the possibility of the future as a project. Nationalism was among the results. As social scientists we must continue to talk about nationalism in an abstract ideal-typical sense. We can only do so, however, in full recognition of the limitations of such a discourse. The 'real' world is full of nationalisms.

Rethinking Ethnicity

I began this book by arguing that although the basic social anthropological model of ethnicity has for a long time been the most useful analytical framework available, its potential has not been fully explored or appreciated. The 'rethinking ethnicity' of the title is my attempt to do some of that exploration and to encourage that appreciation. In the process, I don't, however, lay claim to dramatic innovation. The rethinking that I have done is just that: thinking again about what others have thought about before, building upon what they have done, occasionally rescuing or renovating overlooked insights, developing hints and suggestions into something more substantial, and putting together things that may not, hitherto, have been connected.

The 'basic anthropological model' is a series of loosely linked propositions, thus:

- ethnicity is about cultural differentiation (bearing in mind that identity is always a dialectic between similarity and difference);
- ethnicity is concerned with culture – shared meaning – but it is also rooted in, and the outcome of, social interaction;
- ethnicity is no more fixed than the culture of which it is a component, or the situations in which it is produced and reproduced;
- ethnicity is both collective and individual, externalized in social interaction and internalized in personal self-identification.

All of these propositions still hold. In emphasizing social construction and everyday practice, acknowledging change as well as stability, and allowing us to recognize individuality in experience and agency as well as the sharing of culture and collective identification, they remain fundamental to a rounded understanding of ethnicity.

They are not, however, all there is to be said. Developments and themes have emerged in the course of previous chapters that are worth restating in closing. If some of them are propositions which were put on the agenda by Fredrik Barth in 1969, only to be subsequently sidelined, that is more, rather than less, reason to attend to them now.

And the first is just such an issue. The axiomatic preoccupation with 'group-ness' in the study of ethnicity, post-*Ethnic Groups and Boundaries*, has encouraged the continuing reification of ethnic groups and, particularly, their boundaries. This might be considered a serious enough problem in that it undermines the analytical vision of the social world consistently promoted by Barth himself; a vision of social life as perpetual coalition, fission and negotiation; of collective social forms as emergent patterns generated by the ongoing ins and outs of individuals interacting. Social groups are not 'things'.

There is another problem, however, that is at least as serious. The preoccupation with definite bounded groups focuses largely – if not totally – on their self-identification. This arguably obstructs our better understanding of processes of ethnic identification in all of their complexity. The focus on group identification rather than social categorization is not simply an 'empirical' oversight. It is, if one can use such a word, simply wrong. If ethnic identification is understood as a dialectical process of mutually implicated internal and external definition, then categorization must be included in our analyses, and social categories as well as groups be counted legitimate – and necessary – as building blocks for our arguments. Even if we acknowledge the analytical centrality of group identification – a reasonable enough point of view, given that some self-conscious 'groupness' is necessary for collective mobilization – it is impossible to understand how groups are constituted without a full appreciation of social categorization. There are no groups, ethnic or otherwise, without categorization.

Nor does this line of argument apply only to collective identification. Any social identity – and ethnicity and its allotropes are not exceptions – must mean something to individuals before it can be said to 'exist' in the social world. The collective cannot be 'real' without the individual. With respect to individual meanings and experience, primary socialization is an obvious place to begin. Entering into ethnic identification during childhood is definitively a matter of categorization: we learn who we are because, in the first instance, other people – whether they be co-members or Others – tell us. Socialization *is* categorization. It cannot be otherwise. What is more, categorization continues to contribute in a significant fashion to individual identification throughout adult life. Being categorized is a necessary and foundational part of the individual development and ongoing mobilization of group identifications; it is at the heart of the individual meaning and experience, and the power and force, of ethnic identification. Without categorization, there are no socialized individuals.

To recognize that categorization – as I have defined it – is a vital element in our models of the social construction of ethnicity, is to place issues of power and compulsion – and resistance – at the heart of what we do, rather than uncomfortably regarding them with our peripheral vision. The corner of our analytical eye will not do. If for no other reason, this is because the capacity to define for Others – in the shape of consequences – what it means for them to be identified in a particular way, is part of our group identification and our experience of membership. To put Others in their place is necessarily to claim a place for ourselves (and vice versa).

This also speaks to the particular need – political as much as intellectual – to engage with the difficult relationship between ethnicity and 'race'.

Anthropology has recently, and for too long, neglected this matter. Although 'race' is an allotrope of ethnicity, they are somewhat different social phenomena. Historically speaking, ethnic identity is probably ubiquitous; 'race' is not. With respect to individual identification, the two are qualitatively different. Ethnic identity is the more general, the more basic; it is also the more likely to be embedded within the everyday contexts of culture-in-common such as language and religion. This does not mean, however, that it is more significant. 'Race' is likely to be at least as consequential as ethnicity in everyday experience, and historically it has been an organizing principle of domination almost without parallel. Identifications of 'race' are typically rooted in categorization rather than group identification, in ascription and imposition rather than subscription, in the external rather than the internal moment of identification. Power in this context is the capacity to determine for Others, not just the consequences of identity, but also their nominal identification itself.

The distinction between the nominal and the virtual is basic to the understanding of ethnic – and other – identities which I am proposing. It is homologous to the group-category distinction but not precisely the same. The nominal is the name: English, Welsh, Ulster Protestant, Irish, Danish, etcetera. Nominal identities are often hierarchically segmentary; individuals may thus participate in a plurality of nominal ethnic (or similar) identities. One can be Danish and a 'home German', Welsh and a *gog*; British and Welsh. In fact, to be a 'home German' one must be Danish, to be a *gog* one must be Welsh, and so on.

The virtualities of identification are constituted in consequences and everyday experience. The hierarchical and segmentary organization of the nominal – the classificatory intersection of the communal, the local, the ethnic, the national, the 'racial' – is, at least in part, to be understood in terms of virtual identification. The practical entailments of communal identification are, for example, different from those of local identity; local identification has different consequences from national identity; and so on.

The relationship between the nominal and the virtual is thus always a matter of specifics, to be discovered. Nominal and virtual may be in harmony with each other or they may not. The virtualities of the same nominal identification can differ from situation to situation. The name may stay the same – X, for example – even though the experience of being an X changes dramatically; conversely, the experience may stay relatively stable while the name changes. Both name and experience may change. Individuals may share a nominal identity, but that may mean very different things to them in practice, it may have different consequences for their lives; they may 'do' it differently. And so on across a wide range of possibilities. The virtualities of experience are likely to be central to processes of change; they are certainly likely to be less stable than the nominal. In times of flux, the relationship between the nominal and the virtual may contribute a useful image of continuity; it is just as likely, however, to sow the seeds of confusion and conflict.

Although the nominal and the virtual can be distinguished for analytical purposes, in everyday social reality they are chronically implicated in each other. This brings us back to the consequences of identification by others. My argument here can be understood as in some respects a collective version of the labelling model of individual identity developed within symbolic interactionism. It is a loosely specified processual model of the way in which what goes on at and across the boundary affects the cultural content of identity. Our 'cultural stuff' will, even if only in part, reflect our interactions with Other(s): how those Others categorize and behave towards us, how they label us. Nor is this all. Our categorizations of Others, and the routines that we evolve for dealing with them, are also intrinsic to our cultural repertoire. Social interaction at and across the boundary will necessarily involve categorizations: of 'us' by 'them', and of 'them' by 'us'. Whose categorizations are the more influential, and the balances that are struck between group identification and categorization, are ongoing open questions, emerging out of history and past experience, located within power relations in the here-and-now, and constitutive of the ongoing situation. Whose definition of the situation counts, nominally and virtually, impinges upon the (external) interactional boundary and (internal) cultural content. Taking categorization seriously means taking the cultural stuff seriously too.

The cultural stuff is undeserving of neglect for other reasons. Logically and substantively, similarity and difference are mutually entailed in identification. Difference cannot exist without similarity, and vice versa. If we are to focus on the social construction of cultural differentiation then we also have to take into account the social construction of cultural similarity (which suggests that we should pay attention to the cultural content of identity). Difference and similarity are each imagined; neither is imaginary; both come together in ethnicity. For difference to be socially marked, there has to be something upon which to seize as its marker, no matter how minor, no matter how arbitrary (no matter how imaginary?). For similarity to be identified there has to be something in common. To follow Max Weber and recognize ethnicity as a principle of collective social organization, in the context of group identification, for example, there probably has to be at least mutual intelligibility of behaviour. Even in the context of categorization, the criteria of identification have to possess at least some social relevance: they have to be differences which make a difference to someone. There are local limits to how arbitrary the social construction of identity can be.

This means that we must also take seriously the fact that ethnicity means something to individuals, and that when it matters, it can *really* matter. This doesn't in any sense mean swallowing the primordialist line. It suggests a focus on culture and the everyday constitution of ethnicity, during primary socialization and subsequently. Some kinds of cultural stuff – religion, or language, perhaps – may be of greater affective and personal consequence than others. In principle, it is possible to mobilize around any marker of differentiation – which end of a boiled egg is the right one to open, for example – and the logic of symbolism allows that anything can be signified in this way. In terms of everyday realities, however, some things may be more emotable than others. And, whether one accepts this or not, the character of the cultural content of being an X or a Y is likely to influence the character of the interaction between Xs and Ys (the cultural acceptability of violence as a means for the pursuit of ends is one obvious illustration that comes to mind).

Re-emphasizing the cultural content of ethnicity offers a further way to differentiate among ethnicity and its allotropes: locality, community, national identity, nationality (which is not quite the same thing), and 'race'. They are about somewhat different things, culturally. And so are their respective ideological expressions. Thus looking at content allows us to distinguish, for example, nationalism and racism, or to differentiate between nationalisms and racisms. This is no more than we might expect given that these are fundamentally ideological: ideology, perhaps before it is anything else, is a matter of culture. The cultural stuff concerned is not, what is more, just a matter of élite culture, of culture with a capital 'C'. It is also inescapably a matter of everyday banal social reality. At least in part, the ordinariness of life fuels the extra-ordinariness of collective mobilization and conflict.

Another theme has been implicit in my approach to the comparative discussions of Northern Ireland, Wales and Denmark. I have leaned heavily on history, albeit an amateur's history, dependent upon secondary sources and commentaries, in order to understand these places. A historical perspective is vital if we are to understand the differences between ethnicity and 'race', or between different nationalist impulses. And without taking the long view we can only take the cultural stuff somewhat for granted. The here-and-now of the ethnographic present that is rightly so beloved by anthropologists is – and must remain – a basic datum of our theorizing and exploration. History, however, must be the other.

These issues and themes come together in the recognition that, although ethnic identity is socially constructed, it is not infinitely variable, malleable or negotiable. It may be deeply founded in the more than half forgotten experiences of primary socialization. It is constrained and shaped by its necessary dependence upon the categorization of Others. Its potential is always an immanent emergent property of its cultural content and history. And it all depends upon how much it matters – in terms of costs and benefits if nothing else – to those whose everyday lives are its making, remaking and unmaking.

That there are limits to the plasticity of ethnicity, as well as to its fixity and solidity, is the founding premise for the development of an under-standing of ethnicity which permits us to appreciate that although it is imagined it is not imaginary; to acknowledge its antiquity as well as its modernity. Rethinking demands that we should strike a balanced view of the authenticity of ethnic attachments. Somewhere between irresistible emotion and utter cynicism, neither blindly primordial nor completely manipulable, ethnicity and its allotropes are principles of collective identification and social organization in terms of culture and history, similarity and difference, that show little signs of withering away. In itself this is neither a 'good thing' nor a 'bad thing'. It is probably just very human. It is hard to imagine the social world in their absence.

Notes

Chapter 2 From Tribes to Ethnic Groups

1. For further argument on whether the Nuer are really the Dinka (and vice versa), see the correspondence pages of *Man* (N.S.) 8 (1973), and Burton (1981), Southall (1976).

2. I have placed the word 'race' in inverted commas to signify that it is a contested concept, whose meaning may not be taken for granted. In my own usage it refers simply to folk 'racial' categorization, and no other meaning should be presumed for it.

3. It is moot whether 'ethnic set' – a broad social field within which ethnic categories are significant classificatory and organizational themes – should actually be included in Handelman's typology.

4. For a discussion of local Hutu–Tutsi 'racial' classifications in Rwanda, see Maquet (1972). See also Banks (1996: 164–5) and de Waal (1994) for discussions of more recent, and more anthropologically troubling, aspects of this conflict.

5. The work of Bruce Kapferer (1988) is particularly relevant to the topic under discussion.

Chapter 3 Myths of Pluralism

1. Gluckman, of course, owed much to Coser and Simmel.

2. And not just by anthropologists: see Saggar (1996).

3. Among the major sources for this discussion, Volumes 2–5 of the *Glamorgan County History* (Cardiff: University of Wales Press, various dates) stand out, for those who want to follow up in great detail, and with respect to only one part of the region, many of the points made in the first half of this section. John Davies's single-volume history of Wales (1993) is indispensable. See Rees (1990) for a political argument which complements in some respects my discussion here. The interested reader can also consult the collection to which the original paper upon which this section is based formed the tailpiece (Jenkins and Edwards 1990).

4. This is a reference to Gwyn Alf Williams's *When Was Wales?* (1985) and his thesis that Wales only existed as a nation between the collapse of the Roman Empire and the emergence, as part of the imperialist project, of the British nation.

Chapter 4 Ethnicity etcetera

1. This can, for example, be seen in the pages of the Royal Anthropological Institute's magazine *Anthropology Today*. Recent articles which deal with conflict of a range of types include Danforth 1993; Desjarlais and Kleinman 1994; de Waal 1994. The, mainly anthropological, contributions to *Identities*, a new journal edited in the United States, also illustrate the developing engagement of the discipline with change and conflict.

2. Among other such conceits are the notions that childhood was unknown in earlier times, or that reflexive self-identity is a distinctively modern phenomenon.

Chapter 7   Majority Ethnicity

1. This in itself may seem to be an odd choice of words: haven't Protestants, after all, always been a minority within Ireland? I am, however, referring here to the fact that until the Reformation, the Irish and their conquerors were adherents to the same universal Catholicism.

2. Although it is valid enough, this is of course the kind of generalization to which one has to resort in a short discussion, and there is considerable variation in this pattern.

3. I have summarized the debate about the extent and impact of discrimination in the decades leading up to the 'troubles' elsewhere (Jenkins 1988: 318–19).

4. Among the 'other things' to which I am referring, the Protestant sense of the legitimacy of their own loyalist political violence was undermined, as it was taken outside the law by paramilitary organizations, and, particularly, as it was manifest in the bloodthirsty assassination campaigns of the 1970s.

5. Lest I am even further misunderstood, to say this is not to join Allen Feldman, for example, in objectivizing murder; in reducing extreme violence and death to acts of communication: 'Stiffing [murder] is a graphic act, and the stiff is a political text whose original script of ethnic-spatial symmetry has been effaced by wounding and death. The corpse, its blood, its wounds are quasi-organic signs of a tactile and political contiguity with the other' (Feldman 1991: 78).

Chapter 8   The Cultural Stuff

1. Reported in the *Guardian*, 28 July 1984.

Chapter 9   Violence, Language and Politics

1. Reported, for example, in the *Guardian*, 17 September 1990.

2. This claim was made in a BBC Cymru-Wales documentary in the *Week In – Week Out* series broadcast on 25 May 1993, on the basis of an opinion poll undertaken for the programme by Beaufort Research, Cardiff, in the counties of Dyfed and Gwynedd. I am grateful to both these organizations for making available to me the survey findings.

3. The utter idealism of Kedourie is perhaps most delightfully summed up in his characterization (1985: 147) of Gellner's argument as 'similar to Marxism'.

4. I recognize that is a major oversimplification of a complex picture, historically and today: see, for example, Ennew (1980).

5. The discussion also suggests that, whatever the cultural and linguistic similarities which exist between the Celtic peoples of the European maritime periphery, their different histories of incorporation into the relevant metropolitan nation-states (i.e. the UK and France) will discourage the emergence of the pan-Celtic nationalist movement proposed by Berresford Ellis (1985).

Chapter 10   Nations, Nationalisms

1. Another way of putting this – and arguably a better one – might be to suggest that our notions of where modernity starts might require some revision (along with our ideas about the medieval). So also might our concepts of 'the state'.

2. For what that alternative might be, see D.E. Thomas (1991).

3. Albeit minus the three Ulster counties of Donegal, Monaghan and Cavan which, in reflection of the demography of ethnicity (and political loyalties), became part of the Free State.

4. Apart from sectarian riots, there were two minor northern campaigns by the Irish

Republican Army, a clandestine nationalist organization, illegal on both sides of the border, during the Second World War and in the 1950s (Bardon 1992: 581–6, 604–12).

5. National movements are defined as: 'the efforts of ethnonational groups which cannot be identified with the state to restructure or reshape existing state arrangements' (Elklit and Tonsgaard 1992: 83). Although this is, as the authors admit, a restrictive definition, it is probably less so than Gellner's.

6. In this context, one wonders what the basis might be for Mann's confident assertion about the European Union that, 'the polls show that negative national stereotypes have almost vanished' (1993: 131).

7. An image which has also been used by Tom Nairn (1981: 329–63).

Sources and Acknowledgements

This book derives to a greater or lesser extent from pieces which have been written over a period of more than twelve years. I have accumulated along the way too many debts of gratitude to those who have read and commented on my work to mention them individually in a context such as this. They have all been thanked in the original publications and those thanks remain on record and heartfelt. I am grateful to the editors, publishers and learned societies concerned, for their support in the past, and, where appropriate, their permission to draw upon – for nothing has simply been reprinted – the following pieces. The italics in parentheses after each piece indicate the chapter or chapters in this book where its remains now lie buried:

'Ethnicity and the rise of capitalism in Ulster', in R. Ward and R. Jenkins (eds.), *Ethnic Communities in Business: Strategies for Economic Survival*, Cambridge: Cambridge University Press, 1984, pp. 57–72 [*7*].

'Northern Ireland: in what sense "religions" in conflict?', in R. Jenkins, H. Donnan and G. McFarlane, *The Sectarian Divide in Northern Ireland Today* (Royal Anthropological Institute Occasional Paper No. 41), London, Royal Anthropological Institute, 1986, pp. 1–21 [*8*].

'Social anthropological models of inter-ethnic relations', in J. Rex and D. Mason (eds.), *Theories of Race and Ethnic Relations*, Cambridge, Cambridge University Press, 1986, pp. 170–86 [*2, 3*].

'International perspectives', in R. Jenkins and A. Edwards (eds.), *One Step Forward? South and West Wales towards the Year 2000*, Llandysul: Gwasg Gomer, 1990, pp. 151–60; Swansea, Social Science Research Institute [*3*].

'Violence, language and politics: nationalism in Northern Ireland and Wales', *North Atlantic Studies*, 3 (1), Autumn 1991, pp. 31–40; Aarhus, Centre for North Atlantic Studies [*9*].

'Rethinking ethnicity: identity, categorization and power', *Ethnic and Racial Studies*, 17 (1994), pp. 197–223 [*5*].

'Nations and nationalisms: towards more open models', *Nations and Nationalism*, vol. 1 (1995), pp. 369–90; London, Association for the Study of Ethnicity and Nationalism [*10*].

'"Us" and "them": ethnicity, racism and ideology', in R. Barot (ed.), *The Racism Problematic: Contemporary Sociological Theories on Race and Ethnicity*, Lampeter: Edwin Mellon Press, 1996, pp. 69–88 [*6*].

'Ethnicity etcetera: anthropological points of view', *Ethnic and Racial Studies*, 19 (1996), pp. 807–22 [*1, 4*].

Bibliography

ADAM, H. 1972. *Modernizing Racial Domination*, Berkeley: University of California Press

ADAM, H. and GILIOMEE, H. 1979. *Ethnic Power Mobilized: Can South Africa Change?*, New Haven: Yale University Press

ADRIANSEN, I. 1992. 'Dansk og tysk spejlet i hinanden', in U. Østergård (ed.), *Dansk Identitet?*, Århus: Aarhus Universitetsforlag

AHMED, A. and SHORE, C. 1995. 'Introduction: Is Anthropology Relevant to the Contemporary World?' in A. Ahmed and C. Shore (eds.), *The Future of Anthropology: Its Relevance to the Contemporary World*, London: Athlone

AKENSON, D.H. 1973. *Education and Enmity: The Control of Schooling in Northern Ireland 1920–50*, Newton Abbot: David and Charles

ALTER, P. 1989. *Nationalism*, London: Edward Arnold

ANDERSON, B. 1983. *Imagined Communities: Reflections on the Origin and Spread of Nationalism*, London: Verso

ANDERSON, E. 1978. *A Place on the Corner*, Chicago: University of Chicago Press

ANTHIAS, F. 1992. 'Connecting "race" and ethnic phenomena', *Sociology*, 26, pp. 421–38

BAKER, S.E. 1973. 'Orange and Green Belfast: Belfast, 1832–1912', in H.J. Dyos and M. Wolff (eds.), *The Victorian City: Images and Reality*, London: Routledge and Kegan Paul

BALIBAR, E. 1991. 'Racism and nationalism', in E. Balibar and E. Wallerstein, *Race, Nation, Class: Ambiguous Identities*, London: Verso

BANKS, M. 1996. *Anthropological Constructions of Ethnicity: An Introductory Guide*, London: Routledge

BANTON, M. 1967. *Race Relations*, London: Tavistock

BANTON, M. 1983. *Racial and Ethnic Competition*, Cambridge: Cambridge University Press

BANTON, M. 1986. 'Epistemological assumptions in the study of racial differentiation', in J. Rex and D. Mason (eds.), *Theories of Race and Ethnic Relations*, Cambridge: Cambridge University Press

BANTON, M. 1987. *Racial Theories*, Cambridge: Cambridge University Press

BANTON, M. 1988. *Racial Consciousness*, London: Longman

BARDON, J. 1992. *A History of Ulster*, Belfast: Blackstaff

BARKER, M. 1981. *The New Racism: Conservatives and the Ideology of the Tribe*, London: Junction

BARNES, J.A. 1954. 'Class and committees in a Norwegian island parish', *Human Relations*, 7, pp. 39–58

BARTH, F. 1959. *Political Leadership among Swat Pathans*, London: Athlone

BARTH, F. 1966. *Models of Social Organization* (Occasional Paper No. 23), London: Royal Anthropological Institute

BARTH, F. 1969a. 'Introduction', in Barth 1969b

BARTH, F. (ed.) 1969b. *Ethnic Groups and Boundaries: The Social Organization of Culture Difference*, Oslo: Universitetsforlaget

BARTH, F. 1981. *Process and Form in Social Life: Collected Essays of Fredrik Barth, vol. 1*, London: Routledge and Kegan Paul

BARTH, F. 1984. 'Problems in conceptualizing cultural pluralism, with illustrations from Sohar, Oman', in D. Maybury-Lewis (ed.), *The Prospects for Plural Societies*, Proceedings, American Ethnological Society, Washington, DC

BARTH, F. 1989. 'The analysis of culture in complex societies', *Ethnos*, 54, pp. 120–42

BARTH, F. 1994. 'Enduring and emerging issues in the analysis of ethnicity', in H. Vermeulen and C. Govers (eds.), *The Anthropology of Ethnicity: Beyond 'Ethnic Groups and Boundaries'*, Amsterdam: het Spinhuis

BATLEY, R. 1981. 'The politics of administrative allocation', in R. Forrest, J. Henderson and P. Williams (eds.), *Urban Political Economy and Social Theory*, Aldershot: Gower

BAUMAN, Z. 1989. *Modernity and the Holocaust*, Cambridge: Polity

BAUMAN, Z. 1990. *Thinking Sociologically*, Oxford: Basil Blackwell

BAUMAN, Z. 1992. 'Soil, blood and identity', *Sociological Review*, 40, pp. 675–701

BAX, M. 1976. *Harpstrings and Confessions: Machine-Style Politics in the Irish Republic*, Assen: van Gorcum

BECHER, T. 1989. *Academic Tribes and Territories: Intellectual Enquiry and the Cultures of Disciplines*, Milton Keynes: Open University Press

BECKER, H.S. 1963. *Outsiders: Studies in the Sociology of Deviance*, New York: Free Press

BECKETT, J.C. 1966. *The Making of Modern Ireland, 1603–1923*, London: Faber and Faber

BECKETT, J.C. 1973. 'Introduction', in W.H. Crawford and B. Trainor (eds.), *Aspects of Irish Social History, 1750–1800*, Belfast: HMSO

BENEDICT, R. 1983. *Race and Racism*, London: Routledge and Kegan Paul [first published 1942]

BENTLEY, G.C. 1987. 'Ethnicity and practice', *Comparative Studies in Society and History*, 29 (1), pp. 24–55

BERRESFORD ELLIS, P. 1985. *The Celtic Revolution: A Study in Anti Imperialism*, Talybont: Y. Lolfa

BEW, P., GIBBON, P. and PATTERSON, H. 1979. *The State in Northern Ireland 1921–1972*, Manchester: Manchester University Press

BHAT, A., CARR-HILL, R., OHRI, S., THE RADICAL STATISTICS RACE GROUP, 1988. *Britain's Black Population: A New Perspective*, 2nd edn, Aldershot: Gower

BILLIG, M. 1995. *Banal Nationalism*, London: Sage

BLAKEY, M.L., DUBINSKAS, F., FORMAN, S., MacLENNAN, C., NEWMAN, K.S., PEACOCK, J.L., RAPPAPORT, R., VÉLEZ-IBANEZ, C.G., and WOLFE, A.W. 1994. 'A Statement to the profession', in S. Forman (ed.), *Diagnosing America: Anthropology and Public Engagement*, Ann Arbor: University of Michigan Press

BOAS, F. 1940. *Race, Language and Culture*, New York: Free Press

BOISSEVAIN, J. 1968. 'The place of non-groups in the social sciences', *Man*, 3, pp. 542–56

BOLLOM, C. 1978. 'Attitudes towards second homes in rural Wales', in G. Williams (ed.) *Social and Cultural Change in Contemporary Wales*, London: Routledge and Kegan Paul

BOON, J.A. 1982. *Other Tribes, Other Scribes: Symbolic Anthropology in the Comparative Study of Cultures, Histories, Religions and Texts*, Cambridge: Cambridge University Press

BORISH, S.M. 1991. *The Land of the Living: The Danish Folk High Schools and Denmark's Non-violent Path to Modernization*, Nevada City: Blue Dolphin

BORLAND, J., FEVRE, R. and DENNEY, D. 1992. 'Nationalism and community in North West Wales', *Sociological Review*, 40, pp. 49–72

BORNEMAN, J. 1992. *Belonging in the Two Berlins: Kin, State, Nation*, Cambridge: Cambridge University Press

BOURDIEU, P. 1977. *Outline of a Theory of Practice*, Cambridge: Cambridge University Press

BOURDIEU, P. 1990. *The Logic of Practice*, Cambridge: Polity

BOURNE, J. and SIVANANDAN, A. 1980. 'Cheerleaders and ombudsmen: the sociology of race relations in Britain', *Race and Class*, 21 (4), pp. 331–52

BOWIE, F. 1993. 'Wales from within: conflicting interpretations of Welsh identity', in S. Macdonald (ed.), *Inside European Identities*, Oxford: Berg

BOYCE, D.G. 1991. *Nationalism in Ireland*, 2nd edn, London: Routledge

BOYD, A. 1969. *Holy War in Belfast: A History of the Troubles in Ireland*, Tralee: Anvil

BREUILLY, J. 1985. *Nationalism and the State*, amended edn, Manchester: Manchester University Press

BRODY, H. 1986. *Maps and Dreams: Indians and the British Columbia Frontier*, 2nd edn, London: Faber and Faber

BROWN, R.M. 1975. *Strain of Violence: Historical Studies of American Violence and Vigilantism*, New York: Oxford University Press

BRUCE, S. 1986. *God Save Ulster! The Religion and Politics of Paisleyism*, Oxford: Clarendon Press

BRUCE, S. 1992. *The Red Hand: Protestant Paramilitaries in Northern Ireland*, Oxford: Oxford University Press

BRUCE, S. 1994. *The Edge of the Union: The Ulster Loyalist Political Vision*, Oxford: Oxford University Press

BRUCE, S. and ALDERDICE, F. 1993. 'Religious belief and behaviour', in P. Stringer and G. Robinson (eds.), *Social Attitudes in Northern Ireland: The Third Report*, Belfast: Blackstaff

BRYSON, L. and McCARTNEY, C. 1994. *Clashing Symbols: A Report on the Use of Flags, Anthems and Other National Symbols in Northern Ireland*, Belfast: Institute of Irish Studies

BUCKLAND, P. 1980. *James Craig*, Dublin: Gill and Macmillan

BUCKLEY, A.D. 1982. *A Gentle People: A Study of a Peaceful Community*, Cultra, Co. Down: Ulster Folk and Transport Museum

BUCKLEY, A.D. 1989. '"We're trying to find our identity": uses of history among Ulster Protestants', in E. Tonkin, M. McDonald and M. Chapman (eds.), *History and Ethnicity*, London: Routledge

BUCKLEY, A.D. and KENNY, M.C. 1995. *Negotiating Identity: Rhetoric, Metaphor and Social Drama in Northern Ireland*, Washington, DC: Smithsonian Institution Press

BUFWACK, M.S. 1982. *Village without Violence*, Cambridge, MA: Schenkman

BURLEIGH, M. and WIPPERMANN, W. 1991. *The Racial State: Germany 1933–1945*, Cambridge: Cambridge University Press

BURTON, F. 1978. *The Politics of Legitimacy: Struggles in a Belfast Community*, London: Routledge and Kegan Paul

BURTON, J.W. 1981. 'Ethnicity on the hoof: on the economics of Nuer identity', *Ethnology*, 20, pp. 157–62

CAIRNS, E. 1992. 'Political violence, social values and the generation gap', in P. Stringer and G. Robinson (eds.), *Social Attitudes in Northern Ireland: The Second Report*, Belfast: Blackstaff

CARRITHERS, M. 1992. *Why Humans Have Cultures: Explaining Anthropology and Social Diversity*, Oxford: Oxford University Press

CECIL, R. 1993. 'The marching season in Northern Ireland: an expression of politico-religious identity', in S. Macdonald (ed.), *Inside European Identities*, Oxford: Berg

CHARLES, N. 1990. 'Women – advancing or retreating?', in R. Jenkins and A. Edwards (eds.), *One Step Forward? South and West Wales towards the Year 2000*, Llandysul: Gwasg Gomer

CHRISTENSEN, J.G. 1994. 'Sprog og kultur i europæisk integration', in J. Liep and K. Fog Olwig (eds.), *Komplekse liv: kulturel mangfoldighed i Danmark*, Copenhagen: Akademisk Forlag

CICOUREL, A.V. and KITSUSE, J.I. 1963. *The Educational Decision Makers*, Indianapolis: Bobbs-Merrill

CLARKE, D.M. 1984. *Church and State: Essays in Political Philosophy*, Cork: Cork University Press

CLEWS, R. 1980. *To Dream of Freedom: The Struggle of M.A.C. and the Free Wales Army*, Talybont: Y Lolfa

CLIFFORD, J. and MARCUS, G.E. (eds.) 1986. *Writing Culture: The Poetics and Politics of Ethnography*, Berkeley: University of California Press

COAKLEY, J. 1990. 'Typical case or deviant? Nationalism in Ireland in a European perspective', in M. Hill and S. Barber (eds.), *Aspects of Irish Studies*, Belfast: Institute of Irish Studies

COE, W.E. 1969. *The Engineering Industry in the North of Ireland*, Newton Abbot: David and Charles

COHEN, A. 1974. 'Introduction: the lesson of ethnicity', in A. Cohen (ed.), *Urban Ethnicity*, London: Tavistock

COHEN, A.P. (ed.) 1982. *Belonging: Identity and Social Organisation in British Rural Cultures*, Manchester: Manchester University Press

COHEN, A.P. 1985. *The Symbolic Construction of Community*, London: Ellis Harwood/ Tavistock

COHEN, A.P. (ed.) 1986. *Symbolising Boundaries: Identity and Diversity in British Cultures*, Manchester: Manchester University Press

COHEN, A.P. 1992. 'Self-conscious anthropology', in J. Okely and H. Callaway (eds.), *Anthropology and Autobiography*, London: Routledge

COHEN, A.P. 1994. *Self Consciousness: An Alternative Anthropology of Identity*, London: Routledge

COHEN, R. 1978. 'Ethnicity: problem and focus in anthropology', *Annual Review of Anthropology*, 7, pp. 379–403

COHEN, Y.A. 1969. 'Social boundary systems', *Current Anthropology*, 10, pp. 103–26

COLLEY, L. 1992. *Britons: Forging the Nation 1707–1837*, New Haven: Yale University Press

COLLMANN, J. and HANDELMAN, D. (eds.) 1981. 'Administrative frameworks and clients', special issue of *Social Analysis* (9), *passim*.

COLSON, E. 1953. *The Makah Indians: A Study of an Indian Tribe in Modern American Society*, Manchester: Manchester University Press

COMAROFF, J. and COMAROFF, J. 1992. *Ethnography and the Historical Imagination*, Boulder, CO: Westview Press

CONNOLLY, S.J. 1992. *Religion, Law and Power: The Making of Protestant Ireland 1660–1760*, Oxford: Clarendon Press

CONNOR, W. 1978. 'A nation is a nation, is a state, is an ethnic group, is a . . .', *Ethnic and Racial Studies*, 1, pp. 378–400

CONNOR, W. 1993. 'Beyond reason: the nature of the ethnonational bond', *Ethnic and Racial Studies*, 16, pp. 373–98

CORMACK, R.J. and OSBORNE, R.D. (eds.) 1983. *Religion, Education and Employment: Aspects of Equal Opportunity in Northern Ireland*, Belfast: Appletree Press

CORMACK, R.J. and OSBORNE, R.D. (eds.) 1991. *Discrimination and Public Policy in Northern Ireland*, Oxford: Clarendon Press

CORNELL, S. 1996. 'The variable ties that bind: content and circumstances in ethnic processes', *Ethnic and Racial Studies*, 19, pp. 265–89

COUPLAND, N. AND BALL, M.J. 1989, 'Welsh and English in contemporary Wales: sociolinguistic issues', *Contemporary Wales*, 3, pp. 7–40

CRAWFORD, W.H. 1972. *Domestic Industry in Ireland: The Experience of the Linen Industry*, Dublin: Gill and Macmillan

CRAWFORD, W.H. and TRAINOR, B. (eds.) 1973. *Aspects of Irish Social History, 1750–1800*, Belfast: HMSO

CROTTY, R.D. 1966. *Irish Agricultural Production*, Cork: Cork University Press

CULLEN, L.M. 1969. 'The Irish economy in the eighteenth century', in L.M. Cullen (ed.), *The Formation of the Irish Economy*, Cork: Mercier

DANFORTH, L.M. 1993. 'Claims to Macedonian identity: the Macedonian question and the break-up of Yugoslavia', *Anthropology Today*, 9 (4), pp. 3–10

DAVIES, C. 1973. 'Cymdeithas yr Iaith Gymraeg', in M. Stephens (ed.), *The Welsh Language Today*, Llandysul: Gwasg Gomer

DAVIES, C. 1990. *Ethnic Humor Around the World: A Comparative Analysis*, Bloomington: Indiana University Press

DAVIES, C.A. 1989. *Welsh Nationalism in the Twentieth Century: The Ethnic Option and the Modern State*, New York: Praeger

DAVIES, C.A. 1990. 'Language and nation', in R. Jenkins and A. Edwards (eds.), *One Step Forward? South and West Wales towards the Year 2000*, Llandysul: Gwasg Gomer

DAVIES, J. 1993. *A History of Wales*, Harmondsworth: Penguin (Welsh language edn, 1990: *Hanes Cymru*, Allen Lane The Penguin Press)

DAVIS, J. 1975. 'Beyond the hyphen: some notes and documents on community–state relations in South Italy', in J. Boissevain and J. Friedl (eds.), *Beyond the Community*, The Hague: Ministry of Education and Science

DAY, G. 1989. '"A million on the move"?: population change and rural Wales', *Contemporary Wales*, 3, pp. 137–59

DAY, G. and REES, G. (eds.) 1989. *Contemporary Wales*, vol. 3, special issue devoted to linguistic and cultural change

DENNEY, D., BORLAND, J. and FEVRE, R. 1991. 'The social construction of nationalism: racism and conflict in Wales', *Contemporary Wales*, 4, pp. 149–65

DEPARTMENT OF MANPOWER SERVICES 1974. *Industrial Relations in Northern Ireland: Report of a Review Body 1971–74*, Belfast: HMSO

DEPARTMENT OF MANPOWER SERVICES 1979. *Northern Ireland Labour Market: A Guide in Graphs and Charts*, Belfast: DMS

DESJARLAIS, R. and KLEINMAN, A. 1994. 'Violence and demoralization in the new world disorder', *Anthropology Today*, 10 (5), pp. 9–12

De WAAL, A. 1994. 'Genocide in Rwanda', *Anthropology Today*, 10 (3), pp. 1–2

DIKÖTTER, F. 1992. *The Discourse of Race in Modern China*, London: Hurst

DILLON, M. and LEHANE, D. 1973. *Political Murder in Northern Ireland*, Harmondsworth: Penguin

DOLLARD, J. 1957. *Caste and Class in a Southern Town*, 3rd edn, New York: Doubleday

DONNAN, H. and McFARLANE, G. 1983. 'Informal social organisation', in J. Darby (ed.), *Northern Ireland: The Background to the Conflict*, Belfast: Appletree Press

DOORNBOS, M. 1991. 'Linking the future to the past: ethnicity and pluralism', *Review of African Political Economy*, 52, pp. 53–65

DOUGLAS, M. 1975. *Implicit Meanings: Essays in Anthropology*, London: Routledge and Kegan Paul

DRUCKER, H.M. and BROWN, G. 1980. *The Politics of Nationalism and Devolution*, London: Longman

DUARA, P. 1993. 'De-constructing the Chinese nation', *Australian Journal of Chinese Affairs*, 30, pp. 1–26

DUNN, J. 1988. *The Beginnings of Social Understanding*, Oxford: Basil Blackwell

EASTHOPE, G. 1976. 'Religious war in Northern Ireland', *Sociology*, 10, pp. 427–50

EIDHEIM, H. 1969. 'When ethnic identity is a social stigma', in F. Barth (ed.), *Ethnic Groups and Boundaries*, Oslo: Universitetsforlaget

ELKLIT, J. and TONSGAARD, O. 1992. 'The absence of nationalist movements: the case of the Nordic area', in J. Coakley (ed.), *The Social Origins of Nationalist Movements: The West European Experience*, London: Sage

ELLER, J.D. and COUGHLAN, R.M. 1993. 'The poverty of primordialism: the demystification of ethnic attachments', *Ethnic and Racial Studies*, 16 (2), pp. 185–202

ENNEW, J. 1980. *The Western Isles Today*, Cambridge: Cambridge University Press

ENOCH, Y. 1994. 'The intolerance of a tolerant people: ethnic relations in Denmark', *Ethnic and Racial Studies*, 17, pp. 282–300

EPSTEIN, A.L. (ed.) 1967. *The Craft of Social Anthropology*, London: Tavistock

EPSTEIN, A.L. 1978. *Ethos and Identity: Three Studies in Ethnicity*, London: Tavistock

ERICKSON, F. 1976. 'Gatekeeping encounters: a social selection process', in P.R. Sanday (ed.), *Anthropology and the Public Interest*, New York: Academic Press

ERIKSEN, T.H. 1991. 'The cultural contexts of ethnic differences', *Man*, 26, pp. 127–44

ERIKSEN, T.H. 1993a. *Ethnicity and Nationalism: Anthropological Perspectives*, London: Pluto

ERIKSEN, T.H. 1993b. 'Formal and informal nationalism', *Ethnic and Racial Studies*, 16, pp. 1–25

ERIKSEN, T.H. 1993c. 'A future-oriented, non-ethnic nationalism? Mauritius as an exemplary case', *Ethnos*, 58, pp. 197–221

EVANS, G. 1973. *Non-violent Nationalism*, New Malden: Fellowship of Reconciliation

EVANS-PRITCHARD, E.E. 1940. *The Nuer*, Oxford: Clarendon Press

EVENS, T.M.S. 1977. 'The predication of the individual in anthropological interactionism', *American Ethnologist*, 79, pp. 579–97

FARRELL, M. 1976. *Northern Ireland: The Orange State*, London: Pluto

FELDMAN, A. 1991. *Formations of Violence: The Narratives of the Body and Political Terror in Northern Ireland*, Chicago: University of Chicago Press

FINLAYSON, A. 1996. 'Nationalism as an ideological interpellation: the case of Ulster Loyalism', *Ethnic and Racial Studies*, 19, pp. 88–112

FIRTH, R. 1958. *Human Types: An Introduction to Social Anthropology*, New York: Mentor

FIRTH, R. 1961. *Elements of Social Organization*, 3rd edn, London: Watts

FLETT, H. 1979. 'Bureaucracy and ethnicity: notions of eligibility to public housing', in S. Wallman (ed.), *Ethnicity at Work*, London: Macmillan

FORMAN, S. (ed.) 1994. *Diagnosing America: Anthropology and Public Engagement*, Ann Arbor: University of Michigan Press

FOUCAULT, M. 1979. *Discipline and Punish: The Birth of the Prison*, Harmondsworth: Peregrine

FRANK, A.G. and GILLS, B.K. (eds.) 1993. *The World System: Five Hundred Years or Five Thousand?*, London: Routledge

FRIEDMAN, J. 1990. 'Being in the world: globalization and localization', in M. Featherstone (ed.), *Global Culture: Nationalism, Globalization and Modernity*, London: Sage

FRIEDMAN, J. 1994. *Cultural Identity and Global Process*, London: Sage

FULTON, J. 1991. *The Tragedy of Belief: Division, Politics, and Religion in Ireland*, Oxford: Clarendon Press

FURNIVALL, J.S. 1948. *Colonial Policy and Practice*, Cambridge: Cambridge University Press

GALLAGHER, A.M. and DUNN, S. 1991. 'Community relations in Northern Ireland: attitudes to contact and integration', in P. Stringer and G. Robinson (eds.), *Social Attitudes in Northern Ireland: 1990–91 Edition*, Belfast: Blackstaff

GEERTZ, C. 1973. *The Interpretation of Cultures*, New York: Basic Books

GELLNER, E. 1983. *Nations and Nationalism*, Oxford: Basil Blackwell

GERHOLM, L. and GERHOLM, T. 1990. 'The cultural study of Scandinavia: where are the frontiers?', *Anthropological Journal on European Cultures*, 1 (1), pp. 83–108

GIBBON, P. 1975. *The Origins of Ulster Unionism*, Manchester: Manchester University Press

GIDDENS, A. 1979. *Central Problems in Social Theory: Action, Structure and Contradiction in Social Analysis*, London: Macmillan

GIDDENS, A. 1984. *The Constitution of Society*, Cambridge: Polity

GIDDENS, A. 1985. *The Nation-State and Violence*, Cambridge: Polity

GIDDENS, A. 1991. *Modernity and Self-Identity: Self and Society in the Late Modern Age*, Cambridge: Polity

GIGGS, J. and PATTIE, C. 1992. 'Wales as a plural society', *Contemporary Wales*, 5, pp. 25–63

GILES, H. and TAYLOR, D.M. 1978. 'National identity in south Wales: some preliminary data', in G. Williams (ed.), *Social and Cultural Change in Contemporary Wales*, London: Routledge and Kegan Paul

GILL, O. 1925. *The Rise of the Irish Linen Industry*, Oxford: Oxford University Press

GLASSIE, H. 1982. *Passing the Time in Ballymenone*, Philadelphia: University of Pennsylvania Press

GLICKMAN, M. 1972. 'The Nuer and the Dinka: a further note', *Man*, 7, pp. 586–94

GLUCKMAN, M. 1956. *Custom and Conflict in Africa*, Oxford: Basil Blackwell

GLUCKMAN, M. 1965. *Politics, Law and Ritual in Tribal Society*, Oxford: Basil Blackwell

GOFFMAN, E. 1969. *The Presentation of Self in Everyday Life*, London: Allen Lane

GOFFMAN, E. 1983. 'The interaction order', *American Sociological Review*, 48, pp. 1–17

GOODMAN, M.E. 1964. *Race Awareness in Young Children*, rev. edn, New York: Collier

GOODY, J. 1977. *The Domestication of the Savage Mind*, Cambridge: Cambridge University Press

GOUDSBLOM, J. 1967. *Dutch Society*, New York: Random House

GRAY, J. 1985. *City in Revolt: James Larkin and the Belfast Dock Strike of 1907*, Belfast: Blackstaff

GRILLO, R.D. 1980. 'Introduction', in R.D. Grillo (ed.), *'Nation' and 'State' in Europe: Anthropological Perspectives*, London: Academic Press

GRILLO, R.D. 1985. *Ideologies and Institutions in Urban France: The Representation of Immigrants*, Cambridge: Cambridge University Press

GRIMSHAW, A. and HART, K. 1995. 'The rise and fall of scientific ethnography', in A. Ahmed and C. Shore (eds.), *The Future of Anthropology: Its Relevance to the Contemporary World*, London: Athlone

GROSBY, S. 1995. 'Territoriality: the transcendental, primordial feature of modern societies', *Nations and Nationalism*, 1, pp. 143–62

GULLESTAD, M. 1989. 'Small facts and large issues: the anthropology of contemporary Scandinavian society', *Annual Review of Anthropology*, 18, pp. 71–93

HAGENDOORN, L. 1993. 'Ethnic categorization and outgroup exclusion: cultural values and social stereotypes in the construction of ethnic hierarchies', *Ethnic and Racial Studies*, 16, pp. 27–51

HALL, J.A. 1993. 'Nationalisms: classified and explained', *Daedalus*, 122 (3), pp. 1–28

HALL, S. 1990. 'Cultural identity and diaspora', in J. Rutherford (ed.), *Identity: Community, Culture, Difference*, London: Lawrence and Wishart

HALL, S. 1991. 'The local and and the global: globalization and ethnicity', in Anthony D. King (ed.), *Culture, Globalization and the World-System*, London: Macmillan

HALL, S. 1992. 'Our mongrel selves', *New Statesman and Society*, supplement, 19 June, pp. 6–8

HALL, S., CRITCHER, C., JEFFERSON, T., CLARKE, J. and ROBERTS, B. 1978. *Policing the Crisis: Mugging, the State, and Law and Order*, London: Macmillan

HAMILTON, A., McCARTNEY, C., ANDERSON, T. and FINN, A. 1990. *Violence and Communities: The Impact of Political Violence in Northern Ireland on Intra-community, Inter-community and Community–State Relationships*, Coleraine: Centre for the Study of Conflict, University of Ulster

HANDELMAN, D. 1977. 'The organization of ethnicity', *Ethnic Groups*, 1, pp. 187–200

HANNERZ, U. 1969. *Soulside: Inquiries into Ghetto Life and Culture*, New York: Columbia University Press

HANNERZ, U. 1990. 'Cosmopolitans and locals in world culture', in M. Featherstone (ed.), *Global Culture: Nationalism, Globalization and Modernity*, London: Sage

HANNERZ, U. 1992. *Cultural Complexity: Studies in the Social Organization of Meaning*, New York: Columbia University Press

HARBINSON, J.F. 1973. *The Ulster Unionist Party 1883–1973*, Belfast: Blackstaff

HARBSMEIER, M. 1986. 'Danmark: Nation, kultur og køn', *Stofskifte*, 13, pp. 47–73

HARDING, P. and JENKINS, R. 1989. *The Myth of the Hidden Economy: Towards a New Understanding of Informal Economic Activity*, Milton Keynes: Open University Press

HARRIS, C.C. 1990. 'Religion', in R. Jenkins and A. Edwards (eds.), *One Step Forward? South and West Wales towards the Year 2000*, Llandysul: Gwasg Gomer

HARRIS, R. 1972. *Prejudice and Tolerance in Ulster: 'Neighbours' and 'Strangers' in a Border Community*, Manchester: Manchester University Press

HECHTER, M. 1975. *Internal Colonialism: The Celtic Fringe in British National Development, 1536–1966*, London: Routledge and Kegan Paul

HECHTER, M. and LEVI, M. 1979. 'The comparative study of ethno-regional movements', *Ethnic and Racial Studies*, 2, pp. 260–74

HESKIN, K. 1980. *Northern Ireland: A Psychological Analysis*, Dublin: Gill and Macmillan

HEURLIN, B. (ed.) 1994. *Danmark og Den Europæisk Union*, Copenhagen: Forlaget Politiske Studier

HICKEY, J. 1984. *Religion and the Northern Ireland Problem*, Dublin: Gill and Macmillan

HILLYARD, P. and PERCY-SMITH, J. 1988. *The Coercive State: The Decline of Democracy in Britain*, London: Fontana

HINDLEY, R. 1990. *The Death of the Irish Language: A Qualified Obituary*, London: Routledge

HOBSBAWM, E.J. 1990. *Nations and Nationalism since 1780: Programme, Myth, Reality*, Cambridge: Cambridge University Press

HOBSBAWM, E.J. 1992. 'Ethnicity and nationalism in Europe today', *Anthropology Today*, 8 (1), pp. 3–8

HOBSBAWM, E.J. and RANGER, T. (eds.) 1983. *The Invention of Tradition*, Cambridge: Cambridge University Press

HOROWITZ, D.L. 1985. *Ethnic Groups in Conflict*, Berkeley: University of California Press

HOWE, L.E.A. 1985. 'The deserving and the undeserving: practice in an urban, local social security office', *Journal of Social Policy*, 14, pp. 49–72

HOWELL, D.L. 1994. 'Ainu ethnicity and the boundaries of the early modern Japanese state', *Past and Present*, 142, pp. 69–93

HOWELL, D.W. and BABER, C. 1990. 'Wales', in F.M.L. Thompson (ed.), *The Cambridge Social History of Britain 1750–1950, vol. I: Regions and Communities*, Cambridge: Cambridge University Press

HUGHES, E.C. 1994. *On Work, Race and the Sociological Imagination*, ed. L.A. Coser, Chicago: University of Chicago Press

HUTCHINSON, J. 1987. *The Dynamics of Cultural Nationalism: The Gaelic Revival and the Creation of the Irish Nation State*, London: Allen and Unwin

HUTCHINSON, J. 1994. *Modern Nationalism*, London: Fontana

HUTSON, J. 1990. 'Rural life', in R. Jenkins and A. Edwards (eds.), *One Step Forward? South and West Wales towards the Year 2000*, Llandysul: Gwasg Gomer

IRVINE, M. 1991. *Northern Ireland: Faith and Faction*, London: Routledge

JACKSON, A. (ed.) 1987. *Anthropology at Home*, London: Tavistock

JACOBSEN, H.S. 1986. *An Outline History of Denmark*, Copenhagen: Høs

JEDREJ, C. and NUTTALL, M. 1996. *White Settlers: The Impact of Rural Repopulation in Scotland*, Luxembourg: Harwood

JENKINS, R. 1982. *Hightown Rules: Growing up in a Belfast Housing Estate*, Leicester: National Youth Bureau

JENKINS, R. 1983. *Lads, Citizens and Ordinary Kids: Working-class Youth Life-styles in Belfast*, London: Routledge and Kegan Paul

JENKINS, R. 1984. 'Understanding Northern Ireland', *Sociology*, 19, pp. 253–64

JENKINS, R. 1986a. *Racism and Recruitment: Managers, Organisations and Equal Opportunity in the Labour Market*, Cambridge: Cambridge University Press

JENKINS, R. 1986b. 'Northern Ireland: in what sense "religions" in conflict?', in R. Jenkins, H. Donnan and G. McFarlane, *The Sectarian Divide in Northern Ireland Today* (Occasional Paper no. 41), London: Royal Anthropological Institute

JENKINS, R. 1987. 'Countering prejudice – anthropological and otherwise', *Anthropology Today*, 3 (2), pp. 3–4

JENKINS, R. 1988. 'Discrimination and equal opportunity in employment: ethnicity and "race" in the United Kingdom', in D. Gallie (ed.), *Employment in Britain*, Oxford: Basil Blackwell

JENKINS, R. 1996. *Social Identity*, London: Routledge

JENKINS, R. forthcoming. 'From criminology to anthropology: identity, normality, and morality in the social construction of deviance', in S. Holdaway and P. Rock (eds.), *The Social Theory of Modern Criminology*, London: UCL Press

JENKINS, R. and EDWARDS, A. (eds.) 1990. *One Step Forward? South and West Wales towards the Year 2000*, Llandysul: Gwasg Gomer

JONES, B. 1988. 'The development of Welsh territorial institutions: modernization theory revisited', *Contemporary Wales*, 2, pp. 47–61

JONES, D.G. 1973. 'The Welsh Language Movement', in M. Stephens (ed.), *The Welsh Language Today*, Llandysul: Gwasg Gomer

JONES, W.G. 1986. *Denmark: A Modern History*, London: Croom Helm

KAPFERER, B. (ed.) 1976. *Transaction and Meaning*, Philadelphia: ISHI

KAPFERER, B. 1988. *Legends of People, Myths of State: Violence, Intolerance and Political Culture in Sri Lanka and Australia*, Washington, DC: Smithsonian Institution Press

KARN, V. 1983. 'Race and housing in Britain: the role of the major institutions', in N. Glazer and K. Young (eds.), *Ethnic Pluralism and Public Policy: Achieving Equality in the United States and Britain*, London: Heinemann

KAYE, K. 1982. *The Mental and Social Life of Babies: How Parents Create Persons*, Brighton: Harvester

KEDOURIE, E. 1985. *Nationalism*, revised edn, London: Hutchinson

KUPER, A. 1988. *The Invention of Primitive Society: Transformations of an Illusion*, London: Routledge

KUPER, L. 1971. 'Political change in plural societies', *International Social Science Journal*, 23, pp. 594–607

KUPER, L. and SMITH, M.G. (eds.) 1969. *Pluralism in Africa*, Berkeley: University of California Press

LA FONTAINE, J. 1986. 'Countering racial prejudice: a better starting point', *Anthropology Today*, 2 (6), pp. 1–2

LAING, R.D. 1971. *Self and Others*, Harmondsworth: Pelican

LANE, C. 1981. *The Rites of Rulers: Ritual and Industrial Society – the Soviet Case*, Cambridge: Cambridge University Press

LARSEN, S.S. 1982. 'The Glorious Twelfth: the politics of legitimation in Kilbroney', in A.P. Cohen (ed.), *Belonging: Identity and Social Organisation in British Rural Cultures*, Manchester: Manchester University Press

LEACH, E. 1954. *Political Systems of Highland Burma: A Study of Kachin Social Structure*, London: Athlone

LEACH, E. 1961. *Rethinking Anthropology*, London: Athlone

LEE, R.M. 1981. 'Inter-religious courtship and marriage in Northern Ireland', PhD thesis, University of Edinburgh

LEE, S.M. 1993. 'Racial classifications in the US census: 1890–1990', *Ethnic and Racial Studies*, 16, pp. 75–94

LEMERT, E.M. 1972. *Human Deviance, Social Problems and Social Control*, 2nd edn, Englewood Cliffs, NJ: Prentice-Hall

LENTZ, C. 1994. '"They must be Dagaba first and any other thing second . . ." The colonial and post-colonial creation of ethnic identities in north-western Ghana', *African Studies*, 53 (2), pp. 57–91

LENTZ, C. 1995. '"Tribalism" and ethnicity in Africa: a review of four decades of anglophone research', *Cahiers des Sciences humaines*, 31 (2), pp. 303–28

LÉVI-STRAUSS, C. 1952. *The Race Question in Modern Science*, Paris: UNESCO

LIDDIARD, M. and HUTSON, S. 1991. 'Homeless young people and runaways – agency definitions and processes', *Journal of Social Policy*, 20, pp. 365–88

LIEBOW, E. 1967. *Tally's Corner: A Study of Negro Streetcorner Men*, Boston: Little, Brown

LINDE-LAURSEN, A. 1993. 'The nationalization of trivialities: how cleaning becomes an identity marker in the encounter of Swedes and Danes', *Ethnos*, 58 (3–4), pp. 275–93

LIPSKY, M. 1980. *Street-Level Bureaucracy: Dilemmas of the Individual in Public Services*, New York: Russell Sage Foundation

LLOBERA, J. 1994. *The God of Modernity: The Development of Nationalism in Western Europe*, Oxford: Berg

LOFTUS, B. 1994. *Mirrors: Orange and Green*, Dundrum: Picture Press

LYCK, L. 1992. 'Denmark and the Maastricht agreement: perspectives for Denmark, EC and Europe', in L. Lyck (ed.), *Denmark and EC Membership Evaluated*, London: Pinter

LYONS, F.S.L. 1973. *Ireland since the Famine*, London: Fontana

McALLISTER, I. 1982. 'The Devil, miracles and the afterlife: the political sociology of religion in Northern Ireland', *British Journal of Sociology*, 33, pp. 330–47

McFARLANE, W.G. 1979. '"Mixed" marriages in Ballycuan, Northern Ireland', *Journal of Comparative Family Studies*, 10, pp. 191–205

McFARLANE, W.G. 1986. '"It's not as simple as that": the expression of the Catholic and Protestant boundary in Northern Irish rural communities', in A.P. Cohen (ed.), *Symbolizing Boundaries: Identity and Diversity in British Culture*, Manchester: Manchester University Press

McKERNAN, J. 1982. 'Value systems and race relations in Northern Ireland and America', *Ethnic and Racial Studies*, 5, pp. 156–74

MacLEOD, J. 1987. *Ain't No Makin' It: Levelled Aspirations in a Low-Income Neighbourhood*, London: Tavistock

MAINWARING, L. 1990. 'The economy', in R. Jenkins and A. Edwards (eds.), *One Step Forward? South and West Wales towards the Year 2000*, Llandysul: Gwasg Gomer

MALINOWSKI, B. 1922. *Argonauts of the Western Pacific*, London: Kegan Paul, Trench, Trubner

MANN, M. 1993. 'Nation-states in Europe and other continents: diversifying, developing, not dying', *Daedalus*, 122 (3), pp. 115–40

MANNICHE, P. 1969. *Denmark: A Social Laboratory*, Oxford: Pergamon

MANSERGH, N. 1936. *The Government of Northern Ireland*, London: George Allen and Unwin

MAQUET, J. 1972. 'Inborn differences and the premise of inequality', in P. Baxter and B. Sansom (eds.), *Race and Social Difference*, Harmondsworth: Penguin

MARCUS, G. 1992. 'Past, present and emergent identities: requirements for ethnographies of late twentieth-century modernity', in S. Lash and J. Friedman (eds.), *Modernity and Identity*, Oxford: Basil Blackwell

MARCUS, G. and FISCHER, M.M.J. 1986. *Anthropology as Cultural Critique: An Experimental Moment in the Human Sciences*, Chicago: University of Chicago Press

MASON, D. 1994. 'On the dangers of disconnecting race and racism', *Sociology*, 28, pp. 845–58

MATZA, D. 1969. *Becoming Deviant*, Englewood Cliffs, NJ: Prentice-Hall

MAYBURY-LEWIS, D. (ed.) 1984. *The Prospects for Plural Societies*, Washington, DC: American Ethnological Society

MAYER, A. 1966. 'The significance of quasi-groups in the study of complex societies', in M. Banton (ed.), *The Social Anthropology of Complex Societies*, London: Tavistock

MEAD, G.H. 1934. *Mind, Self and Society from the Standpoint of a Social Behaviorist*, Chicago: University of Chicago Press

MIDMORE, P., HUGHES, G. and BATEMAN, D. 1994. 'Agriculture and the rural economy: problems, policies and prospects', *Contemporary Wales*, 6, pp. 7–32

MILES, R. 1982. *Racism and Migrant Labour*, London: Routledge and Kegan Paul

MILES, R. 1989. *Racism*, London: Routledge

MILES, R. 1996. 'Racism and nationalism in the British Isles: a view from the periphery', in R. Barot (ed.), *The Racism Problematic: Contemporary Sociological Debates on Race and Ethnicity*, Lampeter: Edwin Mellon Press

MILLER, D. (ed.) 1995. *Worlds Apart: Modernity through the Prism of the Local*, London: Routledge

MILNER, D. 1975. *Children and Race*, Harmondsworth: Penguin

MITCHELL, J.C. (ed.), 1969. *Social Networks in Urban Situations*, Manchester: Manchester University Press

MOERMAN, M. 1965. 'Ethnic identification in a complex civilization: who are the Lue?', *American Anthropologist*, 67, pp. 1215–30

MOODY, T.W. 1974. *The Ulster Question 1603–1973*, Cork: Mercier

MOORE, R. 1972. 'Race relations in the six counties: Colonialism, industrialization and stratification in Ireland', *Race*, 14, pp. 21–42

MOORE, R.I. 1987. *The Formation of a Persecuting Society: Power and Deviance in Western Europe, 950–1250*, Oxford: Basil Blackwell

MORGAN, K.O. 1981. *Rebirth of a Nation: Wales 1880–1980*, Oxford: Clarendon Press

MORGAN, P. 1983. 'From a death to a view: the hunt for the Welsh past in the Romantic period', in E. Hobsbawm and T. Ranger (eds.), *The Invention of Tradition*, Cambridge: Cambridge University Press

MOXON-BROWNE, E. 1983. *Nation, Class and Creed in Northern Ireland*, Aldershot: Gower

MOXON-BROWNE, E. 1991. 'National identity in Northern Ireland', in P. Stringer and G. Robinson (eds.), *Social Attitudes in Northern Ireland: 1990–91 Edition*, Belfast: Blackstaff

MÜLLER-HILL, B. 1988. *Murderous Science: Elimination by Scientific Selection of Jews, Gypsies and Others, Germany 1933–1945*, Oxford: Oxford University Press

MUNCK, R. and ROLSTON, B. 1987. *Belfast in the Thirties: An Oral History*, Belfast: Blackstaff

MURRAY, D. 1983. 'School and conflict', in J. Darby (ed.), *Northern Ireland: The Background to the Conflict*, Belfast: Appletree

NAIRN, T. 1981. *The Break-Up of Britain: Crisis and Neo-Nationalism*, 2nd edn, London: New Left Books

NASH, J. and OGAN, E. 1990. 'The red and the black: Bougainvillean perceptions of other Papuan New Guineans', *Pacific Studies*, 13 (2), pp. 1–17

NELSON, S. 1975. 'Protestant "ideology" reconsidered: the case of "discrimination"', *British Political Sociology Yearbook*, 2, pp. 155–87

NEWCOMER, P.J. 1972. 'The Nuer are Dinka: an essay on origins and environmental determinism', *Man*, 7, pp. 5–11

O'DONNELL, E.E. 1977. *Northern Irish Stereotypes*, Dublin: College of Industrial Relations

O'DOWD, L., ROLSTON, B. and TOMLINSON, M. 1980. *Northern Ireland: Between Civil Rights and Civil War*, London: CSE Books

OKELY, J. 1983. *The Traveller-Gypsies*, Cambridge: Cambridge University Press

O'LEARY, B. and McGARRY, J. (eds.) 1993. *The Politics of Antagonism: Understanding Northern Ireland*, London: Athlone

O'REILLY, E. 1992. *Masterminds of the Right*, Dublin: Attic

O'SULLIVAN SEE, K. 1986. *First World Nationalisms: Class and Ethnic Politics in Northern Ireland and Quebec*, Chicago: University of Chicago Press

ØSTERGÅRD, U. 1992a. 'What is national and ethnic identity?', in P. Bilde, T. Engberg-Pedersen, L. Hannestad and J. Zahle (eds.), *Ethnicity in Hellenistic Egypt*, Århus: Aarhus University Press

ØSTERGÅRD, U. 1992b. *Europas Ansigter: Nationale stater og politiske kulturer i en ny, gammel verden*, Copenhagen: Rosinante

ØSTERGÅRD, U. 1992c. 'Danish identity: European, Nordic or peasant?', in L. Lyck (ed.), *Denmark and EC Membership Evaluated*, London: Pinter

ØSTERGÅRD, U. (ed.) 1992d. *Dansk Identitet?*, Århus: Aarhus Universitetsforlag

ØSTERGÅRD, U. 1992e. 'Peasants and Danes: the Danish national identity and political culture', *Comparative Studies in Society and History*, 34, pp. 3–27

ØSTERGÅRD, U. 1995. 'Dansk mindretals politik i praksis' (Arbejdspapir, 24–95), Århus: Center for Kulturforskning

PAINE, R. 1974. *Second Thoughts about Barth's Models* (Occasional Paper No. 32), London: Royal Anthropological Institute

PATTERSON, H. 1980. *Class Conflict and Sectarianism: The Protestant Working Class and the Belfast Labour Movement*, Belfast: Blackstaff

PELTO, P.J. and PELTO, G.H. 1978. *Anthropological Research: The Structure of Inquiry*, 2nd edn, Cambridge: Cambridge University Press

PHOENIX, E. 1994. *Northern Nationalism: Nationalist Politics, Partition and the Catholic Minority in Northern Ireland 1890–1940*, Belfast: Ulster Historical Foundation

PORTER, E. 1996. 'Culture, community and responsibilities: abortion in Ireland', *Sociology*, 30, pp. 279–98

PROTTAS, J.M. 1979. *People Processing: The Street-Level Bureaucrat in Public Service Bureaucracies*, Lexington, MA: Lexington Books

PRYCE, K. 1979. *Endless Pressure: A Study of West-Indian Life-styles in Bristol*, Harmondsworth: Penguin

RADCLIFFE-BROWN, A.R. 1952. *Structure and Function in Primitive Society: Essays and Addresses*, London: Cohen and West

RAPPORT, N. 1995. 'Migrant selves and stereotypes: personal context in a postmodern world', in S. Pile and N. Thrift (eds.), *Mapping the Subject: Geographies of Cultural Transformation*, London: Routledge

REDDY, G.P. 1993. *Danes Are Like That! Perspectives of an Indian Anthropologist on the Danish Society*, Mørke: Grevas

REES, I.B. 1975. *The Welsh Political Tradition*, Cardiff: Plaid Cymru

REES, I.B. 1990. 'Wales today: nation or market?', *Planet*, 79, pp. 56–91

REID, A. 1980. 'Skilled workers in the shipbuilding industry 1880–1920: a labour aristocracy', in A. Morgan and B. Purdie (eds.), *Ireland: Divided Nation, Divided Class*, London: Ink Links

REX, J. 1973. *Race, Colonialism and the City*, London: Oxford University Press

REX, J. 1986. *Race and Ethnicity*, Milton Keynes: Open University Press

REX, J. 1991. *Ethnic Identity and Ethnic Mobilization in Britain*, Warwick: ESRC Centre for Research in Ethnic Relations

REYNOLDS, S. 1984. *Kingdoms and Communities in Western Europe 900–1300*, Oxford: Clarendon Press

RICHARDS, M.P.M. (ed.) 1974. *The Integration of a Child into a Social World*. Cambridge: Cambridge University Press

RIST, R.C. 1977. 'On understanding the processes of schooling: the contributions of labelling theory', in J. Karabel and A.H. Halsey (eds.), *Power and Ideology in Education*, New York: Oxford University Press

ROBERTS, B. 1994. 'Welsh identity in a former mining valley: social images and imagined communities', *Contemporary Wales*, 7, pp. 77–95

ROBERTSON, R. 1992. *Globalization: Social Theory and Global Culture*, London: Sage

ROLSTON, B. 1991. *Politics and Painting: Murals and Conflict in Northern Ireland*, Rutherford: Fairleigh Dickinson University Press

ROLSTON, B. 1992. *Drawing Support: Murals in the North of Ireland*, Belfast: Beyond the Pale

ROSE, R. 1971. *Governing without Consensus*, London: Faber and Faber

RUANE, J. and TODD, J. 1992. 'The social origins of nationalism in a contested region: the case of Northern Ireland', in J. Coakley (ed.), *The Social Origins of Nationalism: The West European Experience*, London: Sage

RUNCIMAN, S. 1958. *The Sicilian Vespers: A History of the Mediterranean World in the Later Thirteenth Century*, Cambridge: Cambridge University Press

RUTHERFORD, J. (ed.) 1990. *Identity: Community, Culture, Difference*, London: Lawrence and Wishart

RYLE, G. 1963. *The Concept of Mind*, Harmondsworth: Peregrine (first published 1949)

SACKS, P.M. 1976. *The Donegal Mafia*, New Haven: Yale University Press

SAGGAR, S. 1996. 'The politics of racial pluralism in Britain: problems of evaluation', in R. Barot (ed.), *The Racism Problematic*, Lampeter: Edwin Mellon Press

SAHLINS, M. 1972. *Stone Age Economics*, London: Tavistock

SAMUEL, R. and THOMPSON, P. (eds.) 1990. *The Myths We Live By*, London: Routledge

SCHERMERHORN, R.A. 1978. *Comparative Ethnic Relations: A Framework for Theory and Research*, 2nd edn, Chicago: University of Chicago Press

SCHLEE, G. 1989. *Identities on the Move: Clanship and Pastoralism in Northern Kenya*, Manchester: Manchester University Press

SCHUTZ, A. 1967. *The Phenomenology of the Social World*, Evanston, IL: Northwestern University Press

SCHUTZ, A. and LUCKMANN, T. 1973. *The Structures of the Life-World*, Evanston, IL: Northwestern University Press

SCOTT, R.A. 1970. 'The construction of conceptions of stigma by professional experts', in J.D. Douglas (ed.), *Deviance and Respectability: The Social Construction of Moral Meanings*, New York: Basic Books

SENIOR, H. 1966. *Orangeism in Ireland and Britain, 1795–1836*, London: Routledge and Kegan Paul

SKOVGAARD-PETERSEN, E. 1994. 'Stemmer om Maastricht', in J. Liep and K. Fog Olwig (eds.), *Komplekse liv: kulturel mangfoldighed i Danmark*, Copenhagen: Akademisk Forlag

SLUKA, J.A. 1989. *Hearts and Minds, Water and Fish: Support for the IRA and INLA in a Northern Irish Ghetto*, Greenwich: JAI Press

SMITH, A.D. 1981. *The Ethnic Revival in the Modern World*, Cambridge: Cambridge University Press

SMITH, A.D. 1986. *The Ethnic Origins of Nations*, Oxford: Basil Blackwell

SMITH, A.D. 1991. *National Identity*, Harmondsworth: Penguin

SMITH, A.D. 1994. 'The problem of national identity: ancient, medieval and modern?', *Ethnic and Racial Studies*, 17, pp. 375–99

SMITH, D.J. and CHAMBERS, G. 1991. *Inequality in Northern Ireland*, Oxford: Clarendon Press

SMITH, M.G. 1960. *Government in Zazzau 1800–1950*, London: Oxford University Press for the International African Institute

SMITH, M.G. 1965. *The Plural Society in the British West Indies*, Berkeley: University of California Press

SMITH, M.G. 1974. *Corporations and Society*, London: Duckworth

SMITH, M.G. 1986. 'Pluralism, race and ethnicity in selected African countries', in J. Rex and D. Mason (eds.), *Theories of Race and Ethnic Relations*, Cambridge: Cambridge University Press

SOLOMOS, J. 1988. *Black Youth, Racism and the State: The Politics of Ideology and Policy*, Cambridge: Cambridge University Press

SØRENSEN, H. and VÆVER, O. 1992. 'State, society and democracy and the effect of the EC', in L. Lyck (ed.), *Denmark and EC Membership Evaluated*, London: Pinter

SOUTHALL, A. 1976. 'Nuer and Dinka are people: ecology, economy and logical possibility', *Man*, 11, pp. 463–91

SPEAR, T. and WALLER, R. (eds.) 1993. *Being Maasai: Ethnicity and Identity in East Africa*, London: James Currey

STEAD, P. 1990. 'The quest for political power', in R. Jenkins and A. Edwards (eds.), *One Step Forward? South and West Wales towards the Year 2000*, Llandysul: Gwasg Gomer

STERN, D.N. 1985. *The Interpersonal World of the Infant: A View from Psychoanalysis and Developmental Psychology*, New York: Basic Books

STONE, J. 1996. 'Ethnicity', in A. Kuper and J. Kuper (eds.), *The Social Science Encyclopedia*, 2nd edn, London: Routledge

STONE, M. 1981. *The Education of the Black Child in Britain*, London: Fontana

STUCHLIK, M. 1976. *Life on a Half Share: Mechanisms of Social Recruitment among the Mapuche of Southern Chile*, London: C. Hurst

STUCHLIK, M. 1979. 'Chilean native policies and the image of the Mapuche Indians', in D. Riches (ed.), *The Conceptualisation and Explanation of Processes of Social Change* (Queen's University Papers in Social Anthropology, vol. 3), Belfast

SYMONDS, A. 1990. 'Migration, communities and social change', in R. Jenkins and A. Edwards (eds.), *One Step Forward? South and West Wales towards the Year 2000*, Llandysul: Gwasg Gomer

TÄGIL, S. (ed.) 1995. *Ethnicity and Nation Building in the Nordic World*, London: Hurst

THOMAS, D.E. 1991. 'The Constitution of Wales', in B. Crick (ed.), *National Identities: The Constitution of the United Kingdom*, Oxford: Basil Blackwell

THOMAS, N. 1991. *The Welsh Extremist: Modern Welsh Politics, Literature and Society*, 2nd edn, Talybont: Y Lolfa

TROYNA, B. and HATCHER, R. 1992. *Racism in Children's Lives: A Study of Mainly White Primary Schools*, London: Routledge

VAN DEN BERGHE, P.L. 1967. *Race and Racism: A Comparative Perspective*, New York: Wiley

VAN DEN BERGHE, P.L. 1981. *The Ethnic Phenomenon*, New York: Elsevier

VAN DEN BERGHE, P.L. 1986. 'Ethnicity and the socio-biology debate', in J. Rex and D. Mason (eds.), *Theories of Race and Ethnic Relations*, Cambridge: Cambridge University Press

VAN DEN BERGHE, P.L. 1995. 'Does race matter?', *Nations and Nationalism*, 1, pp. 357–68

VERDERY, K. 1993. 'Whither "nation" and "nationalism"?', *Daedalus*, 122 (3), pp. 37–45

VERDERY, K. 1994. 'Ethnicity, nationalism and state-making. *Ethnic Groups and Boundaries*: past and future', in H. Vermeulen and C. Govers (eds.), *The Anthropology of Ethnicity: Beyond 'Ethnic Groups and Boundaries'*, Amsterdam: het Spinhuis

VERMEULEN, H. and GOVERS, C. 1994. 'Introduction', in H. Vermeulen and C. Govers (eds.), *The Anthropology of Ethnicity: Beyond 'Ethnic Groups and Boundaries'*, Amsterdam: het Spinhuis

WADE, P. 1993. '"Race", nature and culture', *Man*, 28, pp. 17–34

WALLMAN, S. 1978. 'The boundaries of race: processes of ethnicity in England', *Man*, 13, pp. 200–17

WALLMAN, S. 1979. 'Introduction: the scope for ethnicity', in S. Wallman (ed.), *Ethnicity at Work*, London: Macmillan

WALLMAN, S. 1986. 'Ethnicity and the boundary process in context', in J. Rex and D. Mason (eds.), *Theories of Race and Ethnic Relations*, Cambridge: Cambridge University Press

WATERS, M. 1995. *Globalization*, London: Routledge

WEBER, M. 1978. *Economy and Society*, ed. G. Roth and C. Wittich, Berkeley: University of California Press

WHYTE, J.H. 1980. *Church and State in Modern Ireland 1923–1979*, Dublin: Gill and Macmillan

WHYTE, J.H. 1990. *Understanding Northern Ireland*, Oxford: Clarendon Press

WILK, R.R. 1993. 'Beauty and the feast: official and visceral nationalism in Belize', *Ethnos*, 58, pp. 294–316

WILLIAMS, B. 1989. 'A class act: anthropology and the race to nation across ethnic terrain', *Annual Review of Anthropology*, 18, pp. 401–44

WILLIAMS, C.H. 1989. 'New domains of the Welsh language: education, planning and the law', *Contemporary Wales*, 3, pp. 41–76

WILLIAMS, G. 1994. 'Discourses on "nation" and "race": a response to Denney et al.', *Contemporary Wales*, 6, pp. 87–103

WILLIAMS, G.A. 1985. *When Was Wales?*, Harmondsworth: Penguin

WILLIS, P. 1977. *Learning to Labour: How Working Class Kids Get Working Class Jobs*, Farnborough: Saxon House

WILSON, T. 1955. 'Conclusions: devolution and partition', in T. Wilson (ed.), *Ulster under Home Rule*, London: Oxford University Press

WILSON, T. 1989. *Ulster: Conflict and Consensus*, Oxford: Basil Blackwell

WOLF, E.R. 1994. 'Perilous ideas: race, culture, people', *Current Anthropology*, 35, pp. 1–12

Index